COMMANDO

COMMANDO

The Illustrated History of Britain's Green Berets

DAVID REYNOLDS

FOREWORD BY COUNTESS MOUNTBATTEN OF BURMA

SUTTON PUBLISHING LIMITED

Dedicated to

Jack Reynolds

First published in 2001 by
Sutton Publishing Limited · Phoenix Mill
Thrupp · Stroud · Gloucestershire · GL5 2BU

British Library Cataloguing in Publication Data
A catalogue record for this book is available from the British Library

ISBN 0 7509 2209 5

Endpapers: *Front*: Royal Marine Commandos mount a cliff assault raid during an exercise on the rugged Cornish coast. Today's Green Berets maintain the raiding skills that the Army Commandos pioneered in the early days. *Back*: Royal Marine Commandos mount a dawn attack aboard rigid raiding craft (RRC) during an exercise in northern Norway.

Frontispiece: A Commando in Sierra Leone, 2000.

Typeset in Sabon 11/14pt.
Typesetting and origination by
Sutton Publishing Limited.
Printed and bound in England by
J.H. Haynes & Co. Ltd, Sparkford.

CONTENTS

FOREWORD

COUNTESS MOUNTBATTEN OF BURMA CBE CD JP DL

The Commandos were formed in 1940 to conduct raids, initially against the coast of occupied France and later throughout enemy-held territory. At first they were all volunteers from the Army and later, in 1942, they were joined by Royal Marines.

My father took over responsibility for the Commandos when he became Chief of Combined Operations in October 1941 where he was closely involved in their development and later, as Supreme Allied Commander South-East Asia, in their employment in that theatre.

Having myself served for fifteen months of my three years' wartime service in the Women's Royal Naval Service in a Combined Operations base near Southampton (HMS *Tormentor*), I still remember the embarkation of several thousand of those brave Commandos for the D-Day invasion in June 1944.

The Army Commandos were formally disbanded in 1945 but the role lived on in the Royal Marines, of whom my father was the Life Colonel Commandant until his assassination in 1979. He maintained a close interest in serving and former members of both organisations and I was delighted to be invited to be Patron of the Commando Association to retain our family link.

Many unique photographs have been brought together here to illustrate the story of the Commandos, ranging from their training for the earliest raids in the dark days of 1940 to the amphibious operations of the present day. The Commandos have a distinguished place in military history. This book is a fitting tribute, not only as a record of their achievements but also as a source of inspiration, in particular to the young men of today, proud to follow in the footsteps of their remarkable predecessors who first wore the green beret.

PREFACE

THE COMMANDANT-GENERAL ROYAL MARINES
MAJOR-GENERAL R.H.G. FULTON RM

This book traces the development of the Commandos from their formation in 1940 to the present. Those remarkable volunteers, whose bravery, resourcefulness and skill illuminated the darkest days of the Second World War, laid the foundations of the Commando idea and paved the way for a style of warfare that allowed the enemy no respite.

As that war progressed and the Allies were able to move onto the offensive, the task of the Commandos developed away from small-scale raids and towards the support of amphibious operations and large armies.

While an innovative approach to different operations demanded new skills, the personal standards learned at Achnacarry Castle in the Highlands of Scotland stayed constant and the qualities of leadership, unselfishness, high professional standards and cheerfulness in adversity remain the Commando touchstone to this day.

Today's Commandos are drawn from all three Services and their role is to provide the nation's amphibious forces and associated specialist units. The Royal Marines are proud to be the current guardians of the Commando ideal, yet it is the spirit that burns within the individual man, of whatever Service – the same spirit that inspired those early volunteers – that is the true Commando Spirit. Our role is to nurture it and develop it. Those who wish to follow in the footsteps of those first Commandos do not wear the green beret without displaying the same mental resolve, physical robustness and military skill.

Today the responsibility of each man is twofold – firstly, to live up to the example and standards of his predecessors in order to ensure that such endeavour and sacrifice were not in vain and, secondly, to set his own example for the next generation.

Introduction

The Commandos

'We need specially trained troops of the hunter class, who can develop a reign of terror down these [enemy-occupied] coasts.'

Prime Minister Winston Churchill, 1940

The Commandos owe their creation to Winston Churchill, who in June 1940, just weeks after taking office as Prime Minister, sought military options to strike back at strategic German targets. His decision followed the fall of France and the setback at Dunkirk which had almost crippled the British Army. It was volunteers from across the Army who formed the first Commando units and these pioneers developed the role of the force throughout the war. The first Royal Marine Commando unit was raised in February 1942. The Royal Marines, known to those who have served as the 'Corps', were formed on 28 October 1664 and by the Second World War had established a proven reputation for tackling the unusual – boarding ships at close quarters, scaling cliffs and attacking enemy vessels in well-defended harbours. It was therefore a natural progression that they should become involved in Commando operations. It was the success of these wartime units that ensured the role was retained after the war and maintained today by 3 Commando Brigade RM.

The word 'commando' can be traced back to the Boer War in 1899 when farmers of Dutch descent fought the British in what was initially perceived to be just another colonial battle. In fact, this conflict was to have a profound influence on future warfare: it saw the creation of the 'commando' tactic which was used to mount a successful guerrilla war. Each community across South Africa provided men for a 'Commando'. Armed and carrying everything they needed on their backs, these small units were mounted on horseback and were totally self-sustained. Throughout the Boer War they planned and executed highly successful raids against the British, using the element of surprise as a key factor in their attacks. Their unconventional approach to warfare caught the British off guard and they soon struck fear into infantry regiments in the Transvaal.

The British, having witnessed the success of the Boers' style of warfare, adopted the concept in 1940 and the first 'independent Commando companies' were raised to mount small raids aimed to strike at enemy fortifications. It was believed that in addition to damaging German fortifications, such a tactic would boost civilian morale

Opposite: A Royal Marine Commando sniper pictured at a training site. Snipers have played a key role in Commando operations since the Second World War.

in Britain. Successful raids by Army Commandos against the Lofoten islands off Norway in March 1941, Vaagso (also off Norway) in December 1941 and St Nazaire in France in March 1942 provided the testing grounds for the Commando role and indicated it was appropriate for broader deployment. In addition, the successful seaborne assault against the Vichy French naval base at Diego-Suarez in Madagascar by No. 5 Commando in spring 1942 renewed belief in the capability of amphibious assaults, which had been shunned by commanders since the failure of the Gallipoli landings of 1915.

In the early days of Commando operations soldiers continued to wear their own regimental headdress and cap badge. At one point there were more than seventy-nine different regiments represented in No. 1 Commando – almost double the number in today's Army. Towards the end of 1942 senior officers of No. 1 Commando decided that headdress should become standard across all ranks and chose the beret as the most practical option. The Royal Tank Regiment had worn a black beret for many years and the recently formed Parachute Regiment and airborne forces had chosen a maroon one. No. 1 Commando's flash was a green salamander moving through fire which made a choice between green, red and yellow logical for the beret. Green was deemed the most suitable and a firm of tam-o'-shanter makers at Irvine in Scotland produced a beret of the kind of green cloth that is still worn today.

As the war continued more Royal Marine units converted, after training, to the commando role. From Dieppe through to the D-Day landings, as well as at the vital campaigns in Sicily, Italy, the Balkans then into India and Burma and across the Far East, the newly formed Royal Marine Commando units played a leading role in the development of seaborne operations. After the Second World War the Commando role was exclusively passed to the Royal Marines and No. 3 Commando Brigade was retained. However, with hostilities over, capital investment in the military was not a priority and wartime weapons and equipment were not upgraded for many years. In general, the effectiveness of the Royal Navy was allowed to deteriorate and there was little scope for building new ships.

The Boer's commando tactic was not the only aspect of South African military life embraced by the British. During the Second World War South African troops serving in the Corps introduced the 'Sarie Marais' – the song of the Boer commandos. In 1952, it was officially adopted by the Royal Marines as one of three official marches, the other two being 'A Life on the Ocean Wave' and 'The Preobrajensky March' (the regimental slow march presented by Lord Mountbatten in 1964).

In the postwar years the Commandos were constantly in action in Palestine, Korea, the jungles of the Far East, Cyprus and Suez. In the latter operation the Green Berets made history when they mounted the first helicopter assault, but they still lacked dedicated assault shipping. After Suez further reviews of defence spending threatened to cut back the already small Commando force. Then in the mid-1960s a decision was made to build two assault ships. These 'Fearless'-class ships, named HMS *Fearless* and HMS *Intrepid*, entered service in 1965 and 1967 respectively, ready to significantly

ommandos return to a port on the south
ast after an early raid. During the
rmative Commando years men wore
ool hats, steel helmets and their own
gimental headdress before a decision
as taken to adopt the green beret.

e wartime Royal Marine units who
nsferred to the Commando role carried the
efix RM after their unit number. After the
ar the Commando role was handed
clusively to the Royal Marines and in
946 the designation was changed — the
ters RM were placed after the Commando.
day, Royal Marine Commandos can be
entified by their green beret and a shoulder
sh on their combat uniforms. In addition,
ose serving in a Commando unit wear the
mmando qualification badge on their left
m. Army personnel who pass the
mmando course are entitled to wear the
mmando dagger for the rest of their
reers. The first women to attend the
mmando course joined Commando
aining Centre in April 2001.

enhance the amphibious capability of 3 Commando Brigade RM. The vessels had the capacity to operate an enclosed harbour at their stern, carry helicopters and coordinate an amphibious assault via a dedicated command-and-control cell. But the Cold War restricted their deployment to the transit of troops to northern Norway for winter training with NATO and they never reached their full potential until the Falklands War in 1982, by which time they were ready for replacement.

During the 1970s the Admiralty attempted to appease senior Commando commanders, who were pressing for ships that could operate helicopters, by commissioning refits for old aircraft carriers so that they could fulfil the Commando role. The age of the ships determined that these 'second career' projects would always have a short life. Defence cutbacks continued to threaten the Commandos' future and while verbal promises of new assault ships and a helicopter carrier were made, no hard steel was being fabricated for these projects. In the 1980s the Corps faced an uncertain future.

Then suddenly the Cold War ended and while it promised the world a new peace it also opened up global opportunities for the Royal Marine Commandos in their role as a lead element of the UK's new Joint Rapid Reaction Force (JRRF). During the Cold War, political tension was concentrated on the superpowers and provided an uncomfortable but stable global environment. Now the world is dotted with potential flashpoints as countries intimidate their neighbours with military power in the race for regional dominance and control of resources. From a military perspective the potential requirement for amphibious operations is illustrated by the fact that more than 70 per cent of the world's surface is covered by oceans and 80 per cent of countries have a coastline, while the majority of the global population lives within 300 miles of the sea. The so-called 'new world order' has left Britain needing strong amphibious forces that can deploy in an expeditionary role to protect British interests overseas and be ready to mount a wide range of new military operations. In the twenty-first century the Commandos' role focuses on Peace Support Operations (PSO) and the evacuation of UK citizens from crisis areas. During the first year of the new century leading elements of the JRRF were on standby to deploy and evacuate British nationals from three countries, highlighting the level of insecurity in the world in the post-Cold War climate.

Since its selection as a key force within the JRRF in 1996, 3 Commando Brigade has seen its readiness for deployment increase and its global commitments steadily expand. Examples include the deployment of Marines to prepare an evacuation of British nationals from Albania in 1995 and in October 1996 45 Commando RM was put on standby to go to Zaire. The mission, codenamed Operation 'Purposeful', was part of a multinational humanitarian operation to save thousands of starving refugees who had been displaced from their villages by armed tribesmen and had fled to remote areas of the jungle. Defence Secretary Michael Portillo ordered the mission after the world's media focused on starving refugees in the central African state. Difficult terrain prevented any immediate overland assistance and speed was essential. A parachute insertion by the lead battlegroup of 5 Airborne Brigade was therefore approved by the

During the late 1980s the Commando Brigade faced an uncertain future. The Royal Navy's dedicated amphibious shipping was 'past its sell by date' – the converted Commando carriers had all been retired and aircraft carriers were being used as 'occasional ferries' for the force. But lack of space resulted in vehicles being lashed on the flight deck and helicopter assaults, as pictured, curtailed the carrier's ability to operate fixed-wing aircraft.

Permanent Joint Head Quarters (PJHQ) in Northwood, London. This was to be followed by a Tactical Air Land Operation (TALO) by 45 Commando RM. A major problem identified by planning staff at Northwood was the fact that the refugees had disappeared into the bush and could not initially be located by satellite. The air plan for the operation included more than twenty C-130 Hercules, twelve of which would carry the leading elements of the force into Zaire. Flying from the UK they would land in Cyprus at night and then in Africa at first light the following day. But just as the Commandos prepared to say goodbye to their families, news came that the refugees had been located and within twenty-four hours the international aid agencies announced there was no longer a requirement for a military intervention force. The mission was cancelled, but it had demonstrated 45 Commando RM's high level of readiness.

A year later, in 1997, a company of 40 Commando RM and a boat group of 539 Assault Squadron RM deployed to the Congo to prepare for a potential evacuation of British nationals. At the same time Tactical Air Control Parties (TACP), small highly trained teams of forward aircraft controllers (FACs), were back in Bosnia where they had been working since the first British troops moved into the region in 1992.

It was during the busy decade of the 1990s that a little-known unit was created under the operational direction of the Royal Navy at Fleet Headquarters, also based in Northwood. The concept for the unit, called the Fleet Standby Rifle Troop (FSRT),

In the post-Falklands years the amphibious role gained credibility, but specialist shipping was still limited. During Exercise 'Purple Warrior' in Scotland a Landing Ship Logistics (LSL) made one of the few direct beach landings since Suez, disgorging its load of vehicles directly onto the shore. Such a landing has not taken place since.

A Commando-trained Navy doctor treats a young baby after 45 Commando RM and elements of the Royal Netherlands Marine Corps were deployed from HMS *Ocean* to provide aid in South America after a hurricane had caused widespread devastation in 1999. The Commando Brigade can be called on to mount humanitarian operations.

emerged in 1996. It consists of six Royal Marine protection parties (RMPPS) drawn from Commando units within the Brigade which are held at high readiness to be deployed to flashpoints across the globe via RN surface ships (generally destroyers and frigates). Since its inception, the FSRT has been deployed on more than thirteen different operations on warships all over the world. Royal Marine Commandos from this small unit deployed to Albania and into Sierra Leone (before the highly publicised Operation 'Palliser' in 1999), as well as East Timor. But its demanding drain on the Brigade's limited resources resulted in it being assigned to Comacchio Group, a specialist Royal Marine security unit, which now provides the manpower for the FSRT. Comacchio was renamed Fleet Royal Marines Protection Group (FPMPG) in October 2000.

At the end of the twentieth century the Royal Navy's focus of operations was redirected towards amphibious warfare with the introduction of a dedicated helicopter carrier and new assault ships designed specially to carry Royal Marines into action.

In a concept similar to the American system of regularly deploying US Marine units aboard ships in groups known as Marine Expeditionary Forces (MEFs) to areas of potential conflict, the Royal Navy formed its own task group known as the Amphibious Ready Group (ARG). This is based around a Commando battlegroup which includes artillery and engineer support and can be sited aboard the helicopter HMS *Ocean* or one of the new assault ships. The ARG is scheduled to deploy twice a year and will provide the UK with a highly mobile, on-call, rapid reaction force.

As the Royal Marines look to the future, new assault ships and a helicopter carrier are the first phase of an entire equipment and tactical transition which will take place over the next fifteen years to ensure that 3 Commando Brigade will remain highly capable. At the top end of the procurement chain the government is expected to order two super aircraft carriers which will carry the new Joint Strike Fighter and will provide the air power capability to support amphibious operations in 2020. New landing ships will replace the two naval support Royal Fleet Auxiliary (RFA) Landing Ships Logistic (LSL) *Sir Percival* and *Sir Geraint*. The new ships, expected to be at least 10,000 tonnes each, will be much larger, more capable and flexible than existing RFA LSLs and will provide a major increase in the capability of the RFA to support amphibious operations and other military tasks, such as peacekeeping duties and disaster relief. Improvements to the existing LSLs are expected to include a bigger flight deck strong enough to handle Chinook and Merlin helicopters and the US Marine Corps' V-22 Osprey. The new vessels will also have the ability to carry more troops, equipment and stores, as well as wide assault routes to permit fully equipped troops to reach embarkation areas quickly. Existing LSLs were designed to be capable of beaching and landing tanks and vehicles through bow doors directly on to the shore. The new ships will operate over the horizon initially, and will land troops and equipment by landing craft, helicopter and Mexeflote-powered craft. They will not have a beaching capability.

The Apache helicopter gunship will join the air assets of the new ARG, replacing the Lynx which has been used in an anti-tank role. A replacement for the Sea King helicopter is also scheduled to be commissioned – the troop-carrying variant entered service in 1979 and is overdue for replacement.

Future amphibious warfare will be based on 'sea denial', according to Brigadier Rob Fry, commander of 3 Commando Brigade RM, who also suggests that the tactics of 'man and the bayonet' are fast being replaced by crew-served weapons – mobile, mounted, heavy machine guns, anti-tank systems, and fire-and-forget missiles. The Commando Brigade is also looking to change its approach to amphibious assault with the acquisition of 108 armoured all-terrain tracked vehicles known as all-terrain vehicle protected or ATV(P). The fibreglass variant of this vehicle has been used in Norway for many years and its procurement in the armoured role will provide limited protection for troops 'crossing the beach', the most dangerous part of any seaborne assault. While no decision has yet been formalised, it is anticipated that all 108 vehicles will be assigned to one Commando unit.

New roll-on roll-off landing craft (LCU Mk10s) have been developed and will embark aboard the first Landing Platform Dock Replacement (LPDR), HMS *Albion*. The introduction of hovercraft has also enhanced the Brigade's amphibious capability. In addition, the Brigade's air defence unit is also to be strengthened with a Rapier battery and is due to become an integral part of the organisation in place of the current system of an assigned unit deploying on operations.

But despite the fact that new equipment is vital to ensure that the Commandos are a force for the twenty-first century, the training package designed to produce high-calibre

The arrival of the helicopter carrier HMS *Ocean* has presented the opportunity for RAF Chinooks (left) to operate from the ship's large deck and support the Commandos. The new Apache helicopter gunship (right), manned by the Army Air Corps, will be assigned to the Brigade to operate from HMS *Ocean* for specific operations.

Royal Marine Commandos is the Brigade's most important asset. As soon as the Brigade was established it was identified that the Commandos needed specialist training and a selection course was established at Achnacarry in Scotland. Today, a high standard of training continues to be maintained at the Corps' Lympstone base where young men undergo a gruelling selection process to win the coveted green beret. Today, the professional standard of Commando training is as important as it was during the Second World War. Across the armed forces personnel who have passed the Commando course carry a hallmark of military quality with them for the rest of their careers.

Teams at the Commando Training Centre at Lympstone have seen generations come and go and have adjusted their programme to ensure that the Corps gets the best out of each recruit so that by the time they reach selection week they are ready and prepared to pass the tests. The Commando course is the longest infantry selection programme of any unit in Europe, possibly the world. Lympstone produces what many observers have described as the best-trained soldiers in the UK, more experienced in a variety of military skills than their Army counterparts. Brigadier Rob Fry believes that standards must be maintained so that the Commando Brigade can continue to function fully. 'We need people that are trained for purpose, trained to operational performance and ready to deploy. There is no time to teach people once they have arrived. They must be fully trained', he said.

The military benefit of maintaining such a long and exhaustive training programme was highlighted in June 2000 when young recruits who had just passed out of the

course were drafted to 42 Commando and quickly found themselves on the streets of Freetown in Sierra Leone. Because training for a Royal Marine Commando includes helicopter drills and instruction in the full spectrum of infantry support weapons, as well as all aspects of radio procedure, these young Marines needed no 'continuation training' and were able to go straight into action. Other recruits passed out of Lympstone and joined 40 Commando RM on operations in Northern Ireland, while some headed for the Balkans with 45 Commando RM.

It is important to state in this introduction that the Royal Marine Commandos are a unique breed whose character is developed by a gruelling physical training programme. It demands winners: a recruit must be totally committed to winning the green beret – just as the pioneers of the role were at Achnacarry in the Second World War. Commando training is not just about physical ability and military skills: many super-fit recruits have failed because they have not been able to grasp the principles of the Commando Spirit which encourages determination, leadership, courage, cheerfulness under adversity and high professional standards. This ethos produces fit, capable, highly trained, thinking soldiers who develop an analytical approach to their planning which puts them ahead of the enemy in the decision-making process – it also inspires the confidence to succeed in business in later life, as many Marines do. A high percentage of former Royal Marines who leave the Corps excel in their second careers, often combining adventure with business, like former Marine-turned-yachtsman Pete Goss. The claim that Royal Marine Commandos who leave the Corps also have success in other military careers is supported by many cases, although Dick

Left: Potential Royal Marine officers pictured at the end of the 30-miler – a demanding yomp across Dartmoor. Across the armed forces, personnel who have passed the Commando course carry a hallmark of military quality with them for the rest of their careers – the green beret. *Above*: A section from the Reconnaissance Troop of 42 Commando after being dropped by a Sea King helicopter at Lyngen fjord, north of Tromso in northern Norway. The Marines are carrying skis and the lead man on the left of the picture is armed with an L42 sniper rifle.

Arthur's is a special one. He joined the SAS and was second-in-command of the unit during the Gulf War. Lieutenant-Colonel Arthur also took part in the Iranian Embassy siege.

Aspects of the Commando Spirit play a fundamental role in most military evolutions, from a routine patrol in Northern Ireland where leadership and professional standards are paramount to success, to the detailed planning and execution of a full-scale amphibious assault. There are numerous examples that demonstrate the values of this spirit. In the Second World War when 40 RM Commando landed at Dieppe the commanding officer Lieutenant-Colonel Joseph Picton-Phillips disregarded his own safety and stood on the beach waving at landing craft to abort the assault. During the fireman's strike in 1977, Marines from 40 Commando RM were sent to the West Midlands to man 'green goddess' fire engines. On one occasion a senior NCO arrived at a burning council house to discover that another military unit was already on the scene but had assessed that it was too dangerous to go in. Aware there were children inside, he threw himself through the front-room window in an attempt to reach them. For him there was still a chance they could be alive and his training would not allow him to stand around – he had to do something positive, although sadly the children died. The Commando Spirit was also clearly demonstrated by Marine Tom Rivenberg who lost both legs in an IRA bomb attack in Belfast, but refused to let his injuries ruin his big day. The young Royal Marine borrowed a set of bandsman's blues and with false legs walked down the aisle to marry his bride. In 1981 the then Commandant-General, Lieutenant-General Sir Steuart Pringle, was caught in an IRA explosion but despite severe injuries, which included the loss of a leg, he continued in his position at the head of the Corps. He visited recruits at Lympstone and Commando units across the Brigade – his fighting spirit was an inspiration to his men. In 2000 Corporal Alan Chambers and Marine Charlie Paton Black showed outstanding fortitude and determination when they yomped across the ice to the North Pole in extreme weather conditions.

But there is a fine line between confidence and arrogance, which should not be confused with the Commando Spirit, as a young Royal Marine in 45 Commando RM discovered when he arrived at Condor (45's barracks in Arbroath) full of pride and eager to enforce some of the skills he had learned in training. As a car approached the main gate he stepped out in front and flagged it down. 'Could I see some ID please', the young Marine barked.

'Do you know who I am', replied the driver.

'No, sorry and I would like to see that ID', added the Marine.

'I'm your commanding officer and when I come through here I expect you to clip your heels together and salute me', responded the irate CO driving the car. The Marine promptly brought himself up to attention, took one pace back and announced,

'Well I am sorry about that sir, take two.' He proceeded to raise both arms and saluted the Colonel with both hands.

Of course all regiments and corps have special internal bonds but, without wishing to denigrate any other formation, the Commando Spirit is unique, not only because all

The requirement to maintain the high standard of Commando training has never been higher than it is in the twenty-first century — a time when the Brigade faces more operational commitments and challenges than at any time since the Second World War.

Marines of the Mountain and Arctic Warfare Cadre which reverted to its original instructor status in the 1990s and was renamed Brigade Patrol Troop. Steve Last is pictured far left with 'Fossy' Foster on the right.

officers and Marines undergo the same gruelling training, but also because the jargon used by the Corps is a language in itself, often not understood by others. At a dinner one evening a former Royal Marine officer was talking to an Army audience about his early days in 45 Commando RM and described himself as a 'young bit of skin'. Just two people knew what he was talking about and laughed – both were former Royal Marines – the remainder of the audience sat with glazed smiles on their faces as though they had missed the joke. (The expression is often used to describe a handsome young marine.)

The bond between Royal Marine Commandos is perhaps best described as a 'frequency' – all who have served are tuned in to it for the rest of their lives. Being a marine is a state of mind – 'once a marine, always a marine'.

This is true of the US Marines, Dutch Marines and indeed marines of many other nationalities who form an international brotherhood. Many people have tried to define the marine commando and perhaps he is best summed up in the words of Rudyard Kipling in his poem 'Soldier and Sailor':

> An' after I met 'im all over the world, a-doin' all kinds of things,
> Like landin' 'isself with a Gatlin' gun to talk to them 'eathen kings;
> 'E sleeps in an 'ammick instead of a cot, an' 'e drills with the deck on a slew,
> An' 'e sweats like a Jolly – 'Er Majesty's Jolly – soldier an' sailor too!
> For there isn't a job on the top o' the earth the beggar don't know, nor do –
> You can leave 'im at night on a bald man's 'ead, to paddle 'is own canoe –
> 'E's a sort of a bloomin' cosmopolouse – soldier an' sailor too.

ONE

FORMATION AND FIRST OPERATIONS

'I can still see that scene on White Beach. It was bloody chaos.'

Marine Alan Saunders, Dieppe

The formation of the Commandos called for a special breed of soldier to volunteer for a new concept in warfare that could not afford to fail. Britain faced its 'darkest hour' and desperately needed a force to strike back at the enemy who had inflicted so much damage. In 1940 the Germans trapped the British Expeditionary Force (BEF) in France and forced it to withdraw to Dunkirk, but fortunately they had failed to close in on the coastal ports and the Royal Navy was able to mount an evacuation. In the nine days before 4 June an armada of small boats worked around the clock to lift the stranded soldiers from the beach. In total 338,226 men, including 120,000 French, were rescued in Operation 'Dynamo'. Hitler's Luftwaffe made repeated attempts to annihilate the evacuation, but the intervention of the RAF, which shot down 129 aircraft, prevented the German airforce from achieving its aim.

As the BEF arrived back in Britain the German High Command was convinced that the sight of a defeated British force and the fall of France would be enough to make Britain agree to a peace deal. Britain was certainly hurting. During the first months of the war its forces had been seriously bruised and the nation's morale severely dented – Europe had been lost with the evacuation from Dunkirk, and the Desert Army had been driven back into Egypt. To many observers the German offensive across Europe seemed unstoppable and there were doubts that Britain could ever recover. Churchill was well aware that something needed to be done in order to boost the country's military effectiveness, as well as the nation's morale, and that it had to come within weeks of the setback at Dunkirk.

It quickly became clear to Hitler that Britain was not going to agree to his peace deal and he ordered his High Command to draw up a scheme for a seaborne invasion of the UK. Operation 'Sealion' was to involve twenty divisions and was based on the Luftwaffe winning the air war against the RAF. The German plan was for an invasion of the south coast of England in a combined airborne and seaborne assault, the latter using amphibious shipping based on a collection of steamers and barges. However, the Luftwaffe was defeated in the Battle of Britain in September 1940 and 'Sealion' was cancelled.

Army volunteers undergo initial Commando training in Scotland. Volunteers for Commando operations came from regiments across the Army. Then in February 1942 the first Royal Marine unit was assigned to Commando training and 40 RM Commando was raised.

Churchill had reviewed dozens of plans to strike back at Germany and was particularly inspired by the concept of Commando action. In mid-1940 the Prime Minister called for a new force to be created to carry out amphibious raids on enemy territory. In Whitehall a proposal to adopt the commando style of warfare had been made by two officers assigned to a small research team within the War Office in the late 1930s. Their task was to review tactics and develop new concepts that could be adopted by British forces. Lieutenant-Colonel John Holland, a Royal Engineer officer, and Major Colin Gubbins of the Royal Artillery (later Major-General Sir) had identified the success of the guerrilla units which played such havoc against the British Army during the Boer War; these groups were formed into small units known as 'commandos'. They ignored contemporary principles of conventional warfare, which involved face-to-face combat, and instead mounted surprise hit-and-run operations.

Holland and Gubbins also highlighted the German use of small units of highly trained 'shock' troops, deployed in the First World War to attack heavily defended positions on the Western Front. They suggested the style of 'raids' used by the Germans and the Boers could be adopted by the British. In addition, it was argued that aggressive commando-type operations would fracture the enemy's cohesion and begin the restoration of national morale.

One of Churchill's staff officers, Lieutenant-Colonel Dudley Clarke, proposed the formation of special units of elite infantry that could operate from landing craft and the Prime Minister quickly approved the concept. The Army rose to the challenge and raised the manpower from volunteers across all regiments who were posted to Scotland for commando and amphibious training. In fact, just months before Churchill became Prime Minister the War Office had approved the formation of ten independent companies who underwent rigorous training in preparation for the abortive Expeditionary Force to Finland. These units trained near Fort William and were mainly drawn from Army volunteer reservists and in concept they were to be the forerunners of the Commandos.

As the Commandos began training, plans were already under way for the invasion of Europe and it was considered that every operation could provide more experience and knowledge to incorporate into the ultimate seaborne assault. At this time there was still very little specialist shipping available to support major amphibious operations. Between the wars there had been little enthusiasm for substantial investment in the capability, primarily because of the failure of the Gallipoli landings in 1915 which saw Allied troops, including Royal Marines, pinned down by enemy fire in the Dardanelles. The Gallipoli assault was a bold plan aimed at seizing the Dardanelles to open a route for the capture of Constantinople. It had all the characteristics of a modern amphibious operation, but lacked detailed planning and preparation. This resulted in calamity and the landing force found itself trapped on the beaches. A catalogue of fundamental errors crippled the operation: there was inadequate reconnaissance, the element of surprise had been lost, and command and control was muddled. By contrast the withdrawal was brilliantly executed; the commanders had learned much from the mistakes of the earlier landings.

Gallipoli highlighted the risk of failure in mounting poorly planned amphibious operations and resulted in the widely held view that such operations were not feasible in the face of the enemy. An exception was the raid on Zeebrugge in 1918 by a battalion of Royal Marines. The use of an amphibious force on the heavily defended mole at Zeebrugge was an outstanding success, but the legacy of Dardanelles still inhibited any real enthusiasm for such operations. It was perhaps not a surprise, therefore, that by 1939 Britain had little more than a doctrine for 'Combined Operations' and a few experimental landing craft.

Although the Army Commandos had been raised in 1940 it was not until Lord Louis Mountbatten succeeded Admiral Sir Roger Keyes as Director of Combined

The classic Commando image. Armed with a Thompson sub-machine gun this sergeant scales a mountain during training in Scotland. The first operations for this special new force took place late 1941 and were then followed with raids in Norway and at St Nazaire.

Operations on 27 October 1941 that they mounted their first major raid. Unlike most military operations, which follow the maxim that 'no plan sustains contact with the enemy', this first raid went almost exactly to schedule. Operation 'Archery' took place in late December 1941. It was a high-risk mission based on an amphibious assault on German-occupied Norway. The area was not heavily defended and provided the first opportunity for Britain's new Commando force to prove it could hit back hard at the enemy.

The targets of the raid were two islands on the coast of Norway – Vaagso and Maaloy. The prime aim of the operation was to demonstrate that Britain was still capable of offensive action. Its tactical objectives were to destroy a German coastal battery on Maaloy, kill as many Germans as possible, and then demolish the main fish factories and a German radio station in Vaagso. No. 3 Commando was selected for the operation. The unit had formed at Plymouth in July 1940 with a strength of 35 officers and 500 men, all Army volunteers, under the command of Lieutenant-Colonel John Durnford-Slater, a stocky Royal Artillery officer who had a 'work hard, play hard' approach to military training. In early December 1941, No. 3 Commando, was reinforced by 100 men of No. 2 Commando and formed the raiding force for the Vaagso islands.

A Royal Navy task force, including the cruiser HMS *Kenya*, the destroyers HMS *Onslow*, HMS *Oribi*, HMS *Offa* and HMS *Chiddingfold*, as well as two infantry support ships HMS *Prince Charles* and

Earl Mountbatten was appointed Director of Combined Operations in October 1941. He was keen to see the Commandos demonstrate their skills as early as possible and in November that year the first operation took place.

The insignia of Combined Operations was retained and is used today.

Training was intense and as well as the physical aspect of the course the Commandos underwent extensive military training to familiarise them with working in small groups. Seaborne assaults in particular were rehearsed time and time again.

HMS *Prince Leopold*, assembled at Scapa Flow where final preparations took place. The Commandos used maps and models to coordinate the details of their attack and on Christmas Day the force sailed for Sullom Voe in the Shetlands. Poor weather delayed the final leg of the deployment, but late on Boxing Day the ships sailed with fighter and bomber support from RAF bases at Wick, Scotland, and Sumburgh in the Shetlands. Early on the morning of 27 December the Commandos launched their attack.

The naval bombardment started at 0848hrs with HMS *Kenya* firing a salvo of starshell (illuminating rounds) which lit up the island of Maaloy. The Commando assault force was divided into five groups: Group 1 landed at Hollevik, Group 2 at south Vaagso, Group 3 on Maaloy, Group 4 was a floating reserve and Group 5 landed at Kapelnoes Point. With naval gunfire supporting the raid, No. 3 Commando assaulted all three targets at once and hit the enemy with the element of surprise. As the men landed naval gunfire was lifted and ten RAF Hampden bombers from No. 50 Squadron swooped in, dropping smoke and high-explosive bombs. But despite their surprise the Germans put up fierce resistance and the Commandos were forced to fight from house to house to secure the island. By 1020hrs the Commando reserves had to be committed.

The coastal gun batteries were silenced and the Commandos had struck at the heart of the German garrison in Vaagso. At 1500hrs as the arctic sun was setting the Commandos were back aboard ship with 71 Norwegian volunteers and 150 German prisoners. They had suffered 19 dead, 52 wounded and had killed more than 100 Germans. The raid was a resounding success, the destroyers sank nine merchant ships and an armed German trawler was captured, along with the ship's secret code books, which provided invaluable intelligence.

German High Command was stunned by the raid and as result sent an additional 30,000 troops to Norway to guard coastal areas against further Commando raids. The concept of using Commando troops in an attack to inflict a significant blow against the Germans and force them to reinforce the area with more troops who could have been deployed elsewhere had proved to be very cost-effective. For the first time since Dunkirk the enemy in Europe had been given a bloody nose. A team from the newly formed Army Film and Photo Unit had joined the Commandos and the success at Vaagso was fully exploited, with pictures in newspapers and film reports at cinemas.

In early 1942 Earl Mountbatten was made an Acting Vice-Admiral, an Honorary Lieutenant-General and an Honorary Air Marshal with a seat on the Chiefs of Staff Committee. He was to become one of the four military commanders in charge of the direction of the war and this marked a new era for Combined Operations. Mountbatten was keen to develop amphibious operations. The Combined Operations Development Centre (CODC) was the source of new ideas and evaluated specialist equipment. The CODC was Mountbatten's brainchild and included the Royal Marines Boom Patrol Detachment who were to mount a remarkable raid on Bordeaux in December 1942. Only a year earlier during the battle for Crete (1941) Mountbatten's ship HMS *Kelly* was sunk and he was picked up from the sea. As Chief of Combined Operations in 1942 he was keen to promote a new wave of Commando raids, the first of which was to be against the German base at St Nazaire.

One of the major benefits the Germans had gained in overrunning France in 1940 was the ability to use the French Atlantic ports to intensify the attack against Britain's vital supply lines. The focus for Combined Operations now centred on these ports, particularly St Nazaire. The German naval campaign had inflicted serious losses on the Royal Navy in the Channel and St Nazaire with its massive dry dock was of strategic importance as a maintenance base so that the powerful battleships, including the *Tirpitz*, or the battle cruisers *Scharnhorst* and *Gneisenau*, could break out into the Atlantic.

Plans for a pure Commando raid were abandoned because of the geographical location of the base and its dry docks, which stood on an estuary of the River Loire with only one deep-water channel covered by four coastal gun batteries. The difficulties of approach included the problem of overcoming mudflats, only possible at high tide with a very shallow draft craft. St Nazaire was the only base where the large German ships could be maintained in dry dock. It was also the most heavily defended port on the Atlantic coast and a force of 6,000 German troops was garrisoned there. Captain John Hughes-Hallet of the naval planning staff reported that any vessel used in an operation at St Nazaire would have to be 'lightened' so that she could steam straight up the Loire and over its sandbanks. Aerial photographs showed there was no boom protecting the dry-dock gate, nor were there any barbed-wire entanglements.

In February 1942, Lieutenant-Colonel Augustus Charles Newman was selected to command and plan the raid, codenamed Operation 'Chariot', while demolition parties were formed of volunteers from Nos 1, 3, 4, 5, 9 and 12 Commandos. The objective was to land a small task force of Commandos in a daring night raid on the U-boat and dry-dock base, destroy it and inflict as much damage as possible on the port. The Germans believed St Nazaire was secure from assault and considered any plan to attack it as 'suicidal'. However, Combined Operations listed the dry dock as the prime target. The members of the unit involved in the operation had been warned of the high risks and were given the invitation to stand down. None did.

HMS *Campbeltown*, a former US Navy destroyer, was the key to the plan. The warship was stripped inside to reduce her draught in the water. She was to ram the dry-dock gates and the explosives in her hull would be ignited later. Army Commando teams aboard support vessels would travel with *Campbeltown* and as the destroyer hit the dock gates the force would assault prearranged targets. Additional Commando groups aboard the warship and the crew of the vessel were to abandon it. Timers would be set to explode hours later.

The Commandos moved to Falmouth in Cornwall for their final preparations. But Combined Operations staff were concerned that the mission might be compromised by German spies in the UK. Working in close liaison with the Special Operations Executive they created an elaborate deception plan which indicated that the Commandos were in fact heading for operations overseas.

It was vital that each team knew the exact details of its role in the real raid. Dress rehearsals were held at Devonport Dockyard in Plymouth, the closest in appearance and layout to St Nazaire. Then late on 27 March the force, headed by HMS *Campbeltown* with eighteen gunboats in support, all packed with Commandos, sailed into the Loire estuary. The profile of the warship, a fifty-year-old US destroyer, had been altered to make her look like a German vessel. She also flew the German ensign. As HMS *Campbeltown* approached the port in darkness she came under intense fire, but made it to the dry-dock gates against the odds. Many of the supporting fleet launches were hit by gunfire and a number of Commandos were killed. The destroyer also took heavy casualties during her approach, but rammed the dry-dock gates at 0134 on 28 March. Just after the impact demolition parties set their charges, while the assault parties attacked German gun emplacements. Once the charges were set, the Commandos and the destroyer's crew attempted to withdraw to rendezvous with motor launches. Against overwhelming enemy fire the raiding force suffered heavy losses. Many men were injured or captured, while a handful escaped. As the battle ended the Germans boarded the warship to search for more Commandos. They thought the raid was over, but then at 2330hrs the explosives ignited. *Campbeltown* was full of Germans and it was later revealed that more than 400 died in the explosion. The armada of 18 gunboats that escorted the *Campbeltown* had been decimated – just 7 returned to Falmouth in Cornwall. The Royal Navy lost 85 men killed and 106 captured, and of the 241 Commandos involved 59 were reported killed or missing and 109 were captured.

The outstanding achievement of Operation 'Chariot' was acknowledged with the awarding of five Victoria Crosses to participants of the mission. They were: the commanding officer of HMS *Campbeltown* Lieutenant-Commander Sam Beattie, who was praised for his gallant seamanship; Sergeant Tom Durrant, who received a posthumous VC for his outstanding courage and valour in defending his colleagues; Lieutenant-Colonel Charles Newman, who headed the Commandos; and Commander Robert Ryder, who led the Navy element. All four received their VCs for their perseverance under fire. The final VC was awarded to Able Seaman William Savage who silenced every gun aboard a harbour defence boat which was attacking *Campbeltown*. His medal was also posthumous.

'Chariot' is still described as 'the greatest raid of all time', primarily for the geographical and tactical hurdles which the planners and raiders had to overcome in order to achieve their mission. British losses at St Nazaire were very high but the raid had crippled the Germans' ability to maintain their front-line warhips. The dry dock was not repaired until 1952.

After the success of 'Chariot', a similar raid was planned for June 1942 on St Valéry-en-Caux. It was codenamed Operation 'Foxrock'. A hundred men from No. 12 Commando were to destroy dock gates and other installations, but the operation was aborted when German aircraft spotted the assault force crossing the Channel.

In 1942 the largest seaborne landings yet undertaken by the British were mounted against the Vichy French naval base at Diego-Suarez in Madagascar. This was no raid but a full-scale invasion with three brigades supported by carrier-based aircraft and naval gunfire. The idea for an operation using Commandos had been germinating since December 1941 when Winston Churchill had suggested seizing Madagascar from Vichy France in order to use it as a possible naval base after the fall of Singapore. Plans for taking the island were drawn up in March 1942 under the codename Operation 'Ironclad'. Men of No. 5 Commando were assigned as part of the assault force and sailed on 23 March, arriving at Durban in South Africa on 22 April.

No. 5 Commando's mission during the operation was to come ashore a few hours ahead of the main assault force and silence two artillery batteries. This task was successfully accomplished; the Commandos took the Germans by complete surprise and captured some 300 prisoners. They then assisted in taking the port of Diego-Suarez. However, additional amphibious landings proved necessary before the entire island could be seized. Some Commandos carried out feints to distract attention away from these landings. Others helped capture the port of Tananarive. Some even acquired horses and formed a 'Commando Cavalry'. By the time the French on Madagascar finally surrendered in November 1942, No. 5 Commando had returned to the UK where they prepared for other operations. The success of Operation 'Ironclad' prevented the chance of the island falling into the hands of the Japanese who, as a

Major-General Robert Laycock, who has been described by many as one of the outstanding wartime leaders, headed Layforce (initially known as Force Z) one of the early Commando units of the war which operated in the Mediterranean and North Africa and into Syria. The unit was disbanded in August 1951 with many of its members forming the nucleus of the SAS in the Middle East. Laycock returned to the UK, took command of Special Operations and succeeded Mountbatten as Chief of Combined Operations in 1943. His brother later headed a separate Commando unit as Layforce 11.

result of their campaign in the Pacific, were beginning to threaten Allied shipping in the Indian Ocean.

Despite this early success, Churchill recognised that it was necessary to mount a larger-scale operation to gain further experience and expand the Commando role before the main invasion of Europe could be launched. Initially, the men who formed the Commando units had been drawn solely from Army regiments, but then on 14 February 1942 the first Royal Marine Commando, No. 40, was raised and more followed in 1943. (The first Royal Marines units were titled with a number followed by the words 'Royal Marine Commando'. Then in 1946 the titles changed to the unit number followed by 'Commando Royal Marines'.)

In early 1942 with just one Royal Marine Commando unit in existence, the main body of the Royal Marines Corps provided manpower for ships of the Fleet, as well as operating a Mobile Naval Base Defence Organisation. The latter force was deployed to Crete to build up defences on the island following the British evacuation from Greece, but soon had to fight its way out after a major German air and seaborne invasion.

Elsewhere a Royal Marines unit called 'Viper Force' was deployed to Rangoon for coastal patrolling. It also had to fight its way out after the Japanese invaded Burma in 1942. Only 58 survivors made it to Calcutta out of the original 107.

The Combined Operations organisation was now beginning to take shape under Lord Mountbatten's direction, and amphibious equipment was slowly being improved. However, there was still a major shortage of specialist shipping and assault craft.

Within just six months of being raised 40 RM Commando saw its first action, but with almost disastrous results. The operation was officially described as a 'reconnaissance in force' and was planned to be no more than a 24-hour raid to see if a port deemed essential to the success of any invasion of Europe could be seized intact. The small fishing port of Dieppe was selected. Its narrow streets and chalk cliffs, almost 100 feet high, were to be the intended target of a Commando and RM Division raid as soon as sufficient craft could be available for the landing. This operation was considered essential because it would test the Allies' amphibious techniques. Later, the RM Division was withdrawn from the plan when direction of the raid passed to the Army's UK Home Forces Command and a political decision resulted in the Marines being replaced by Canadian forces. In addition, a planned intensive aerial bombardment of Dieppe was cancelled, much against the advice of Lord Mountbatten.

Planning staff developed two tactical plans for the Dieppe raid. Both were ambitious. The first involved landing seven battalions of Canadian units on various beaches to the east and west of the town, while the second developed the idea of dropping parachute forces on the flanks in conjunction with a direct assault from the sea on the town itself. As planning continued, the main objective was still to assess the potential for seizing a port and evaluating Britain's amphibious capability.

The final strategy for the attack on Dieppe was submitted to the Chiefs of Staff by Lord Mountbatten on 11 May 1942 and approved by them two days later, with the date for the raid, codenamed Operation 'Rutter', provisionally set for the night of 20/21 June. However, a rehearsal on the Dorset coast on the night of 11/12 June did not go well and a further period of training was considered necessary. The landing forces were assembled for intensive training on the Isle of Wight, and a second rehearsal at the end of June went much better. The raid was then rescheduled for the night of 4 July. The troops embarked on 2 July, but then the weather broke, with strong gales in the Channel which continued unabated until 8 July. The initial raid on Dieppe now cancelled, there was concern that details of the operation would leak out and compromise security, but the raid was quickly rescheduled for August and renamed Operation 'Jubilee'.

Before the cancellation, certain modifications were made to the original plan. Since it was obvious that the weather would be a critical factor, the idea of using parachute troops for the outer flanking landings was rejected, and Nos 3 and 4 Commandos were substituted. They would assault from the sea. It was also decided that because of the risk of heavy casualties among the French civilian population of Dieppe, there could be no preliminary bombardment from the air or by capital ships. The success of the plan would therefore rest entirely on surprise.

On the evening of 18 August, the force weighed anchor and set sail from the shelter of the Solent, from Shoreham and from the little port of Newhaven. The bay at Newhaven was packed with ships: their journey would take all night. The forces employed at Dieppe were far larger than any used on previous raiding operations. The landing included six battalions of Canadian infantry and a Canadian tank regiment, all from the 2nd Canadian Division, three British Commando units, including the newly formed Royal Marine Commando, elements of the American Rangers, men from No. 10 (Inter-Allied) Commando, and a Royal Engineer unit. The naval force consisted of 237 ships and landing craft plus two flotillas of minesweepers, and included no fewer than eight destroyers for convoy work and inshore supporting fire.

This direct assault was charged with destroying German defences within the town, capturing German barges in the inner harbour and sailing them back to England if possible. The barges were to have been used in Hitler's Operation 'Sealion' plan to assault southern England. In 1942 it was feared that they might still be deployed. Further objectives included the destruction of radar installations, the airfield at St Aubin 3 miles inland, and an attack on a German divisional HQ at Arques-la-Bataille, 6 miles inland. The time allotted for these tasks, from landing to withdrawal, was seven hours.

Poor intelligence and a lack of reconnaissance failed to identify the strength of German fortifications in and around Dieppe, and while the Allies were aware of gun batteries that protected the sea approaches into the port, the level of reinforcement of these positions had been underestimated. Anyone approaching Dieppe cannot fail to notice the high cliffs around the port. In 1942 enemy bunkers had been built on these natural vantage points and provided an excellent defence against any seaborne assault. The extent of their reinforcement was immense – they were in effect the first stage of Hitler's developing Atlantic Wall – and even today two of the bunkers on the left of the road are a reminder of the Dieppe operation.

The final plan for the assault called for landings on eight separate beaches, with two outer-flank attacks, two inner-flank attacks and a landing in force by Canadian infantry and tanks directly across the beach, against the port of Dieppe itself. The Allies were aware of the defences covering the sea approaches to Dieppe where two batteries, each with 150mm guns, could traverse through 360 degrees and had a range of 12 miles. They were supported by numerous machine-gun teams.

To secure the flanks, No. 3 Commando's mission was to destroy the coastal defences at Yellow Beach 1 and the Goebbels battery at Yellow Beach 2, while No. 4 Commando was tasked to land and then destroy the Hess battery on Orange Beach 2 and the coastal defences at Vasterival-sur-mer above Orange Beach 1 and behind Dieppe's lighthouse. The Royal Regiment of Canada was to land at Blue Beach and the Essex Scottish Regiment on Red Beach, supported by Canadian armour. Both Red and Blue beaches were overlooked by more coastal defences which were heavily dug in and defended on the high ground. The Royal Hamilton Regiment was scheduled to land at White Beach, while the South Saskatchewan Regiment and the Queen's Own Cameron Highlanders would go ashore at Green Beach. 40 RM Commando would go ashore in support of the Canadians. Marine Alan Saunders who served with X Company, 40 RM Commando and landed at Dieppe, said: 'The plans changed and changed. There has been comment that 40 RM Commando were a reserve force, but we were never a reserve. We were always scheduled to go ashore on White Beach. Our landing at White Beach was delayed because the Canadians were under heavy fire.'

The beach in front of the town was made up of stone and shingle. It was also fairly steep. To this natural defensive site the Germans had added wire and mines. In addition, it was shadowed by coastal guns which could trap any invaders in the water before they had time to get ashore.

H-hour for the first troops to land was 0450 on Wednesday 19 August 1942. All went well until 0345, when the invasion fleet was only 7 miles from the French coast and still completely undetected. Then, quite without warning, a starshell illuminated the small group of landing craft carrying No. 3 Commando onto Yellow Beach 1 at Berneval. They had run into a small German convoy and the element of surprise was totally lost. The convoy, escorted by armed trawlers, opened heavy and accurate fire on the landing craft and their escort vessel, the steam gunboat SGB5. Within a few minutes SGB5 was badly damaged and the landing force compelled to scatter. To make matters worse the battle had raised the alarm on shore.

Only seven of the twenty-three craft carrying 3 Commando managed to get ashore at Berneval, and of the men who landed, no fewer than 120 were killed, wounded or captured. Major Peter Young (later Brigadier), the second-in-command of No. 3 Commando, and eighteen of his men were in the only craft to reach Yellow 2. With great courage he decided that if the Commandos could not silence the guns then they should harass them as much as possible with sniper fire. The men of No. 3 Commando stalked their way towards the huge weapons, hid in wheat fields and sniped at the coastal guns from within their arcs of fire. The Germans directed their huge artillery towards the Commandos, but the guns could not be depressed sufficiently to fire at the necessary 150-yard range and the blast passed over the heads of Major Young's men. The 18-strong force had pinned down more than 200 Germans and had ensured that the battery was sufficiently 'tied up' to prevent it adding to the firepower directed at the main seaborne assault forces. It was an outstanding action.

The six-gun battery near Varengeville was situated almost 1,000 yards inland near Orange 1 and the weapons above Orange 2 were the target of No. 4 Commando, commanded by Lieutenant-Colonel the Lord Lovat. Earlier he had mounted rehearsals at Lulworth Cove in Dorset. The plan was to assault the guns with two forces. The first was under the command of Major Derek Mills-Roberts and would land on Orange 2 to attack the position from woods at Vasterival. At the same time Lord Lovat and his team would land at Orange 2 near Quiberville and sweep behind the battery from where they would launch a charge.

The planning and preparation paid off for Lovat and his men and their operation went well, although it was a very bloody assault. After intense mortar and small-arms fire from Group 1, who laid down smoke to confuse the enemy and give Lord Lovat's Group 2 the

Dieppe was the first raid for the newly formed
40 RM Commando. The unit travelled in
French gunboats and transferred to landing
craft for the final approach and assault on
White Beach. They were ordered ashore to
support the Canadians who had been trapped
by German gunfire on the beach. As they
started their assault on White Beach, they too
came under intense bombardment. Landing
craft were hit and only a few actually made it
to the shore. It was here that the unit's
commanding officer Lieutenant-Colonel Pictor
Phillips put on a pair of white gloves and
semaphored the other assault boats to turn
back. He was killed. *Top*: French gunboats
can be seen; *centre*: the scene off Dieppe;
bottom: a Canadian tank lies abandoned on
the beach.

cover to attack, Lovat fired a series of white Very lights to signal the start of the assault. With bayonets fixed, B and F Troops led by Captain F. Gordon Webb and Captain Pat Porteous charged the gun emplacement. Webb's right hand was shattered by a mortar fragment and he was left firing his pistol with his left. The assault teams quickly placed charges on the weapons' breech blocks and underground magazines. The battery was then set alight. It had been a costly operation with many Commandos killed, but this aspect of Dieppe was a success. Lovat and his men made their way back to Orange 1 under constant and heavy fire, and eventually made the rendezvous with their landing craft.

In Dieppe itself the advantage of surprise was lost. The cliffs on the flanks of the town were heavily defended and the main force, attempting to land on Dieppe beach with inadequate fire support, was badly mauled even before it reached the shore. The men had barely got out of their landing craft before suffering casualties. To add to the chaos the force commander, Major-General Roberts, had received conflicting radio reports about the progress of the assault and the German air force was now active overhead. It was clear that all was not well, but details of what was actually happening were very difficult to obtain, not least because the beaches were obscured by the heavy smokescreen laid to shield the offshore fleet from the coastal batteries.

A decision was made to commit 40 RM Commando to White Beach on the understanding that the Canadians had established a foothold and were doing well.

Commandos pictured returning from an early raid. In the formative years equipment and weapons varied a lot. Many of these early raids were named after their commander, such as Fynn Force of No. 12 Commando, which was named after its South African Captain Fynn. The Royal Navy played a key role in getting these raiding forces to their objectives and bringing them home again.

Then it suddenly became clear that the Canadians had not secured White and in fact were in serious trouble. It was decided that any attempt by HMS *Locust* and the Royal Marine Commandos to enter the port was to be abandoned, but the Marines on *Locust* were already attempting to close Dieppe when this order was given. 40 RM Commando prepared to land in support of the Canadian Royal Hamilton Light Infantry on White Beach, quickly transferred from the French gunboats into assault landing craft and were escorted into Dieppe by HMS *Locust*.

The Marines were now in seven landing craft with their commanding officer Lieutenant-Colonel Joseph Picton-Phillips leading the way. The small force quickly came under accurate fire; a Royal Navy officer described the assault as a seaborne version of the Charge of the Light Brigade with shell blasts constantly hitting the waters around the flotilla as it made its way towards White Beach. Near the shoreline the firepower increased and it became clear that any attempt to reach the beach would end in death, but the Colonel refused to turn back until he had made every possible effort to land. His lead craft ran onto the shore as the others remained in the water. The Colonel knew the situation was hopeless. Enemy gunfire controlled every aspect of the beach and in an outstanding act of bravery Picton-Phillips put on a pair of white gloves and semaphored to the other assault boats to turn back. He was shot and killed

Royal Marines who served with 40 RM Commando at Dieppe parade at Norton Manor camp in Taunton, home of today's 40 Commando RM, to remember their colleagues. Lieutenant-Colonel Graham Dunlop and his RSM WO1 Willy Stocks are on the left.

in a matter of seconds. Alan Saunders, from X Company, 40 RM Commando, takes up the story:

The operation had been cancelled in June and we thought we were going on an exercise until we saw live ammunition. We sailed on the night of 18 August and once aboard the briefing started. It was a lovely evening, calm and a flat sea. After some nosh we checked our ammunition and grenades and checked it again before trying to get a bit of sleep. In the early hours we heard some gunfire. No. 3 Commando we later learnt had been hit by a coastal convoy.

Our briefing orders had focused on bringing the naval barges back to the UK and breaking into a naval intelligence centre and recovering some documents from a safe. We were to go ashore in French boats and everyone was very confident. The French *chasseurs* were laying off their entrance to the Channel and the plan was that HMS *Locust* would sail ahead of us and smash the boom across the harbour. She was under heavy fire, but made at least three attempts to crash the boom.

By now the firepower was increasing and the order came to transfer from the *chasseurs* into LCAs and land on White Beach. We understood that the Canadians had broken through and established a foothold on White Beach, but they hadn't. As we approached the beach I was firing my Bren, but we had little chance. The Canadians who had tried to make it in had been hit hard and the sea was full of burning landing craft and every few seconds another shell landed. It was hell. We wore battledress and steel helmets – the only action in which we wore them as I remember. We carried 100 rounds of ammunition, six grenades, a toggle rope and scaling ladders. We were just two hundred yards off the shore when our LCA was hit and burst into flames. Some of us reached the shore, but realised there was nothing we could do but get the hell out of it.

I can still see that scene in White Beach. It was bloody chaos, bodies floating everywhere, debris across the beach and the constant rattle of gunfire being aimed at us. I suppose you would call it the killing fields. I was in a group tasked to get into the German naval headquarters and secure sensitive papers which the intelligence boys had highlighted, but obviously it never happened.

Our little group swam back out to sea and hung onto floating debris. We were picked up four hours later by HMS *Brocklesby* having ditched our ammo boots, helmets and anything else that was too heavy. The *Brocklesby* was on survivor patrol and so we stayed in the area for some time and then the Germans started to direct their fire at us, which was the last thing we needed. But there were some lighter moments.

The ship picked up our Quarter Master Wiggie Bennett, who obviously looked after all our stores, and guess what? He was still wearing every bit of his kit including steel helmet and ammunition boots – we couldn't believe it.

When we finally got back to Pompey we gave our names to the sailor manning the survivors' registry and went off to be debriefed. We looked a strange bunch in

Survivors of the Dieppe operation return to Britain. Losses had been terrible: of the total landing force of 6,100 more than 60 per cent were injured or killed. Those who had made it ashore were shot or taken prisoner. A few others swam to safety and were picked up by Royal Navy ships.

borrowed sailors' clothing, but the personalities of those of us who came back had changed at White Beach. The Commando had been blooded.

Ken Morris was also serving with 40 RM Commando at Dieppe, although he never got ashore. He recalls: 'I was aboard the *Locust* and as I remember very few made it to the beach and most of those were taken prisoner. Others swam away and were picked up by the Navy.'

The total landing force at Dieppe was 6,100. Of those, 4,963 were Canadians. In human terms, with a casualty rate of more than 60 per cent the operation was a tragedy. However, the lessons learned were to prove vital to the success of the landings at Normandy two years later. The principal legacy of Dieppe was the realisation that it would not be feasible to capture a port by frontal attack. Thus the seeds of the idea for the prefabricated Mulberry harbours used in the Normandy assault were sown. Dieppe also highlighted the fact that considerable firepower would be required to support any future landings. After the disaster at Dieppe Mountbatten faced criticism for the heavy losses but the vital lessons learned in Operation 'Jubilee' made a significant impact on the success of Operations 'Neptune' and 'Overlord' two years later in Normandy.

In 1943 Mountbatten was appointed Commander South-East Asia and concentrated on the reconquest of Burma. The battle was primarily land based and was conducted by General Slim with initial victories at Imphal and Kohima. The Commandos played a vital role in the Arakan, the coastal region of Burma that offered a route to the centre of the country.

The Dieppe raid and the constant stream of Commando attacks infuriated Hitler and the German command. On 18 October 1942 the Führer issued an instruction to his senior field officers which in essence directed that any Commando soldier captured should be shot whether he was carrying arms or not. Known as the Commando Order it read: 'From now on all men operating against German troops in so-called Commando operations are to be annihilated to the last man. This action is to be carried out whether they are soldiers in uniform, or soldiers with or without arms, whether fighting, surrendered or seeking to escape, whether they come into action by ship, aircraft, or parachute. No quarter is to be given.' Despite an instruction that the order was for senior commanders only and that it was classified 'not to fall into enemy hands', the text of the document soon leaked out and gave the British military a clear indication of the impact these operations were having on the German military machine. The order was savagely implemented by the Germans who murdered many Commando soldiers taken prisoner in the course of the war, including the Royal Marines captured on Operation 'Frankton' – the daring 'Cockleshell Heroes' canoe raid on shipping at Bordeaux. The canoe raid took place in December 1942. It was the first raid for the newly raised Royal Marines Boom Patrol Detachment (the forerunners of today's Special Boat Service): their mission was to canoe 71 miles up the Gironde river and attack German shipping. These enemy vessels were valuable and important targets as they were bringing in vital supplies from the Far East and the majority had evaded Royal Navy submarines.

While Dieppe had seen the first action of Royal Marine Commandos, in 1942 the Royal Marines as a whole were not being fully utilised. Apart from a few amphibious raids and its Fleet commitment, the RM Division, as it was called, lay idle. 'I have heard nothing of the Royal Marine Division since the Royal Marine Brigades went on the Dakar Expedition', wrote Churchill in a minute dated 3 June 1942. 'What are the plans for its employment?' The Admiralty got the hint, and under pressure from Lord Mountbatten, the Chiefs of Staff Committee broke up the Royal Marines Division and the Mobile Naval Base Defence Organisation and in April 1943 started to form them into Commando units. (In 1940 Royal Marines had been sent to capture Dakar in an attempt to persuade the French African colonies to support de Gaulle. The attack was called off, partly because the Marines did not have adequate craft.)

The Commando Training Centre at Achnacarry near Fort William had already been established in 1942 to provide a specialist training package for Army volunteers. The camp was isolated in the Scottish Highlands and provided the perfect location for a rugged and realistic training. Lieutenant-Colonel Charles Vaughan, who was serving with the Commandos, was selected to command the centre and assigned a strong team of officers and NCOs who worked as instructors. Soon the name Achnacarry became well known throughout the military; it was regarded as the most strenuous training centre run by any of the Allied forces.

Fresh recruits at Achnacarry. The lead soldier, a warrant officer, carries a Thompson sub-machine gun. After training many Commandos discarded their helmets and wore a woolly hat or their green beret, although at Dieppe and other operations some Commandos chose to retain their helmets.

Following the establishment of Achnacarry, no soldier could join a Commando unit or wear the coveted green beret without passing a six-week gruelling physical course. During the three years of its existence thousands of troops from all regiments of the British Army, the Royal Marines and Allied forces, including the US Rangers, completed the Commando course. All recruits who arrived at Achnacarry were volunteers and the first units of Commandos were made up of officers and soldiers from all regiments and corps of the British Army. Among the instructors were Captains Fairbairn and Sykes – two former Shanghai police officers who had returned to England to act as unarmed combat instructors. Calling on their experience in the Far East, they devised a new fighting knife and recommended it to the War Office. The first batch was made by Wilkinson Sword in January 1941 and the weapon was named after its creators. The Fairbairn-Sykes was issued to all Commando units and was based on a 7-inch carbon steel blade and a ringed handle grip.

Achnacarry had a single aim – to produce fit, tough, disciplined soldiers who could work in small teams. They needed to be highly motivated and able to work on their own initiative. Like today's Royal Marine Commando trainers, the wartime instructors strove to encourage the volunteers to have confidence in their ability. Speed marching was a high priority: they ran, on average, 7 miles in an hour, carrying full equipment and rifle. Their equipment was cumbersome and very basic compared to comfortable modern combat clothing and the equipment issued to today's Commandos.

One of the tests the volunteers faced was an endurance course that included a 5-mile run followed by an assault course and then a range test in which their shooting ability was measured. Today the Commando Training Centre at Lympstone still uses this selection test, although in an adapted format.

Scotland offered excellent natural training facilities – Ben Nevis, Britain's biggest mountain, was on Achnacarry's doorstep. There was plenty of potential for river-crossing training and all types of boats and landing craft could be deployed on Loch Lochy. In addition, a limited

The Fairbairn-Sykes fighting knife. During the war, the knife was issued to all Commando units. This picture, posed for the War Office, was taken in 1943 and clearly shows the shaped handle and the 7-inch blade.

phase of survival training was included in the course and the remoteness of the camp allowed live ammunition and explosives to be used.

After six weeks, the successful volunteers were awarded their green berets and the newly fledged Commando soldiers marched away from Achnacarry to Spean Bridge railway station and then on to join their units. They often went straight overseas and into action. Throughout 1942 and for the rest of the war Royal Marines joined their Army colleagues on the course. Many never returned to Britain, but all are remembered at the memorial at Spean Bridge. Today a special illustrated display is maintained at the Spean Bridge Hotel. The area also has strong links with surviving Commandos. (In 1993 the Commando Association was awarded the Freedom of Fort William and Lochaber.)

The Commando Training School at Achnacarry turned out 40, 42, 43, 44, 45, 46, 47 and 48 RM Commandos – 40 and 43 to serve in Italy, 42 and 44 to Burma and the remainder to work up for the invasion of France. This operation was a significant development in Royal Marines history as it marked the transition from pure 'sea soldiers' and infantry to Commando forces.

It is important to mention here another wing of Royal Marine operations that was vital in the support of the amphibious assaults that delivered the Commandos into action. As staff at Combined Operations developed their doctrine it was clear they would need to expand their support units, including landing craft crews and engineers. They formed a Royal Marines Armoured Support Group, in which troops manned 'Centaur' tanks. These could fire from landing craft while approaching the shore, then land and deploy from the beaches in support of troops.

Throughout this period amphibious operations continued to be developed. In November 1942 the biggest amphibious operation to date took place: the invasion of

Vichy French North Africa in Operation 'Torch'. British and US seaborne landings took place along the coast from Casablanca to Algiers. While the landings were relatively lightly opposed, valuable experience was gained from their sheer scale. The operation was the first to be supported by tri-Service beach groups who directed naval gunfire support from the shore. Combined Operations Pilot Parties (COPP) were also used for beach reconnaissance and communications.

'Torch' had been planned to link up quickly with the British 8th Army and capture Tunis, but in reality progress was slow. The Germans flew in reinforcements from Sicily and it was not until May 1943 that the Allies secured North Africa. There was now an urgent requirement to get a foothold in Europe. Allied commanders considered two strategic options. The first involved an assault on Sardinia, opening up opportunities for a strike into southern France and central Italy, while the second plan focused on an invasion of Sicily and then a push into southern Italy. Having studied the ground, the Allies took the second option. Fundamental to this plan was the fact that an assault on Sicily would draw German forces further away from their supply routes and compel the enemy to stretch their logistics resources. In addition, Allied fighter aircraft based in Malta were within range of some areas of Sicily and would be able to give greater protection to a seaborne assault on the island.

The capture of Sicily, Operation 'Husky', was planned as a pincer movement, with the US 7th Army invading on the west coast between Licata and Scoglitti and the British 8th Army on the east coast south of Syracuse. Both 40 and 41 RM Commando units were to land on the left flank of the Canadians with No. 3 Commando landing on the north-east extremity of the invasion, tasked to neutralise machine guns overlooking the beaches where 5th Division was to land.

The Marines of 40 RM Commando had undergone extensive amphibious training in Scotland in which they perfected their landing skills, particularly at night. They were billeted around Kilwinning in Ayrshire with other Commandos under Brigadier Robert Laycock's command. Laycock, a Royal Horse Artillery officer, had commanded Nos 7, 8 and 11 Army Commandos, who had mounted raids in the Mediterranean and were named 'Layforce'. The force made numerous raids before being disbanded in 1943 when Laycock was promoted to the command of Combined Operations.

40 RM Commando sailed from the Clyde at the end of June 1943 ready for their role in Operation 'Husky'. This was the first major opposed assault of the Italian campaign and many who took part were surprised that enemy opposition was initially light. Alan Saunders, who was serving with 40 RM Commando, remembers Sicily well:

We went to Ayrshire in March 1943 to prepare for Sicily and took part in numerous exercises. We were very much a unit having been blooded at Dieppe and presented with our green berets at Weymouth in the October of 1942. After extensive training we embarked in the MV *Derbyshire* off the Isle of Arran and sailed for Sicily. It was a bloody mess, we landed on the wrong beach and I was shot up. On the second day I was hit by mortar shrapnel and eventually evacuated to Algiers and later back to the UK.

For this Marine the war was over and a couple of years later he was medically discharged, which was a great shock. He said: 'It was the most bitter day of my life when I left. I loved the Corps and would have stayed as long as possible, but it wasn't to be.'

By August 1943 Sicily had fallen to the Allies and subsequent landings were planned for the Italian mainland at Reggio, Salerno, Termoli and Anzio. However, because the long Italian coastline was ideal for bold outflanking amphibious operations, the campaign was characterised by missed opportunities, of which the landings at Anzio were the prime example.

In September 1943 the 8th Army crossed the Messina gap, a 3-mile stretch of water between Sicily and the toe of mainland Italy. There was little opposition to the landings because the Germans had withdrawn to defensive positions. As part of the Salerno plan 41 RM Commando and No. 2 Commando were tasked to land near the village of Vietri, silence the coastal batteries and then move inland to seize the narrow pass at La Molina, which would give the Allies control of the road running between Salerno and Naples. Meanwhile, US Rangers would land at the fishing village of Maiori and move 6 miles inland into the hills to hold the Nocera defile, overlooking the road to Naples. The US 5th Army, commanded by General Mark Clark, which was composed of the 10th British Corps and the US VI Corps, would then sweep through the mountains and cut off Salerno from Naples by D+4. But the German commander, Field Marshal Kesselring, was convinced that Salerno was the main objective of the Allies and reinforced the area with forces from the eight combat divisions available to him. This included a panzer division which he ordered to dig in on the high ground overlooking Salerno Bay.

Both 41 RM Commando and No. 2 Commando embarked on the *Prince Albert* and went ashore in the early hours of 9 September 1943, No. 2 Commando landing first at Marina Cove beaches, followed by 41 RM Commando. No. 2 Commando, commanded by Major Jack Churchill, led the initial assault to the gun battery on the high ground above the beach and quickly captured six prisoners. Then as dawn broke the Commandos began to meet heavy and sustained resistance. They pushed on and took positions around two viaducts near the village of Vietri and the Molina Pass, which was flanked by several hills. These became known to the Commandos as Castle Hill, Hospital Hill and White Cross Hill.

German resistance was fierce and the Commandos held their initial positions but were then forced to withdraw. The Commandos attacked the position again and this time the Germans withdrew. This skirmishing continued for several days as 41 RM Commando and No. 2 were forced to hold on without reinforcements while the main landings came under intense fire, particularly from the German panzers dug in and overlooking the bay.

Casualties mounted. Regular fire fights took place as the Commandos fought to control the various hills and the Molina Pass. After one intense battle in which 41 RM

Commando sustained heavy casualties, several troops of No. 2 Commando scaled the steep-sided Dragone Hill, driving out German machine-gunners who had inflicted the losses. But the respite was short-lived. The Germans pounded the hill with mortar shells and were able to bring in more machine guns. The Commandos only regained the feature after another bloody fight that cost 100 lives. Later, they were withdrawn and replaced by 43 RM Commando and No. 9 Commando who had now landed in Italy. In the words of one Marine who served with 41 RM Commando: 'At Salerno we had an easy landing but then it was lively, the hardest time 41 had had, or ever had. Losses were very heavy.' In fact, of the 738 Commandos of 41 and No. 2 who went ashore in mainland Italy on 9 September 1943 only 372 returned to Sicily.

The Germans had established a defensive line running across Italy from the north of the Garigliano river through to Cassino and across the Apennines to a point south of Ortona. After the US 5th Army's breakout from Salerno beachhead and the advance of the British 8th Army from Taranto, the Germans fell back to this line and put up a stubborn defence. As the enemy retreated from Salerno it was decided that the Commandos should seize the port of Termoli on the estuary of the River Biferno. It was thought that the Germans might make a stand here and if they could be outflanked they would be forced to continue their withdrawal, allowing the Allies to maintain their advance. In September 40 RM Commando and No. 3 Commando, having been withdrawn after landing near Reggio, were selected to carry out the operation with elements of the Special Raiding Force. The small force sailed from Sicily and reached Bari on 30 September where they were briefed.

The mission was daring and demonstrated what could be achieved by using an amphibious force to leapfrog forward. At this point the 8th Army was in contact with the enemy south of the Biferno. The Commandos were tasked to take the port and hold it until the 8th Army could cover the 15 miles to Termoli and link up with the landing force. On 3 October the Commandos came ashore and caught the Germans totally by surprise. It had been a rough night and the enemy had not expected a landing, let alone under such conditions. There was little German opposition, although 40 RM Commando was involved in a series of skirmishes throughout the town before digging in at various locations. By dawn the Commandos had taken 500 prisoners. A number of German Army supply trucks driving towards Termoli were ambushed by the unit as more British forces arrived. They included the 56th Recce Regiment and advanced units of the British 78th Division and the Argyll and Sutherland Highlanders.

Then there was a lull of almost a day until the enemy counterattack commenced with a vengeance: the Germans were determined to retake Termoli. The enemy assault began on D+2 and the situation deteriorated very quickly. Heavy rain washed away the bridge erected over the Biferno by the British engineers and Termoli was cut off from the 8th Army. The recce unit had taken a prisoner from 26th Panzer Division who indicated the combat capability of enemy forces in the area. The Argylls, who were dug in around a church, were forced back and German tanks rolled towards the Commandos' position in an olive grove. An artillery barrage on the enemy was called in; later that day Kittihawks strafed the German positions and bombed the tanks. The Commandos were ordered back into the town as the remnants of 16 Panzer Division moved into the olive groves and dug in for the night.

The next day, 6 October, 40 RM Commando held off the final German attack. The 38th Irish Brigade arrived in Termoli, the Germans were rounded up and the route was open for the Allies to push towards the Gustav Line. General Bernard Montgomery arrived to congratulate the Commandos and told them they had saved the situation.

C/Sergeant Ken Morris recalls his time at Termoli:

We went ashore in KDs [khaki drill] as I recall. The weather wasn't very good but it wasn't that bad. We didn't expect it to be so quiet, but there was a fair bit of skirmishing. Many of the Germans were packed aboard trains waiting to travel north on leave. They had been retreating through Italy and used their armour to destroy bridges and roads so as to make life difficult for us. They knew exactly what they were

Commando training was at its busiest during the first couple of years of the war as Achnacarry aimed to train sufficient numbers of men to join units bound for operations in Sicily, Italy and Burma as well as those preparing for the invasion of Europe.

Green Berets of No. 9 Commando pictured aboard a Jeep at Anzio in 1944. No. 9 Commando took part in the action at Garigliano River estuary in December 1943 and worked extensively alongside 43 RM Commando.

doing. When their panzers advanced on us it could have easily been a different story, but by then the Army had linked up with us. It was a tough few days. Later we went into Yugoslavia, Greece, Corfu and Albania. In fact I believe apart from No. 2 Commando, we [40 RM Commando] were the only British troops to fight in Albania.

Despite the fact that it was the first Allied step back onto continental Europe, the Italian campaign was seen as less important than the establishment of the long-awaited second front in France. With the enemy withdrawing to prepare positions across the Italian peninsula two Allied divisions were landed at Anzio in January 1944 behind the German defensive front. The landings themselves took the Germans by surprise but because of indecision and vacillation the Allies remained on the beachhead too long and failed to break out. This gave the enemy time to mount a heavy counterattack and within two months the assault had bogged down into a stalemate which was only broken when a link up with the main Allied force was achieved.

The wealth of experience collected in the amphibious assaults in Norway, France and Italy was to provide the knowledge necessary for the successful planning of the D-Day landings in June 1944. D-Day came just two days after the Allies liberated Rome.

TWO

FROM D-DAY TO VJ DAY

'As we sat in the landing craft, I think it is fair to say that everyone was scared stiff.'

Corporal Ken Parker

The greatest amphibious assault in history, the Allied invasion of German-occupied Normandy, was launched on 6 June 1944. It had taken four years to plan and with the Commandos at the forefront Operation 'Neptune', the naval assault phase of 'Overlord', punched a hole in the enemy's defences that eventually provided the route to victory in Europe. Since Dunkirk in 1940 preparations had been under way for the invasion of Europe and the Commandos had played their role, striking along the enemy-held coastline, mounting deception attacks to distract Hitler's commanders and, of course, launching the raid on Dieppe in August 1942, which provided valuable lessons for D-Day.

The detailed planning for a cross-Channel amphibious operation began in late April 1942 under the codename 'Round-Up'. Admiral Sir Bertram Ramsay was appointed naval commander, although he soon left to plan and command the 1942–3 series of Mediterranean amphibious operations. A small staff continued to establish the necessary UK infrastructure requirements for 'Neptune', providing headquarters at Portsmouth and Plymouth, landing craft bases, maintenance facilities and loading yards.

In May 1943 Prime Minister Winston Churchill met President Franklin D. Roosevelt in Washington at the Trident Conference where they confirmed their decision to undertake a full-scale invasion of Europe. Now it was up to the military commanders to select an invasion site. The Germans expected any invasion to strike around Calais and the Allies decided to utilise the enemy's suspicions. An elaborate deception plan was drawn up to indicate that the Pas de Calais had been selected as the site for an Allied landing. The charade included phoney reconnaissance raids, the formation of dummy British Army units in south-east England with fake landing craft and inflatable tanks, and an elaborate covert campaign to hoodwink enemy spies in the UK.

German commanders poured more resources into the Calais area to reinforce it. By the time the Allies were ready to mount the invasion nearly 45 per cent of the enemy's strength, which would otherwise have been deployed on the Eastern Front, had been drawn west to guard against a potential invasion. Meanwhile, Allied planners looked further down the coast for their 'real' invasion beaches. They selected stretches of land between Cherbourg and Le Havre as the key sites for the assault. These areas were within easy reach of Allied air bases in southern England and the sea crossing for the amphibious force was the shortest available if the Pas de Calais was ruled out.

In May 1943 the Commander-in-Chief, Portsmouth, Admiral Sir Charles Little, was appointed Naval Commander-in-Chief (Designate) for the invasion of Europe and was made responsible for the preparation of the naval plan. At the end of June, a conference (codenamed 'Rattle') was held in London, chaired by Vice-Admiral Lord Louis Mountbatten and attended by, among others, US and Canadian Army representatives. This conference reached definite conclusions about the planning, training and equipment required for 'Neptune', including the need for artificial harbours. Later, in August, the strategy based on the information and conclusions generated by 'Rattle' was approved by the Combined Chiefs of Staff at the Quebec Conference.

As planning for the operation continued, a number of Commando raids were launched in 1943 against the French coast, aimed at gathering intelligence and capturing prisoners who could provide vital information for the Allied assault. In autumn the same year further raids were made in Norway which forced the Germans to divert troops from their fortifications along the French coast, particularly in Normandy, to reinforce their units in parts of Norway. These attacks helped to confuse and distract the enemy and supported the overall deception plan intended to convince the German High Command that any Allied invasion would focus on the Calais area.

Admiral Ramsay became Allied Naval Commander Expeditionary Force (ANCXF) of the operation in October 1943 and with General Montgomery, who was now Commander-in-Chief of the 21st Army Group, he spent weeks heading planning conferences that reported to General Dwight Eisenhower, the overall Supreme Allied Commander of 'Overlord'.

The initial joint plan (which covered all aspects of naval, army and air force units assigned to the operation) was issued on 1 February 1944, followed on 15 February by the naval outline. Provisional naval orders were issued on 2 April and, on a very limited scale, sealed orders on 24 April. By now preparations were well advanced and an exercise, codenamed 'Fabius', was staged to test the basic embarkation arrangements. 'Fabius' covered ports on the south coast from Felixstowe in Suffolk to Plymouth in Devon and round to South Wales. While the planning went well, bad weather meant the exercise had to be cut short. There was now just a month before the invasion was due to take place.

As planning for 'Neptune'/'Overlord' intensified, forces moved closer to the coast and in May Admiral Ramsay and Montgomery moved to Eisenhower's headquarters at Southwick House. This former stately home, hidden away in its own grounds at Portsdown Hill near Portsmouth, was now the communications nerve centre for the main embarkation.

On 8 May, Ramsay informed General Eisenhower that 5 or 6 June were the earliest acceptable days for launching 'Neptune', with 7 June as a standby in extreme

The Germans' Atlantic Wall consisted of beach defences and coastal gun emplacements. These wooden stakes, designed to prevent vehicles and armour advancing, were wired together and Teller mines were distributed to delay any assault further.

circumstances. Officers were told to open their operational orders on 25 May and three days later were informed that the Supreme Commander had decided on 5 June as 'D-Day'. Then at 0415 on 4 June as storms raged in the Channel the decision was taken to delay by twenty-four hours in the hope that the weather would improve.

The Germans believed, as had the British at one stage, that the Allies could never mount a successful major invasion without first capturing a port. As a result German coastal defence was centred around the Channel ports. Nevertheless, they had not neglected to fortify the Normandy beaches which were protected by a series of defensive obstacles that formed part of the Atlantic Wall. The initial fortifications were built in late 1941, but from 1942 a stronger line was constructed along the coast, similar to the Siegfried Line on the Franco-German frontier. The key ports were greatly reinforced, while tank traps and fortified gun positions covered the intervening coastline. On the beaches themselves obstacles were installed below the high-water mark to trap assault craft before they could land their troops. These ranged from projecting stakes to 9 feet high steel and concrete tetrahedrons linked by a network of minefields. However, they proved less formidable than originally planned and by June 1944 were still not complete.

The perceived threat of an Allied seaborne landing around the Pas de Calais continued to tie down large numbers of enemy troops and vital resources. The number of phoney radio messages was increased to convince the Germans that any indication of landings in Normandy must be a feint. Thus, a substantial part of the German Army's reserves was held back awaiting the expected main assault on Calais.

However, in spite of the deception plans, the preparation and the experience of the previous four years doubts still remained. An attack by the US Marines in the previous November on the tiny Pacific island of Betio in the Tarawa atoll reminded the Allies of the casualties that could be suffered in an assault on a well-defended beach. On an island the size of New York's Central Park the Marines lost more than 1,000 men and double that figure were wounded in a 76-hour running battle before the Japanese defenders were overcome.

Tarawa and the legacy of Dieppe made it clear that it was essential to ensure that the Allies got ashore and off the Normandy beaches as quickly as possible. This meant confirming that the beaches would allow the landing craft to get in close enough to disembark their troops and determining whether the sands would be firm enough to support armoured vehicles. It was also necessary to establish the exact layout and extent of the underwater obstacles. Therefore, long before the invasion, frogmen and Combined Operations Pilotage Parties carried out recces of the enemy coastline to obtain this data. The information was vital to the invasion force and in the months prior to D-Day it allowed planners to modify and adapt drills and procedures. Those involved in 'Neptune'/'Overlord' rehearsed each part of the landings from the loading of vehicles and stores to the beach assault itself. As little as three months before Operation 'Neptune' was launched landing trials were still taking place at a site in north Devon which had been specifically chosen because of its similarity to the Normandy beaches. Here, at Instow, the Combined Operations Experimental Establishment's (COXE) techniques for waterproofing vehicles and handling stores were developed. Copies of the Normandy obstacles were also built and methods devised to overcome them. (The base still exists as a trials and development centre for amphibious operations.)

Principal among the equipment being tested were amphibious armoured vehicles designed to break through beach obstacles and breach static defences. Inspired by Major-General Sir Percy Hobart and developed with knowledge based on the experiences at Dieppe and North Africa, they were known as 'Hobart's funnies'. They included tanks fitted with flame-throwers, mine-clearing flails and fascines or bridges for crossing ditches. Others were designed to lay metal trackways across beaches to prevent following vehicles from bogging down in the sand. This equipment proved highly successful for both the British and the Canadians. In contrast the Americans, who did not adopt the vehicles, experienced greater difficulty in advancing from their beaches.

One of the biggest problems to overcome was the shortage of landing ships. These craft fell into two categories – the LSI (Landing Ship Infantry) and the LST (Landing Ship Tank). Both had been specially developed for assault landings and were mass-produced in the USA for service with the Royal Navy under Lend-Lease agreement. But there was still insufficient specialist shipping for the size of the operation contemplated in Normandy. Winston Churchill telegraphed the US Army Chief of Staff, General George C. Marshall, in early 1944, stating: 'The whole of this difficult question only arises out of the absurd shortage of the LSTs. How it is that the plans of two great empires like Britain and the United States should be so much hamstrung and limited by a hundred or two of these particular vessels will never be understood by history.' In the drive to resolve the shortage, merchant tankers were converted to landing ships by cutting away their bows and fitting retractable causeways. Specially designed shallow-draft vessels fitted with guns and rockets for close-in fire support were also produced to make up the shortfall in conventional vessels.

Because of the lack of adequate ports along the open stretch of the Normandy coast chosen for the landings and the difficulty in capturing those that did exist, as events at Dieppe had demonstrated, it was necessary to provide shelter and large-scale unloading facilities to support the invasion until such time as a major port could be seized. To meet this requirement artificial 'Corncob' breakwaters and 'Mulberry' harbours were produced in two separate projects. Corncobs provided breakwaters by scuttling old ships – four veteran warships and fifty-four merchant vessels – off the assault beaches. The five shelters these created were codenamed 'Gooseberries' and were to be laid between 7 and 10 June with the aim of forming a lee for the smaller craft and also to serve as bases for maintenance and repair parties. The two Mulberry harbours were far more ambitious in concept and execution. They were designed to preclude the need to capture a port and gave sheltered anchorage in an area equivalent in size to Dover harbour. They could handle 6,000 tons of stores and 1,250 vehicles per day. The life of the two harbours was to be ninety days. (Elements of these structures in fact lasted much longer and half a century later Royal Marine coxswains from the assault ship HMS *Fearless* had to steer their landing craft carefully through the remains of the Mulberry harbours as they spearheaded a D-Day anniversary commemoration in 1994.)

Each Mulberry comprised three main components. The Bombardons were 200-foot floating, steel, cruciform structures moored end-to-end offshore to reduce wave energy and provide shelter for a deepwater anchorage. Phoenixes were concrete caissons, uniformly 200 feet long but varying in displacement between 2,000 and 6,000 tons sunk on the 30-foot line to form breakwaters for the inner harbour. The third element was a

Commandos land on D-Day, 6 June 1944. Prior to the Commandos' arrival, armoured and tracked vehicles landed with the aim of providing firepower for the infantry troops in the main force. When the Commandos came ashore some of the units carried bicycles while some others carried small motorbikes. The motorbikes, as seen here, were used by despatch riders to relay information between Commando units if communications failed.

floating pier known as a Whale. The Phoenixes also provided accommodation and a platform for anti-aircraft gun positions. The Whales, the floating pierheads, piers and roadways within the port, were prefabricated steel and concrete structures which were assembled on arrival. Four Whales were lost as they were towed across the Channel in bad weather. In order to fuel the huge volume of vehicles unloaded from the anchorages, an oil pipeline, codenamed PLUTO (Pipeline Under the Ocean), was laid on the Channel bed. It was hoped that this would reduce the congestion ashore in the landing areas. There would be one Mulberry on Gold beach and one on Omaha. Gold beach, a British bridgehead where the 50th Division landed, was on the right of the British landing points in the centre of the seaborne assault stretching from Les Roquettes through to Arromanches and Port-en-Bessin. Omaha, where the second Mulberry was positioned, covered the area from Port-en-Bessin through to St Laurent and Point du Hoc.

In May 1944 a troop from No. 10 Commando carried out raids along the Pas de Calais coast to gain information on the types of mines being used by the Germans while at the same time continuing the deception plan that any invasion would strike at this part of France.

As the final plans were made ready it was announced that the Allied force was to be commanded by General Dwight Eisenhower, the Supreme Allied Commander for Operation 'Overlord', while General Montgomery would command the landing forces of British, US and Canadian troops. US and British airborne troops were to lead the D-Day landings in a combined parachute and glider assault. Their mission was to secure and protect the flanks of the seaborne assault, seize strategic objectives 6 miles inland and prevent the Germans from trapping the main assault force at the beachhead. US Airborne divisions were tasked to fly in over the Channel and drop 6 miles inland between Quineville and Brevands on the night of 5/6 June. They would be followed at dawn by an infantry division which would land at Utah beach. The British 6th Airborne Division was to drop on the banks of the Orne with a glider unit seizing the Bénouville bridge (Pegasus Bridge) in a *coup de main* shortly after landing. With the flanks secure to protect the seaborne assault, the main invasion force would come ashore under an umbrella of air and naval superiority, but intelligence had highlighted that the beaches were littered with obstacles, many of which would be obscured by the high tide.

By 1944 the Commandos were well organised and assigned to four Special Service Brigades (also known as Commando Brigades). 1st Special Service under the command of Brigadier the Lord Lovat was in Britain preparing for 'Overlord' and included Nos 3, 4 and 6 Army Commandos as well as 45 RM Commando. The 2nd Special Service was in the Mediterranean and consisted of Nos 2 and 9 Army Commandos as well as 40 and 43 RM Commandos. The 3rd Special Service was about to depart for the Far East and included Nos 1 and 5 Army Commandos as well as 42 and 44 RM Commandos. Finally, 4th Special Service was also in the UK and preparing for D-Day under the command of Brigadier 'Jumbo' Leicester. It was a dedicated Royal Marine brigade consisting of 41, 46, 47 and 48 RM Commandos. In total there would be three Army Commando and five Royal Marine Commando units taking part in the landings.

arines of 45 RM Commando check their equipment at a camp prior to departing for Normandy. Many Commandos took bicycles to Normandy to provide an element of limited mobility, though a lot were left on the beaches. 45 RM Commando had to race ashore with Lord Lovat's Brigade to link up with the airborne troops at Pegasus Bridge.

At Normandy the 1st and 4th Brigades were earmarked for quite different tasks. Brigadier Lord Lovat was to land his 1st Brigade on Sword beach on the left flank and seize the port of Ouistreham before pushing forward through German lines to link up with the 6th Airborne Division 6 miles inland. His force would subsequently come under the 6th's command. The men of 4th Special Service Brigade were deployed to the west of their colleagues in 1st Brigade and ordered to seize a number of coastal resorts at Lion-sur-Mer, St Aubin, Luc and Langrune, as well as providing troops to extend and link the flanks of the British and Canadian landings on Gold and Juno beaches and towards the flank of the American landings on Omaha. 47 RM Commando of 4th Special Service Brigade was to operate on the extreme right of the British Army, away from its Brigade. Its mission was to seize the fishing town of Port-en-Bessin. 46 RM Commando was to be a Brigade reserve and would go ashore on 7 June, the day after the main landings.

In the weeks leading up to D-Day a series of events clearly indicated to the men of the task force that the invasion was close. They had been constantly exercising their roles, but now something different was happening. On 1 April 1944 a visitor ban was imposed within 10 miles of the UK's south coast, and foreign, diplomatic and courier movements to and from the UK were suspended. Assembly areas for the vast army were established at almost every port from Falmouth to Dover. Marine Bill Andrews had joined 47 RM Commando at Herne Bay after training with Holding Commando at Wrexham in North Wales. Having completed extensive amphibious exercises to refresh its skills the unit was ordered to move to a concentration area at Southampton known as Camp C19. Andrews said:

We had leave for a couple of days then the Field Security Police sealed the camp – no one out, no one in. The briefing sessions began with scale models, maps and bogus names for the areas we were going. We were to be the link with the Americans on the extreme right of the British and Canadian sectors and had to capture Port-en-Bessin where the undersea pipeline [PLUTO] would come ashore. We were issued with all kinds of escape items – hacksaws that looked like pieces of chewing gum, handkerchiefs with maps overprinted, small pocket compasses and some French money. We were soon on the move and boarded ships anchored off the Isle of Wight. We were surrounded by naval vessels, fast attack craft, destroyers and the new rocket ships which we hadn't seen before.

Before dawn on 6 June small units of naval Commandos landed ahead of the main force to mark the landing sites and ensure that the assaulting units found their designated beaches, while off the coast of Normandy Royal Navy midget submarines got into position on the surface ready to use their navigation lights to provide additional direction for the first assault waves. As the invasion troops headed for France few were aware of the potential for Allied success that lay ahead of them. Their minds were focused on their immediate task after a period of total isolation in the assembly areas.

In the hours before the landings, troop ships, transporters, tank carriers, barges and assault craft quietly slipped anchor and, escorted by warships, were led across the Channel to their objectives. The landings themselves were timed for about 0600hrs but the precise details varied according to the tide. The British, for example, opted for a half-tide landing that presented a longer assault across the beach but also exposed underwater obstacles and defences.

On D-Day daybreak was at 0515hrs with sunrise listed in the orders as at 0600. It was a cold morning. The sea off Normandy was packed with landing craft and assault ships bobbing around as they headed towards their landing beaches. Gunfire support from battleships constantly pounded the enemy on shore, planting a vivid memory of battle for those who took part.

The assault forces assigned to land on the five beaches were given a code: Force S would land at Sword beach, Force J at Juno, Force G at Gold, Force O at Omaha and Force U at Utah. Among some of the first ashore were the obstacle-clearing units and Marine Cyril

Opposite: Neptune, the naval assault phase of the 'Overlord' operation, required months of planning and preparation. The 'Neptune' armada included more than 5,000 warships and amphibious assault craft which landed the troops across five beaches at Sword, Juno, Gold, with the US landing at Omaha and Utah.
Inset: Commandos wearing their green berets and armed with Thompson machine guns on D-Day.

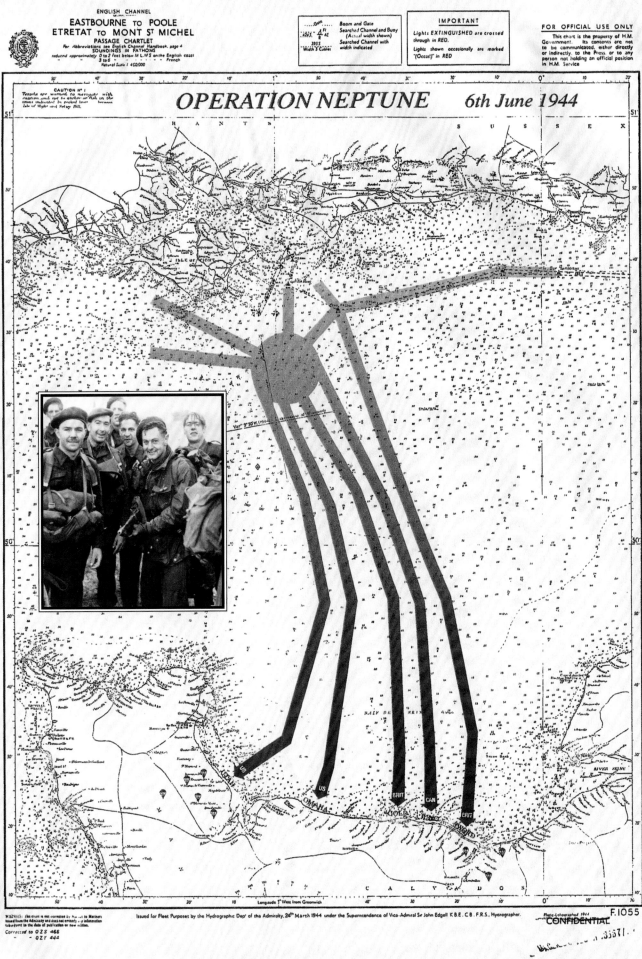

Commandos of the 1st Special Service Brigade (Lord Lovat's force) go ashore at Normandy. Armour that had grounded on the beach or been hit by German guns can be seen ahead of the advancing Commandos. All are wearing their green berets.

'Ichabod' Penberthy, who joined the Royal Marines in 1942, remembers the scene well. His landing craft made for the shore under an intense bombardment of enemy fire from Gold beach as the first assault went in on the morning of 6 June 1944. He said:

I was dead scared. We all were. Make no mistake about it a lot of prayers were said that day. Shells were landing all around us, landing craft were being hit. It was bloody horrendous.

From the beach for almost a quarter of a mile out to sea the water was full of cordite, blood and bodies. The scene I saw that day was a mass of devastation and will always be with me. It impressed my mind and I will never forget it.

When we took in the first wave of infantry the shelling was intense and after we dropped our troops we waited off the beach, but we were being stonked by such heavy enemy fire that the coxswain turned the landing craft away from the beach with the intention of mooring alongside an LST.

Suddenly we were hit and I was in the water. It was all very sudden. I was just going into the engine room when it happened. Another landing craft picked us up, but I couldn't remember anything of the event. I think I had shell shock. Eventually I was shipped back to hospital in Portsmouth and then to a Canadian military hospital in Hampshire.

Several months later when I rejoined my unit a mate of mine was on the main gate and collapsed when he saw me. It turned out they had all been told I was dead and I had been posted missing presumed dead. When the landing craft was hit it turned over and it was believed that the crew were all killed.

The stories of D-Day nearly all include anecdotes of the journey across the Channel and the vivid recollections of cramped conditions aboard the landing ships, the apprehension of what was going to happen and the terrible odour of sea sickness which made others ill. 'Everyone was ill. The smell was awful and if you hadn't been sick you soon were the minute the stench hit you. The mixture of engine oil, being tossed around in the sea and that terrible pong was with me for years. When the ramp went down we couldn't wait to get out and I fell straight into the sea', recalls Wally Manton who served with 48 RM Commando.

In the first sixteen hours of the invasion 132,815 (75,215 British and Canadian and 57,600 American) troops were landed. Allied troops poured onto five beaches codenamed Sword, Juno, Gold, Omaha and Utah. The seaborne assault was mounted from an armada of more than 5,000 ships and amphibious assault craft that packed a 50-mile stretch of the French coastline. The British alone sustained 3,000 casualties, while the US recorded 6,600 injured.

While Commando reconnaissance units were among the first ashore, the main force of Green Berets in the Special Service Brigades were not in the first wave. To penetrate the German defences, known as the Atlantic Wall, the first Allied forces ashore were a mixture of tanks, infantry and special armoured vehicles (including 'Hobart's funnies') allotted the task of seizing beachheads and penetrating coastal defences. The Commandos in fact came ashore more than an hour after the first wave when the beaches should have been secured. Their initial tasks were to overwhelm strongpoints and extend the beachheads to either flank. At Gold beach, east of Omaha, 47 RM Commando was to go ashore with the British 50th Division. Further east on Juno 48 RM Commando would come ashore at St Aubin. Then between St Aubin and Ouistreham 41 and 45 RM Commandos would land with the British 3rd Division, while 46 RM Commando was held back as a reserve.

The commanding officer of 47 Commando, Lieutenant-Colonel Charles Phillips, had the task of capturing the vital harbour of Port-en-Bessin where the undersea pipeline would come ashore. The unit was the last of the Commandos to land in France but its job was probably the most difficult.   The harbour at Port-en-Bessin was surrounded by chalk cliffs between Omaha where the Americans landed and the westerly end of Gold where the British landed. The countryside around the port was heavily defended and a frontal attack was deemed impossible. 47 RM Commando was to land near Arromanches and march more than 10 miles inland through enemy-held terrain to

Commandos of the 1st Special Service Brigade (also known as Commando Brigade) move inland from the beaches on D-Day. This force included Nos 3, 4 and 6 Army Commandos as well as 45 RM Commando.

assault Port-en-Bessin from the rear. The battle was later highlighted by General Sir Brian Horrocks, who commanded XXX Corps in the battle for Normandy and was described by Montgomery as 'one of the best Corps' Commanders of World War Two', as typifying the courage and spirit of the Commandos during the Second World War.

Bill Andrews of 47 RM Commando recalls:

We were about 4 miles from the French coast, the sky was full of black smoke and gunfire which seemed to explode in a crescendo then die down. Over the Tannoy system we heard 'to the landing craft'. I turned to a colleague and wished him the best of luck and we shook hands.

Once in the landing craft and in the water we were signalled into formation and started the run in, which was uneventful until a few hundred yards off the beach. Then it was plain they did not want us to land, as their shells started to come

Royal Marine Commandos move inland from the beaches on D-Day. These Commandos have a number of bicycles with them and it appears some are wearing helmets while others have opted for their berets. More than 3,000 of the British troops landed on 6 June 1944 were injured or killed.

down on us with good accuracy – many hitting the water nearby and exploding on impact.

Suddenly the landing craft bumped and the ramp went down and we were heading out. We saw an armoured bulldozer working like hell, then all of a sudden he got a shell right in the side. We headed for a gap in the sand dunes and passed bodies on the beach – one had a direct hit in the chest. At the time I didn't feel sorry – but I do now.

We came up to an enemy machine gun bunker and a German officer was just sat there, cap and all, dead as a door nail. It was a strange scene. There was a strong smell of diesel fuel and when the shells hit a strong smell of cordite filled the air. Then suddenly the sun would come out for a short period.

Ken Parker, a Corporal with 47 RM Commando, will never forget the intense fire that the landing craft came under as they neared the beach. As well as dodging incoming shells the coxswains had to try to avoid subsurface obstructions and the sand dunes that could suddenly bring a boat to a halt:

As we sat there I think it is fair to say that everyone was scared stiff. I'm not afraid to say that I almost wet my pants and I am sure a few prayers were said that morning. The firepower that the enemy put down was awesome and accurate. It was as if they were expecting us.

Those coxswains were fantastic. They had our lives in their hands and many of them were killed. In fact of the fourteen craft which supported our landing twelve were hit. Then as the ramp went down it was a case of run like hell across the open beach. It was a good 500 yards and as we were still under fire you didn't have time to stop and think, you just ran to the top of the beach for cover.

As you ran though the water you tried to help anyone who had fallen down, but it was an awful scene as the landing craft came into the beach. Some were hitting dunes, others were taking direct hits. It was very intense. As we regrouped we discovered our troop officer, Lieutenant Peter Winter, had been injured and we then came under the command of Captain Pat O'Brien.

A lot of weapons and equipment had been lost in the landing and so it was a case of pick up whatever you could from the beach and prepare to move off through German lines. By now we had lost about sixty of the Commando as we pushed out of the beachhead towards the feature known as Point 72, a large feature which overlooked Port-en-Bessin. By late on the 7 June [D+1] we had liberated the port.

The attack on Port-en-Bessin was a classic operation. The commander used all aspects of support fire to fix the enemy before starting his advance. The assault was timed for 1600hrs and at 1400hrs the naval bombardment began. It was followed at 1550 by a squadron of RAF Typhoons who made their attack on the enemy defences. However, as the Marine Commandos broke cover of Escures they came under heavy sniper fire and while 47 Commando was able to secure the port, the enemy troops on Point 72 mounted a fierce counterattack, killing a number of Marines and taking others prisoner. The following morning a recce patrol was sent in and discovered that the enemy had fled. The battle for Port-en-Bessin cost the lives of at least sixty Royal Marine Commandos and the local community has never forgotten its liberators. The survivors of 47 RM Commando are regularly welcomed back and treated as dignitaries by the fishing community.

As 48 RM Commando went ashore at Juno it also met fierce opposition. The Germans had built concrete strongpoints in the villages and 48 landed right in front of one. Landing craft were crippled by enemy fire as Marines jumped over the side and the beach was littered with casualties. The plan was for 48 to land after the last wave of the Canadians was ashore. Headed by the North Shore Regiment, the Canadians were equipped with tanks and when 48 RM Commando landed it should have simply passed through the Canadian lines and headed towards Langrune where it was due to link up with 41 RM Commando which had landed on Sword.

Lieutenant-Colonel Jim Moulton had taken command of 48 RM Commando just twelve weeks before D-Day. It was a difficult period for the Colonel who had to steer his unit through intensive training before the men went into billets at Gravesend. Then late in May 1944 the unit moved into the Commando marshalling camp for briefings and final rehearsals. On 5 June, 48 RM Commando sailed from Warsash in Hampshire bound for France. Major Dan Flunder was unit adjutant and found himself making the crossing in a wooden landing craft which tossed its occupants around on top of the water instead of sailing through it – everyone was sick. It was a grey, windy morning and as he approached the coast he got his troops on deck to breathe the fresh air and prepare for the assault.

The sea was covered with craft as far as the eye could see, from big ships to small landing craft. The shore line was under bombardment, there were sinking craft which had been hit and things didn't look particularly good.

I didn't realise we were under small arms fire until I saw two men collapse and fall overboard. By then it was too late to beat an undignified retreat behind the superstructure and it was only later that I found the neat group of three bullet holes in the map board across my back. They must have passed between my arm and my body during that period.

The storm had caused the tide to be further in than we had expected, so the beach obstacles were in many cases still covered and craft were hitting them. The CO got our mortars firing smoke from the landing craft. They used sand bags as a baseplate and in a pitching sea hit the beach, sending clouds of smoke scudding down the beach to obscure us from enemy fire.

We hit a submerged obstacle and I wasn't halfway down the ramp before a big wave carried the boat off the obstacle and somersaulted me into the sea. The next thing I remember is finding myself walking up the beach, wet through of course, and with some of my equipment torn off, including my pistol, but still clutching my ash walking stick.

I must have had a blow on the head because some minutes had elapsed. When I got to the top of the beach, I was violently sick from the combined effects of swallowed salt water and inhaled smoke. I found most of the troops I had last seen in the landing craft, with the signallers already trying to establish communication with the rest of the unit.

The beach was covered with casualties, some Canadian, some ours. The surf was an incredible sight with beached and half-sunken landing craft wallowing in each successive wave. Just offshore other craft were stuck on obstacles or sinking and some which had been hit were burning.

Some tanks struggled ashore from a bad beaching and some were bogged down in the shingle. They had their turret lids closed, and those that were moving were heading for a large group of wounded. I was sickened to see one run over two wounded men.

I was furious and ran back down the beach and hammered on the turret to try to get somebody to put his head out. This had no effect at all, so I stuck an anti-tank grenade in its track and threw myself flat while it went off. That stopped the tank and saved the wounded.

The landings on Juno have been described by many as a 'murderous affair', with some landing craft taking direct hits at the beachhead and others disgorging troops who ran straight into the line of fire. A Canadian soldier recalls seeing a landing craft approach and then as the ramp went down a German machine gun opened up, chopping down a row of Royal Marine Commandos before they had a chance to get their feet wet.

As the landing progressed 48 RM Commando suffered heavy losses. The commanding officer lost almost 40 per cent of his manpower through death, injury or troops simply not being able to land. In a situation that could easily have deteriorated into total disaster Lieutenant-Colonel Moulton's leadership gave the Commando the direction it needed. Walking up the beach, almost in defiance of the enemy shelling, he grouped his senior officers at the sea wall and began to take stock of the situation. Suddenly a mortar bomb landed close by and splinters struck him in the arm, hand and leg, but he chose to ignore the injuries and began sorting out his men.

The Commando set off for Langrune determined to meet up with 41. Again the men encountered heavy opposition from enemy strongpoints which slowed them up and resulted in more losses. Finally, the Brigade commander, 'Jumbo' Leicester, ordered the Commando to stop and take up defensive positions in anticipation of an armoured counterattack. Major Flunder remembers the advance to Langrune and the sight of A Troop 48 RM Commando led by its commander Major Mike Reynolds. In spite of being hit in both arms Reynolds led his troop ashore, his battledress soaked in blood. 'It was a quite remarkable sight', said Flunder.

The expected counterattack did not happen and the next day Lieutenant-Colonel Moulton took what was left of his Commando into Langrune to capture the strongpoint. Dan Flunder said:

Men who incredibly had swum ashore straggled in for some time. Among them was RSM Travers, who had been swept a long way to the east, landing right under the guns of the Langrune strongpoint.

Later after Langrune we crossed Pegasus Bridge and took up the positions we occupied with the rest of 4 Commando Brigade and 6th Airborne Division for some weeks on the exposed eastern flank of the invasion force.

When we took over our positions at Sallenelles from 4th Parachute Battalion they had just beaten off a heavy German attack and our first task was to clear up the battlefield and bury a substantial number of German corpses before settling down to improve our positions and start a programme of aggressive patrolling.

We had always believed that the secret of a quiet life was to be thoroughly aggressive and dominate the area, but here it was more necessary than ever to disguise our weakness in numbers.

Commandos come under heavy fire after landing on D-Day. Many of the tanks in the initial wave were trapped by German defensive fire and the Commandos were sometimes forced to push forward on their own.

Our main headquarters was a nearby house which was hit by shell fire on our first day in, wounding the RSM and two of our signallers. It was in our Command Post I sat pressed to the earth wall one evening with Ronnie Grant and two of his signallers, trying to stop my knees trembling while we were heavily shelled.

The heaviness of the shell fire suggested an imminent attack, and anyway it was a wet miserable evening. I was greatly impressed by Ronnie's magnificent calm as we did our best to make normal conversation over the noise and against shuddering earth at our backs.

Many years after the war Ronnie suddenly said to me one day, 'You know, I always meant to say something to you that I've never quite got round to. Do you remember one evening we sat in the Command Post at Sallenelles and were heavily shelled? I've always wanted to say how much I admired your calmness that evening, you seemed totally unaffected.'

I was reluctant to spoil such a charming illusion, but honesty compelled me to tell him about my difficulty in keeping my knees still!

Many of the men in 41 RM Commando had seen service in Italy and Sicily before returning to England to prepare for the Normandy landings. The unit, commanded by Lieutenant-Colonel Tim Gray, had the task of assaulting Lion-sur-Mer on Sword beach – the most easterly of the three British beaches. On D-Day, 41 actually landed almost

200 yards west of the intended site. The men came ashore under heavy fire and the beach was littered with burning tanks and debris. Many of the assault battalions were still on the beach. There were bodies in the water, smoke swept across and shells landed periodically. The plan involved the Commando being split into two assault units. Force 1 was to neutralise the enemy strongpoint at Lion-sur-Mer, while Force 2 had the mission of assaulting a heavily defended château west of the town. The initial attack cost the lives of three officers and it was a further twenty-four hours before the enemy position was captured by the Lancashire Regiment.

Just like 47 and 48 RM Commandos the Marines of 41 will always remember the death and destruction they saw as they landed. The regimental sergeant-major was killed and many Marines were fatally wounded. Marine Frank Nightingale, a Bren gunner, was hit as he came ashore and then took another bullet as he fired his weapon from the beach. He recalls, 'There were dead bodies all over the beach.' Later, as the unit made its way to link up with 48 RM Commando and attack the radar station at Douvres, the CO was wounded and the second-in-command killed. Nevertheless, the Commando surrounded the radar station and with the assistance of a troop of tanks, forced 200 Germans to surrender.

Corporal Arthur Hines landed with 41 RM Commando on D-Day. Like everyone else, his unit had gone into isolation at Southampton and then on 4 June boarded landing craft for the trip across to France along with 46, 47 and 48 RM Commandos. In his memoirs he wrote:

We slipped our moorings in darkness and formed a huge invasion fleet. There were cruisers, destroyers, frigates, minesweepers, in fact any type of naval craft you could think of plus hundreds of landing craft. We started off towards Sword Beach in Normandy which was just west of the River Orne.

About halfway across we heard the roar of aircraft, hundreds and hundreds, some towing gliders. It was the airborne forces going over to secure vital bridges some miles inland. The famous 'Pegasus Bridge' was named after the Airborne division 'Flying Horse'.

As dawn was breaking, we went on deck and we could see the Normandy coast. Suddenly the Navy opened with heavy guns to neutralise the German fortifications which were quite awesome. As we got closer to the shore the German guns opened up on us and a number of ships were hit.

We prepared to land, having avoided all the obstacles and mines, thanks in many cases to the frogmen who had gone ashore earlier to remove as many as they could. We moved up the beach as quickly as we could with our heavy equipment, hoping we did not tread on any mines. I saw some of our chaps had been hit and were dead or wounded.

Shells, mortars and machine guns were coming from all quarters. I suddenly felt a pain in my backside and felt something dripping down my leg. I thought that it was blood but found that a piece of shrapnel had pierced my water bottle. The rest of the shrapnel had ripped the whole of the back of my trousers and they were wide open.

Apart from being a bit numb, I felt alright and joined the rest of my troop in Lion. We dug in and prepared to attack a heavily fortified radar station. We had 50 per cent casualties that first day. The next day I found I had difficulty standing up due to the shrapnel in my backside. I went to a field dressing station and a doctor placed a label around my neck and said I would be going to hospital in the UK.

The shrapnel had lodged near my sciatic nerve and I was shipped back to a Canadian hospital near Ascot. Later I rejoined my Troop and was promoted to Sergeant.

Lieutenant Paddy Stevens and a number of men from 41 RM Commando were cut off from the main body of the force by enemy armour. Stevens led the attack, destroying one tank with a grenade before the Germans fled. He later led a fighting patrol that raided a radar station, gaining vital intelligence papers which were of immense value to the unit's later operations. For his outstanding leadership and initiative he was awarded the Military Cross. A famous photograph taken at Normandy shows men of 41 RM Commando lying flat on the beach and includes a lone standing figure. This was Lieutenant Stevens (later Colonel) who, leading from the front, was assessing the next move for his men.

Also on Sword was 45 RM Commando and the Green Berets of the 1st Special Service Brigade commanded by Brigadier the Lord Lovat. On landing the Commandos of 1st Brigade faced an immediate fight because the troops of the initial assault waves were still under German attack on the beaches. Lord Lovat and his troops, who had been piped ashore by Army Commando Bill Millin, quickly cleared the enemy out of Ouistreham and headed for the Bénouville bridge.

Lieutenant Paddy Stevens, second-in-command of A Troop 41 RM Commando, stands on the beach in front of his men. On 6 June 1944 the unit lost 100 men from a total of 450. The majority seen here are wearing their steel helmets and are armed with Lee Enfield rifles and Bren guns.

Commandos of the 1st Special Service Brigade, which included 45 RM Commando, pictured near Pegasus Bridge after linking up with units of the 6th Airborne Division. In the first few days of Operation 'Overlord' the Commandos suffered heavy losses. For example, 45 RM Commando sustained 35 dead and more than 100 casualties.

The airborne troops had secured the bridges and had fought off a German counterattack but were still under fire. Lovat's Commandos reinforced the Red Berets and came under their command for the rest of the operation. The film *The Longest Day* immortalised the Commandos' arrival and Bill Millin playing the pipes. However, he did not play on the bridge over the Caen Canal as the film shows. Sniper and mortar fire rained down as the Commandos ran over the bridge and it was only when they reached the eastern bank that Lovat ordered Millin to play 'Blue Bonnets over the Border'. He did so as the Commandos marched over the River Orne bridge.

45 RM Commando had been tasked to move inland to the village of Merville and occupy the nearby battery which had been attacked hours earlier by the 9th Parachute Battalion. They had seized it and moved on. The Germans then reoccupied the battery, although the main guns had been spiked. Two Royal Marines had in fact jumped with 9 Para – Lieutenant Winston and Marine Donald – and were to liaise between the two units. Just as 45 RM Commando was about to attack the battery Lord Lovat ordered his men to ignore it, hold the village and deny the ground to any German assault.

On the morning of 7 June (D+1) 45 RM Commando was ordered to take up positions around Hauger. Then later in the day the men were tasked to move again and seize the coastal defences at Franceville, which was situated on the far eastern side of the Orne estuary. This meant that they had to move back towards the coast past the Merville area.

The village of Franceville was a small holiday spot with the numerous properties situated north of a main road that ran directly through the resort. The target for 45 RM Commando was the defences on the beach and those further east. The main road through Franceville was codenamed 'Piccadilly' and was to be a reference point for every Marine in the unit during the assault. The advance to the village was bloody: the unit came under intense fire and sustained numerous casualties. The Commandos fought like lions, but faced a series of counterattacks from the Germans who were supported by heavy artillery. The men responded to these attacks until they had almost run out of ammunition. A final heavy German assault, again with artillery support, resulted in Lord Lovat ordering Major Nicol Gray, who had replaced the injured Lieutenant-Colonel Charles Ries, to withdraw.

In the first three days of the Normandy campaign 45 RM Commando suffered 35 fatalities and at least 100 wounded. Awards made for actions during these same

Lieutenant-Colonel Moulton, the commanding officer of 48 RM Commando directs tank fire on the Langrune strongpoint. On D-Day the unit, which had sailed for Normandy from Warsash in Hampshire, lost 40 per cent of its manpower through death, injury or troops not being able to land.

three days comprised one DSO, three MCs and four MMs. Lord Lovat, the Brigade commander, wrote: 'Franceville could not have been a healthy place and 45 RM Commando did a fine job holding up the Hun's advance along the coastal road while the brigade dug in on the high ground.'

Sergeant Arthur Gray, who was serving with 45 RM Commando as part of 1st Special Service Brigade, arrived at Eastbourne with the unit prior to D-Day and after extensive training in north-west Scotland. He said:

Although talk of invasion was in the air and we thought we would be involved, nothing gave an inkling of the role we would take.

Intensive training commenced with beach landings around Eastbourne, Newhaven, Seaford and Pevensey Bay. These landings were followed by attacks on mock batteries and strong points in and around the villages of Wartling, Westham and Herstmonceux.

In late May 1944 came the move to Southampton. The entire Brigade was under canvas in a heavily protected area and with no contact with the outside world. There followed 10 days of intensive briefings with models, photographs and maps all bearing codenames such as Piccadilly, Freeman Hardy and Willis, and others.

There was a final kit check, then on 5 June we left for Warsash harbour. What a sight. It was full of other naval vessels. We boarded our landing craft and I went off for a briefing and then I knew – France it was to be. Maps were issued and the codenames were gone. Each marine was issued with phrase books in German and French.

45 would land at 'Queen Red beach' in the Sword section two miles west of Ouistreham, rendezvous about 800 yards inland and then fight our way to the River Orne and Caen Canal bridges and link up with the 6th Airborne Division who were to have landed by parachute and glider earlier. We were then to take and hold ground around Le Plein and Amfreville, the second objective being Franceville-Plage.

Final briefings took place. A brew of tea and special hot rations were passed around. Despite attempts at humour and leg pulling, all were very tense. The point of no return was now and all were pondering the future.

My own thoughts were – would I land reasonably dry, the landings being at fairly low water. How strong would the defences be? I slept until 0400hrs. As daylight was approaching we sailed past all sorts of warships. At 0700hrs we were suddenly amongst it. Guns were firing, low flying aircraft skimmed overhead. Force S sailed on. No sign yet of the French coast.

But by now we could see the coastline amongst the haze and smoke. The landing craft prepared to run in. B Troop's craft was hit but sailed on. All crouched on the upper deck, we had to grin and bear it as German artillery and machine guns fired at us.

Now we were there – 'down ramps' came the command. I ran down, then in front of me the blast from a shell landing in the sea nearby blew a marine into three foot of water. I and others pulled him ashore. We quickly cleared the beach and made for the rendezvous. Now came the move to the bridges. E Troop followed by A Troop led as we advanced under heavy mortar fire.

The signal was received that the bridges were captured intact but were still under heavy fire. The commanding officer Lieutenant-Colonel Charles Ries was hit and severely wounded. However, the link-up was achieved, green and red berets mingled and the paras were glad to see us. Then came a change of plan, 45 RM Commando was to be detached as it was not clear whether the battery at Merville was in our hands.

As we entered nearby Sallenelles fire from an enemy strongpoint pinned down a section of E Troop with part of recce. I learnt that the battery had been silenced earlier, but the enemy had returned in strength to the nearby village. After some sharp fighting the village was taken.

Lieutenant-Colonel Peter Young, later Brigadier, commanded No. 3 Commando at Normandy and gave a vivid first-hand account of the landings:

The flotilla is steaming ahead, 45 Commando to the starboard, 3 Commando to the port, the craft leaping about like young lambs. Ahead big guns are flashing but as yet not a sound comes back from them.

Gradually the dawn brightens and the mist begins to clear, ahead big ships are silhouetted against the sky. Now we are moving among the great warships roaring out their broadsides, cruisers first, then the battleship *Ramillies* belching forth 15-inch shells – a sight to remember.

We put on more speed, the soldiers forget to be sea sick and then suddenly, with almost magical precision, the columns of craft form into line abreast. Land ahead now – a hundred yards away a column of water shoots into the air, while to port a tank landing craft burns fiercely, ammunition exploding as the crew go over the side. Ashore is a line of battered houses which look familiar from the photographs. They must surely mark our landing place.

Ouistreham is not much more than a thousand yards to port now. Somewhere on the front are the guns that are shelling us; the flashes are visible every few seconds. The beach at last. The ramps are pushed out and hang for a moment above the water. My weight on the starboard gangway submerges it and I find myself in 5 feet of water splashing ashore. Ahead the sand is marked by the track of one of our swimming tanks which has safely crossed the beach enough to explode any mines that may have been there.

46 RM Commando went ashore on D+1 (7 June) as part of 4th Special Service Brigade. On 11 June the Commando liberated Rots and Le Hamel and every year members of the 46 RM Association, along with other Commando associations, return to France to remember their colleagues who died at Normandy. The respect for British

forces' action during the liberation of France is still overwhelming more than fifty years on. In 1999 the 46 Commando Association laid wreaths at the Bayeux and Ranville cemeteries and then paid their respects at Rots and Le Hamel, only to discover that the local mayor had arranged for a marble plaque to be unveiled in memory of the men of 46 Commando who fell liberating the area on 11 June 1944.

On 10 June, four days after D-Day, Winston Churchill set foot on French soil to visit British troops after General Montgomery had reported that he was sufficiently established to receive a visit. The key to the success of the landings had been the devastating effect of the naval and aerial bombardment. On D-Day 106 warships, ranging in size from battleships to rocket boats, blasted the coastline. Total air superiority also enabled Allied aircraft to wreak havoc on the road and rail network, crippling German logistics. However, as the invasion spread out from the French coast and supply lines lengthened, it became imperative to capture a major port if the 'breakout' was to maintain its momentum. The British and Canadians, for instance, were using 12,000 tons of supplies a day, which could not be sustained as the distance of the advance increased.

Marines of 46 RM Commando advance through Delivrande near Caen on 9 June 1944. A French family watches, as the leading Commando sergeant looks towards the camera, his face gaunt with tiredness and the effects of battle. A day later Prime Minister Winston Churchill set foot on French soil to visit British troops.

On 4 September 1944 the Allies took Antwerp, the second biggest port in Western Europe. It was a significant strategic success and allowed them to maintain supply lines to the 2 million troops who were now advancing on Germany. There was a problem, however. The port sits on the River Scheldt, almost 40 miles inland from the sea. At the mouth of the river the huge estuary entrance to Antwerp was controlled by German fortifications situated on the island of Walcheren, which dominated the area with its coastal batteries. Before Antwerp's docks could be used by the Allies, Walcheren, an artificial island recovered from the sea by the Dutch, and its thirty-plus guns would have to be captured and the riverbanks cleared of the enemy. However, this was one of the most heavily defended sections of Hitler's Atlantic Wall.

The force tasked to take Walcheren and the neighbouring islands consisted of 4th Special Service Brigade (commanded by Brigadier Leicester), 2nd Canadian Division and 52nd British Division. 4th Special Service Brigade was now made up of No. 4 Commando, 41, 47 and 48 RM Commandos plus two troops of No. 10 Commando.

The assault, Operation 'Infatuate', was scheduled for 1 November with No. 4 Commando landing on beaches to the south of the island, its primary mission to take the town of Flushing. The Royal Marine Commandos of 41, 47 and 48 landed at the western side of the island, tasked to assault and seize Westkapelle. Walcheren was a mass of dunes and dykes, and the flat island sat below sea level. Around it was one of the oldest and strongest sea defences in Holland. It was 250 feet wide, rose to 35 feet and ran for 3 miles along Walcheren's western shoreline. RAF raiders bombed the dyke in October 1944 and flooded a large area of western Walcheren. Prior to the operation it had been recognised that the strong coastal defences on the island had to be neutralised if the assault force was to have any chance of a successful landing. Further attacks were due to take place days before 'Infatuate' but unfortunately low cloud and bad visibility prevented many of the aircraft from taking off and the naval bombardment from HMS *Warspite*, HMS *Roberts* and HMS *Erebus* had little effect on the enemy gun batteries. Air attacks finally took place on the day of the assault.

The Commandos' raid on Walcheren was truly of David and Goliath proportions – the Germans with their long-range gun batteries built into strong defences looking out to sea and the Allied force in a variety of landing craft and small ships. The enemy blasted the assault force as it approached the shore and 172 Marines and sailors were killed, with a further 200 injured. The result was one of the bloodiest fights the Commandos had ever faced, with 41, 47 and 48 RM Commandos landing under heavy fire. In covering them, the Landing Craft Support vessels had to fight an unequal artillery duel with the German shore batteries and many were sunk or crippled with heavy losses.

Most survivors who served at Walcheren describe the action as the worst they ever encountered. One Commando said: 'Close your eyes and imagine being in a landing craft heading towards Westkapelle and being scared stiff as shells keep pounding the sea around you. The explosions seem to get closer every time the next one lands. You are not really sure how far you have left to run when the landing craft on your port

Above: Commandos prepare to land at Walcheren. Some of the Buffaloes (amphibious tracked vehicles) in which they went ashore can be seen on deck. 41, 47 and 48 RM Commando faced some of their bloodiest fighting of the war at Walchere

Left: Marines of A Troop 41 RM Commando advance through Westkapelle towards their objective, the lighthouse at Walcheren. The assault was described as a hundred times worse than the D-Day landings the Commandos faced an overwhelming hail of German firepower. Walcheren was fina secured on 8 November.

side suffers what appears to be a direct hit. We later saw that the German defences were immense. They just had to sit there and pick us off.'

Marine Ken Parker, who saw action with 47 RM Commando at Walcheren, clearly remembers the landings and the massive hail of German firepower. He said: 'It was a hundred times worse than D-Day. These guys were firing out to sea and they were very good. The big guns that covered the coast were ready for us. Their firepower was immense. We were open targets with nowhere to hide. The shells just kept coming and coming. Dozens of landing craft were hit, it was a sight I will never forget.'

The gaps made in the dykes by the RAF provided access for the Commandos and after a bloody landing 41 advanced towards the concrete bunkers, the leading elements of the units wearing yellow squares on their backs so that the RAF Typhoon pilots screaming to make attacks on the enemy ahead of the unit could monitor the progress of the men. The rocket attacks by the Typhoons provided the vital close-in support that the Commandos required.

Many of the Commandos also went ashore in amphibious tracked vehicles called Buffaloes which deployed from tank landing craft. These vehicles ensured a dry landing and gave some limited protection – they were, perhaps, the forerunners to the modern Brigade's BVs.

Some elements of 41 landed near Domburg and attacked German battery W18 which contained more than 200 troops. The fighting was intense and after the battery was taken the Germans counterattacked but were beaten off. No. 4 Commando, 47 and 48 met fierce resistance but Walcheren was finally secured on 8 November.

In September 1944 the Allies stood on the borders of Germany. Since June they had landed 2 million men on French soil and inflicted massive damage on the enemy. More than 600,000 German losses were reported while the Allies had lost 40,000. Belgium had been liberated and the final move into Germany involved crossing a complex of rivers and estuaries. More than 2,000 Commandos took part in landings at Walcheren and its capture was vital to the logistics support of British and Canadian forces which had now ground to a halt in Holland. The resupply of stores and munitions had delayed operations and the Rhine crossing could not now take place before March 1945.

In order to secure a continuous advance Montgomery and Eisenhower planned to drop airborne soldiers into Holland in an area stretching from Arnhem to Eindhoven in order to secure the bridges. However, the plan stalled when heavy German resistance trapped parts of the airborne force. Then in December 1944 the Germans mounted an offensive aimed at breaking through the Allied front in the Ardennes to divide the US and British forces and destroy them. Both 47 and 48 RM Commandos were in the Ardennes and in mid-January 1945 47 RM Commando raided the island of Kapelsche Veer in the middle of the Maas, which had been held by German paras. The battle raged all night until 47 ran out of ammunition. It was another two weeks before Kapelsche Veer fell when it was assaulted by two Canadian infantry battalions who found the graves of 150 Germans killed by 47 RM Commando.

Throughout the early winter No. 4 Commando Brigade continued to mount operations in north-west Europe. No. 1 Commando Brigade deployed to the Maas area in January and occupied Maasbracht, while 45 RM Commando secured itself in the village of Montfortebeek. Here the Commando was pinned down by enemy fire from well-prepared positions behind the Montfortebeek dyke. The battle that followed took place in bitterly cold weather and over flat, exposed, snow-covered ground. The Brigade was given the task of clearing the enemy from the Division's left flank between the railway and the River Maas. It also had to capture Maasbracht. While the leading elements of the Commando achieved their objective, the headquarters company and the remainder of the unit were pinned down by heavy shelling, trapped in the open ground.

It was here that Lance-Corporal Thomas Harden of the Royal Army Medical Corps, who was attached to A Troop, won the VC. Several Marines had been hit and lay in the snow seriously wounded. Harden crawled forward, dressed their wounds and carried one man back to his troop before returning with a stretcher party for the other

Marines of 48 RM Commando with a Canadian Army unit embark aboard naval craft for a raid across the River Maas in early 1944. After the push through the Ardennes, and the crossing of the Rhine, it was into Germany and the war in Europe formally came to an end on 7 May 1945.

two. As he helped to evacuate the third wounded Marine he was shot through the head and killed. Harden was awarded a posthumous Victoria Cross for his outstanding bravery. 45 RM Commando received an outstanding commendation from the Divisional commander and was later relieved by No. 6 Commando.

The Commandos continued their advance and in March 1945 the first units cross the Rhine. At Becklingden war cemetery a headstone identifies the first soldier to cross the river – Captain Barry Pierce of 46 RM Commando. He was killed on 13 April, but had served with Y Troop in the operation to cross the Rhine on 23 March 1945.

In early April No. 1 Commando Brigade reached Munster and on the 19th the Brigade arrived in Luneberg and prepared for their final assault – a night crossing of the River Elbe, which runs across Germany from Hamburg to Dresden. The crossing took place on 29 April and was made under heavy fire, but the Brigade pushed through enemy positions and resistance finally ended on the 30th. In the early days of May No. 1 Commando Brigade stood triumphant on the shores of the Baltic.

The success in north-west Europe contrasted with the fighting stalemate in Italy, where the Germans yielded ground but never looked like collapsing totally. Various attempts were made to crack the front. In April 1945 at Lake Comacchio in north-east Italy, 43 and 40 Commandos fought a battle to dislodge the Germans from their strongly held positions. During the winter of 1944 the Allied campaign in Italy ground to a halt along a front just south of Bologna. Ammunition was in short supply and the waterlogged ground allowed no decisive action by either side. In the spring of 1945, however, Field Marshal Sir Harold Alexander, Commander-in-Chief of Allied forces in Italy, was determined to mount an offensive that would finally break German resistance in Italy.

Alexander's plan called for a push north-west to Ferrara by the British 8th Army, using the Argenta Gap, which lay between extensive floodlands to the west and the lagoons of Lake Comacchio on the eastern coast. At the same time, the US 5th Army was to strike north-wards to the west of Bologna. In order to weaken resistance in Bologna a small British Commando force was to strike first at Lake Comacchio, drawing reserves away to the east to ensure that before the 8th Army began its advance the threat posed to its right flank by enemy forces

April 1945, Army and Royal Marine Commandos in the ruins of Osnabruck pose for the camera as they catch up with newspaper reports. The soldier on the left – an Army Commando – is wearing a First World War German Army helmet which he had presumably 'liberated'.

positioned around the lake was removed. The western and northern ends were defended by German units while a long sand spit on the lake's eastern perimeter had numerous gun emplacements manned by the Turkoman Division.

The task of seizing the lake for the Allies was allotted to 2 Commando Brigade. While two Army Commandos, Nos 2 and 9, were to strike at the western shore and the western side of the spit from assault boats, two Royal Marine Commandos supported by the 24th Guards Brigade were to drive northwards over the spit of land, pushing through and destroying the Turkoman positions. It was here that Corporal Tom Hunter charged alone with a Bren gun to draw fire from German machine guns, thus enabling his troop to reach cover. He was killed soon afterwards and was posthumously awarded the Victoria Cross for his gallant action. His citation read: 'Throughout the operation his magnificent courage, leadership and cheerfulness had been an inspiration to his comrades.'

In Burma 42 and 44 RM Commandos took part in the bitter fighting at Akyab, Myebon and Kangaw, as well as raids along the Arakan coast. The Marines found themselves facing fierce fighting: Lord Mountbatten had taken over as Supreme Commander South-East Asia and was looking for a major push against the Japanese.

Early in January 1945, No. 3 Commando Brigade was ordered to carry out an amphibious assault against the Japanese forces holding the Myebon peninsula in north-west Burma. The Brigade was to act in conjunction with elements of the 25th Indian Division to prevent the enemy's 54th Division from withdrawing across the Yomas and into the Irrawaddy valley. At 0830hrs on 12 January assault craft transported 42 RM Commando to the landing beaches, which were secured with little opposition, and then No. 5 Army Commando moved inland to root out the enemy. The Brigade's other two units, No. 1 Army Commando and 44 RM Commando, were put ashore on the wrong beach but eventually got into action.

During the following two days the Brigade fought a series of small-scale battles against the enemy who were forced to retreat into nearby foothills. On 15 January a brigade-strength attack was launched against Japanese positions. Supported by fire from Sherman tanks, the assault troops were able to deal with the defenders. The Brigade's losses amounted to five killed and thirty wounded.

With the clearance of the Myebon peninsula, the only possible escape route for the Japanese lay along the road between Myohuang and Tamandu. To prevent such a move 3 Commando Brigade was ordered to cut the route near the village of Kangaw and on 21 January 1945 the Commandos moved into action. Embarked in landing craft, the formation set sail for the launching position, 6 miles south of Kangaw. Air reconnaissance had identified enemy strongpoints along the Brigade's intended approach to Kangaw. General Christoson, commander of the US XV Corps, decided that the road should be cut, providing the anvil on which to smash the enemy. With the 82nd (West African) Division sweeping down from the north, a bold plan was prepared which involved an amphibious assault in landing craft moving south and east

Opposite, top: Members of No. 2 Commando wait for the word to go into action at Lake Comacchio on 2 April 1945. The Army Commandos embarked in amphibious vehicles called 'Fantails', which took them to the enemy across the lake. They were joined in the battle for Comacchio by 40 and 43 RM Commando units who fought their way north along the sand spit at Scaglioca. *Opposite:* Lieutenant-Colonel Robert Sankey, wearing binoculars, who commanded 40 RM Commando at Comacchio discusses the plan with his signals adviser. Before they could make any advance the Commandos of both 40 and 43 RM Commandos had to cross the River Reno. During the battle Corporal Thomas Hunter of 43 RM Commando saved his troop from a waiting ambush at Scaglioca. He was killed and later awarded a posthumous VC.

3 Commando Brigade wades ashore at Myebon in Burma. The landings took place in January 1945 and those who were there say they will never forget the mud, which took several hours to cross. After Myebon the Brigade was tasked to land at Kangaw.

Marines scour Hill 170 for signs of the enemy. The Japanese attack was fierce and fanatical. After ten days of fighting the enemy was driven out. It was estimated that more than 300 enemy dead were left on Hill 170.

through the narrows of the Thegyan river and then north up the Daingbon Chaung to a beach 2 miles south-west of Kangaw.

Captain John Owen (later Major-General), who had joined the Corps as an enlisted man at Lympstone in January 1942 and went to Achnacarry in 1943, served with 44 RM Commando in the landings at Myebon. He recalled: 'It seemed to be all mangrove swamp. We had to wade four or five hundred yards which took nearly three hours. We were exhausted and covered from head to foot in mud which sucked our boots off.' The direct approach would have been 7 miles long. The selected approach involved motoring 20 miles through waterways in the heart of enemy country. The landings were supported by artillery which was provided by 27 Field Regiment RA who fired 25-pounders from Z craft anchored in Daingbon Chaung. There was also supporting gunfire from the Indian Navy ship *Narbada* lying off Myebon.

The Brigade was to surround the village of Kangaw and defeat the Japanese. One of its principal objectives was a feature known as Hill 170. It was jungle covered, like the entire area, and this slowed the progress of any operation. The Brigade's No. 1 Army Commando landed first and by nightfall most of Hill 170 had been secured. However, as Commandos climbed through the jungle it was very quiet and they feared the Japanese were waiting for them. From its forward position, codenamed 'Pinner', the Brigade could look across at the enemy in Kangaw and see the Japanese ready to attack.

That night the Commandos stood to at last light, then a couple of hours later the Japanese launched a ferocious attack from Kangaw to try to take Hill 170. Mortars and artillery were directed at the Brigade's positions – many Commandos were injured by splinters of bamboo sprayed across the trenches when the shells landed. Captain Owen, who commanded half a troop said: 'As we advanced up Hill 170, along jungle-

Elements of 3 Commando Brigade aboard landing craft as they mount a mission deep into the jungle. The Marines found the Japanese very brave but also discovered that they placed little value on their injured comrades and would leave them behind rather than evacuate them.

covered features, I felt something was building up. We were hot and tired and regrettably many of us did not dig in as well as we should have done. Suddenly all hell was let loose. Shells were bursting everywhere. I remember seeing a Marine hit in the pouch where he had carried a phosphorus grenade – terrible. We lost 60 men. The next day when we were burying them we were attacked again.'

The Japanese made numerous 'fanatical' attacks in which they stormed the Commandos' position. Another ten days of intensive fighting ensued at Kangaw before the Japanese were driven out. It was estimated that the Japanese sustained more than 2,000 casualties during the various battles; 300 of the bodies were found on Hill 170. While the Marines found the Japanese to be brave, they also discovered that they placed little value on their injured comrades and would leave them behind rather than evacuate them.

Meanwhile, Captain Matthew Oliver was in a small unit of Commandos who were part of General Bill Slim's 14th Army – the so-called 'Forgotten Army' – which fought across South-East Asia in Malaya, Burma, Thailand and China. The unit of less than 80 was outnumbered by more than 500 Japanese prisoners whom they had to process in Hong Kong. Captain Oliver said: 'We had only ever seen corpses, usually with enough wounds to kill twice over, because believe me they died hard. We were heavily outnumbered but they'd already had the heart knocked out of them. The heat was terrible, the humidity worse, and it never stopped raining. I was young, determined and more than a little foolish, which I suppose some would see as the ideal qualifications for the Commandos.'

By the time Oliver got to Burma in November 1944 the Japanese were retreating, but they were still putting up stubborn resistance to the fast advancing 14th Army. Nothing in the campaigns across Europe or North Africa could have prepared the Commandos for the fanaticism of the Japanese, who mounted wave after wave of reckless attacks. They had almost no regard for human life and their soldiers were prepared to do anything for their country. Snipers were roped in position in their trees so they could never get out alive and their corpses remained, causing the advancing 14th Army to be vigilant and slowing down its progress.

After Burma, the Commandos began preparing for a seaborne assault on the Malay peninsula, which commanders claimed would make D-Day look like a picnic. 'We were already heading for Malaya when news came through that the atomic bomb had been dropped. There was considerable relief all round', added Captain Oliver. A memorial to the twenty-eight members of 42 Commando who lost their lives during the operations in the Arakan in 1944–5 was erected in the memorial garden at the Royal Marines Museum in 1998.

The surrender of Japan was marked at a ceremony in August 1945 when the union flag was officially hoisted ashore at Yokohama by Major Peter Norcock RM, whose grandfather had carried the Colour with the Royal Marines battalion that landed in 1870. The Corps had played a fitting and heroic part in the Second World War. Its strength reached a peak of 78,000 men, of whom 7,542 were killed or wounded in the conflict.

Opposite: Army and Royal Marine Commandos round up Japanese soldiers who had surrendered in the Fanling areas of Hong Kong. They were shipped by railway to Kowloon on 15 September 1945.

RM SPECIAL FORCES

What we now know as special forces units pre-date the formation of the Royal Marine Commandos in 1942. Various units combining Army and Navy, as well as RM personnel, were formed from late 1941 for beach reconnaissance, small unit raids behind enemy lines, attacks on enemy headquarters and other intelligence roles. They operated off the French coast, in the Mediterranean, and in the Far East against the Japanese. Probably the most famous of these units was the deceptively named RM Boom Patrol Detachment under Major 'Blondie' Haslar, which trained in canoe handling, long-distance swimming and shallow-water diving.

Their attack on German shipping in the Gironde estuary at Bordeaux in 1942 employed a team of two-man canoes which were dropped off the French coast by submarine. The operation has become legend and is the story of the 'Cockleshell Heroes'.

The canoeists travelled by night and laid up during the day on their 70-mile approach to Bordeaux. Limpet mines were placed below the waterline of the ships, and several vessels containing vital German war supplies were sunk. The raid was an important success and the techniques employed were to set the style for many future operations. Only one pair of canoeists survived the attack – Major 'Blondie' Haslar and Marine Bill Sparks. Two other Marines drowned, six were caught by the Germans and shot – murdered despite the fact that they were wearing uniform when they were captured.

These and other special forces units continued to create havoc for the enemy throughout the rest of the war. Parachuting behind German lines, they engaged in clandestine intelligence and sabotage from D-Day onwards, operating across France and Germany ahead of the Allied advance. In the Far East similar small combined service teams continued harassing the Japanese in support of naval operations in Burma, Malaya, Sumatra, Thailand and the Pacific islands.

At the end of the war all of the Army and most of the Navy personnel in these groups, which had achieved the greatest success of all units on either side in the conflict, were disbanded. Many of the remaining Royal Marine operatives joined the newly formed all-Royal Marine Special Boat Squadron. It performed the same, but perhaps more surgical role, and was later renamed the Special Boat Service. It is no longer a Brigade or Royal Marine asset and is commanded and directed by the Director of Special Forces, although the Corps still drafts personnel from the SBS back into Commando units when they have completed their operational tours of duty.

THREE

OPERATIONS IN KOREA, PALESTINE AND MALAYA

'When we weren't fighting the enemy, we were fighting the cold.'

Marine Fred Hayhurst

The postwar agreement to partition Korea and split control between the superpowers created political and social instability that ultimately led to conflict in 1950. The invasion by the Soviet-armed North Korean People's Army (NKPA) across the 38th Parallel signalled the start of a bitter three-year conflict that would involve the deployment of Royal Marine Commandos fighting alongside their cousins in the US Marines in the most extreme weather conditions.

As the Second World War came to an end Japan was occupied by Allied troops and an agreement had been formalised in which America would administer Korea until such time as the country could recover from Japanese rule and form its own government. However, in the last days of the war Russia stepped in on the side of the Allied powers against Japan and then demanded a share in the control of Japan's empire. A hasty and perhaps crude decision was made to divide Korea at the 38th Parallel, cutting the peninsula in two. The Soviets would control the North and the US would hold the South. Both countries stationed military forces in their sectors and passed on weapons, equipment and training packages to the respective Korean forces.

Few people in the West had heard of Korea before this time. The 600-mile peninsula on the border of China had been occupied by Japan since 1905. From 1910 it had been a colony of the Japanese Empire. The entire country was undeveloped and mountainous, many towns were isolated and Korea's major transportation link was a railway on its east coast. The weather offered extremes of scorching sunshine and severe winters.

In 1948 the United Nations held elections to try to unite the country politically – at this time Korea was still technically one nation – but under Soviet direction, the North ignored the poll and only the South took part. In August the South declared itself the Republic of Korea (RoK) and a month later the North became the Democratic People's Republic of Korea – both sides wanted to govern the entire country and claimed they could unite it.

At this point the Americans and Soviets pulled their forces out, leaving training teams to assist the new administrations. But during the next two years there were constant clashes along the border. Both sides blamed each other for the incidents which involved incursions by military forces from both sides. Hundreds were killed and political relations between North and South, as well as between the US and the Soviets, fell to an all-time low. The tension was such that by early 1950 those in the South were fearful that the North, with its Soviet armour, would invade. The United Nations made a second attempt in May to unite the country and met representatives from North Korea. While there was failure to achieve an agreement on unification, the UN was delighted to announce that the North Koreans pledged that they only wanted a peaceful unification of the country. This statement reassured UN officials that there would be no conflict and the imminent threat of invasion was dismissed.

Just three weeks later on 25 June the NKPA rolled across the border, without any previous declaration of its intent, and invaded the South. Seoul, the capital city, fell to the invaders on 30 June. Demands by the UN Security Council for an end to hostilities and worldwide condemnation of the North's action were ignored. Instead the North Koreans simply continued their advance, gaining as much ground as they could before the South could counterattack.

The West saw the invasion as an opportunity for Russia to spread its communist influence. It was feared that the Soviets would roll their tanks across the plains of Europe and into Germany. Now, just five years after the end of the Second World War, East–West relations had broken down and Cold War tension was building. While the superpowers battled in Korea, Western Europe was eager to see the Soviets stopped.

The United Nations called upon its member states to render military assistance to the South and almost immediately US President Harry S. Truman ordered his country's air and sea forces to give support to the Korean government. Prime Minister Clement Attlee added British aid and put all naval forces in the Far East under US command. More than twenty countries offered military and logistical assistance.

The US deployed ground troops that were stationed in Japan as part of the occupation forces and Britain directed two infantry battalions from Hong Kong. But it soon became clear that it would not be easy for the initial force to stop the North Korean advance. The NKPA's invasion of South Korea included eight divisions and was spearheaded by Soviet-built T34 tanks. Later, the Chinese entered the war on the North's side, equipped with US, British and Japanese weapons. In addition the NKPA had adopted Russian tactics. It was a very robust and determined army, willing to die for the cause. By contrast the RoK forces, those from the South, were relatively lightly equipped with US weapons and while they had received military training from the Americans, it had been limited.

Among the advance forces into South Korea was the US 24th Infantry Division, which arrived on 30 June. It was followed from Japan by the 25th Infantry Division and the 1st Cavalry (late in July) who all massed at Pusan, a port on the south-east coast. This initial UN force was limited in its capability and was also vulnerable to attack by the NKPA. It moved out of the bridgehead to establish a foothold in south-east Korea but was soon pushed back. The NKPA moved further south and forced the RoK and UN forces to retreat. In early September the US 24th Infantry Division was driven back to Pusan, having failed to stem the communist advance, but was able to hold the port. This was vital to allow further UN reinforcements to come ashore.

The British 27th Infantry Brigade had arrived in Pusan in late August along with the American 2nd Infantry Division and elements of a provisional US Marine Brigade. This US Marine force would later join up with the 1st US Marine Division and land at Inchon. The first British Royal Marines to serve in Korea (drawn from ships' detachments) also arrived at this time. They came from the Far East Fleet and the small team included six sailors. After initial training they were attached to a US Army raiding company. This first force was commanded by Lieutenant Derek Pounds who flew out from the UK to head the detachment, which later became known as 'Poundforce'. The men spent three weeks at Camp McGill, a US Army base at

Marines of 41 Independent Commando at Bickleigh in August 1950 before flying out to Japan. On the right of the picture is Sergeant Sid Moon, behind him is Marine Gordon Payne – he was nineteen years old on 27 August 1950, the youngest Marine allowed to leave from the UK. Many on the troopship *Devonshire* were originally bound for the Far East and did not reach nineteen until well into 1951 – some did not see their nineteenth birthday at all.

The call to deploy Commandos in Korea came at a time when 3 Commando Brigade was already on operations in the Far East. The Korea force was formed from volunteers from across the Corps.

Takehama near the US naval base of Yokosuka, 50 miles south of Tokyo. Here the team was issued with US clothing and taught how to handle American weapons, although many still favoured their own.

The British Pacific Fleet had been assigned to the UN and operated mainly on the west coast of Korea, while the US 7th Fleet's responsibility included the east coast, which lent itself to amphibious operations. Admiral Sir Patrick Brind, commanding the British Pacific Fleet, offered the Commander of UN Naval Forces, Admiral C.T. Joy, a small raiding force to operate against the communist lines of communication. At the time 3 Commando Brigade was already heavily engaged in the anti-terrorist campaign in Malaya and this committed the Corps to raising a small independent Commando unit for operations in Korea: 41 Commando was reborn, having been disbanded at the end of the Second World War.

At Bickleigh camp (then the Royal Marines Commando School) on the edge of Dartmoor in Devon orders were received in August 1950 to form an independent commando unit to serve with the United Nations forces deployed in Korea. The unit was to be used for special raiding tasks behind enemy lines and would be commanded by Lieutenant-Colonel Douglas B. Drysdale. An initial force of 100 was raised from Royal Marines at establishments across the UK while an additional 100, who had already sailed for the Far East aboard the *Devonshire*, were to join the newly raised unit in Japan. The Independent Commando was officially formed on 16 August 1950. Fred Hayhurst, a Marine who served in 41 Independent Commando, has clear memories of the events. He said: 'The force was formed up at Bickleigh. The size of the unit was about 200 with just 100 flying out from the UK. We were already at sea on the troopship bound for Malaya to join 3 Commando Brigade.'

Lieutenant-Colonel Drysdale and his unit started their journey to Japan on 1 September, bound for Camp McGill. Those who flew out to Japan had to travel in civilian clothing and went via Cairo, Basra, Karachi, Rangoon and Hong Kong. All were under strict orders not to appear as a military party so as not to cause a 'political incident'. The British Embassy in Rangoon sent a 'secret' telegram directing that no indication should be given that the passengers were 'military'. At Hong Kong the party changed into military uniform because the last legs of the journey were over Allied-held territory. Those from the troopship soon joined them. The force was to be under command of the US Navy and at Camp McGill was issued with clothing. It then underwent a period of training on the US weapons to be used in Korea.

Fred Hayhurst said:

We left the ship at Singapore and went straight to RAF Changi. It took several flights over four days to get to Japan which included two nights at Clark Air Force Base in the Philippines. This was our first experience of a US camp and the food was fantastic and unlimited. A real treat after eleven years on wartime rationing. We eventually got to Camp McGill and were all issued with American weapons and equipment, although we continued to wear our green berets at all times. The US kit was good, but there were aspects of our kit which we preferred such as the Vickers machine guns. Despite the US clothing the entire unit had taken their denison smocks with them – which the Americans constantly tried to buy.

By the end of September, with training complete, 41 Independent Commando embarked in a US submarine and two assault personnel destroyers (APDs) heading for the coast of North Korea. At this time the NKPA made a second attempt to seize Pusan. The North Koreans were significantly south of the 38th Parallel and in strong numbers. Their advance was causing serious concern to the UN commander General Douglas MacArthur. He planned a seaborne strike on the west coast at Inchon, still south of the 38th Parallel, but to the rear of the NKPA main effort. If successful it would give the UN the opportunity to establish forces to the north of the advancing NKPA forces in south-east Korea. Tactically it would allow MacArthur's forces to strike at the enemy and drive him out of South Korea while at the same time delivering a psychological blow which could affect the momentum of the NKPA operations around Pusan.

Prior to Inchon the small Royal Marines 'Poundforce' was deployed on operations from the Royal Navy warship HMS *Whitesand Bay*. The Green Berets mounted a diversionary raid alongside the US Army Raiding Company just days before the seaborne assault. They later joined the 1st Marine Division on the road to Seoul.

The Inchon landings took place on 15 September and were mounted by the 1st US Marine Division, which had sailed in from the US west coast. Some of the troops had landed in Japan for training, while the main force headed straight for Inchon. It included the 1st Provisional Marine Brigade which had been one of the early units into Pusan. As the 1st Marine Division landed at Inchon, United Nations forces simultaneously broke out of the Pusan perimeter and the North Korean offensive started to collapse with units withdrawing to the 38th Parallel. The US Marines' landing was an outstanding success and dramatically changed the direction of the war. In total 71,339 men and 230 warships from seven different countries took part in the Inchon operation. The 1st US Marine Division rapidly advanced inland, recapturing Seoul. Along with other United Nations forces they pushed the NKPA out of the South. Then, after the UN Council passed a resolution sanctioning entry to the North, the US Marines chased the NKPA across the 38th Parallel.

After Inchon the 1st US Marine Division was ordered to prepare for two more amphibious operations, but because of a delay in clearing mines the Division made a landing at Wonsan. At Hungnam the Division, which had been put under command of 10th Corps at Inchon, was commanded by Lieutenant-General Almond. He ordered the US Marines of 1st Division to advance 78 miles into the mountains. Yudam-ni was the furthest north they reached before the Chinese attacked. Here the Division had established itself in the mountains around the Chosin reservoir, many miles inland. The commander of the 1st US Marine Division, General Smith, had misgivings about the plan to push his force further forward, concerned that his troops would be isolated high in the mountains without support. However, he managed to concentrate the Division along the single-track road that was to become his vital main supply route. He was therefore in a better position to pull out if his Division was cut off from other UN formations.

Throughout August and September UN forces in Korea had been fighting hard to maintain their ground at Pusan and then mount an offensive to drive the NKPA back over the 38th Parallel. October saw the first operations by 41 Independent Commando which was tasked with a raiding role. Its primary mission was to destroy enemy supply routes, particularly the key rail link. One of the main North–South lines of communication, the railway line ran in and out of tunnels along the east coast between Hamhung and Chongjin.

41 was split into two raiding forces: Group 1 headed by Lieutenant-Colonel Drysdale and Group 2 headed by Major Aldridge. (Poundforce rejoined the Commando and took part in the raids from the USS *Wantuck* and USS *Bass*.) On the night of 1 October, less than a month after arriving in Japan, Lieutenant-Colonel Drysdale headed his men in a raid at Sorye Dong and the railway line. The Commandos of Group 1 were transported aboard the US Navy submarine USS *Perch*, a converted 'Balao'-class submarine which had had its torpedo tubes removed so that

ght: Captain Pat Shuldham runs through the ders sequence with B Troop aboard the USS *rt Marion* prior to a Commando daylight raid.

low: Marines of 41 Independent Commando epare charges on the railway during a mmando daylight raid. They are wearing een berets and British boots but carry US apons jackets and webbing.

it could carry 110 troops. In addition, a small hangar was fitted to the rear of the conning tower to transport a small craft capable of towing inflatable boats ashore. On the raid Lieutenant-Colonel Drysdale's team laid charges and mines under the rails. The detonations were heard as the force extracted itself. On 5/6 October Group 2 under command of Major Aldridge was ferried into action aboard the APDs USS *Wantuck* and USS *Bass*. The two raids on consecutive nights were against stretches of railway line many miles apart. In total 130 Marines from Group 1 and Group 2 were involved and their inflatables were towed ashore by five landing craft.

After the raids the Commandos were shipped back to Japan where they stayed at Camp McGill. The journalist and MP Tom Driberg accompanied both these raids as a war correspondent and wrote a detailed account for the now defunct Sunday newspaper *Reynolds News* and the English *Japanese Times*.

41 Independent Commando was shipped to Hungnam, the rear support base for the 1st US Marine Division. It arrived on 15 November 1950 to be placed under command of the Division. The plan was for the Commando to be used as a reconnaissance force to protect the left flank during the advance from Yudam-ni.

At this time the UN command spoke about the troops being home for Christmas. The NKPA appeared to be broken: UN forces had pushed it out of the South and were dominating most of North Korea. However, the UN had not taken account of a new threat to the conflict – China. The Chinese Communist Forces (CCF) had already expressed concern at the situation and indicated that they would not be willing to see UN forces overrun the North. They now began to mount isolated attacks against South Korean forces and the United Nations troops. Then on 27 November the CCF launched a major offensive, deploying eighteen divisions to attack United Nations forces all along the front west of the Chosin mountain range. The British 8th Army and the US 10th Corps were forced to withdraw, leaving the 1st Marine Division totally isolated.

Prior to the Chinese–North Korean assault the British and American forces, along with UN troops from other countries, held a defensive line with the 8th Army (which included the Argyll and Sutherland Highlanders and the Middlesex Regiment) in the west, 10th US Corps to the east and the US 1st Marine Division in the middle. The centre ground remained 'no man's land'.

The Chinese advanced further south and quickly forced all UN units to retreat as they encircled the 1st US Marine Division with twelve divisions of their own. Isolated and spread out along the main supply route from Hungnam to Yudam-ni, the Marines were unable to mount a counterattack against the overwhelming numbers of Chinese. In addition, the Chinese had captured parts of the road linking the various units of the Division and believed they had their prey trapped. The Chinese general had ordered his troops to 'kill these marines as you would snakes in your home'. The situation was desperate.

Out on a limb and with their force fragmented, the Division's three Marine regiments, with their own engineers, armour and artillery regiments supported by aircraft of the US Marine Air Wing and the US Navy, were operating in the mountainous terrain surrounding the Chosin reservoir. Two regiments were at Yudam-ni, close to the Chinese border while the final regiment was 22 miles south at Koto-ri. Between Chosin and Koto-ri was Divisional headquarters at Hagaru. The men were about to face the fight of their lives.

Before the Chinese assault the Division's commander had requested a reconnaissance force and 41 Commando had already arrived at Hungnam as planned in support of the US Marines whose headquarters was close to Chosin reservoir. The Royal Marines were issued with additional US cold-weather clothing such as fur-lined parkas to combat the conditions of 40 degrees below zero. The severe weather was a constant enemy to both sides. The CCF's clothing looked second rate compared to the US Marines'. However, it is important to note that while the Chinese troops may have looked like a second-rate army in their thick yellow and white quilted cotton uniforms and crêpe-soled canvas shoes they were in fact seasoned fighters. Tactically they were very adept, adopting a policy of fight by night, hide by day – a key factor in Western military doctrine in the twenty-first century.

On 28 November 41 Commando was scheduled to leave Hungnam and drive north to join the Division and support the 7th US Marines at Yudam-ni. The Commando drove up the mountain track and met no enemy. Having ascended 4,000 feet up the Funchilin Pass the Commando arrived at Koto-ri where the 1st Marine Regiment was based. The unit was greeted with the news that the CCF had blocked the road to the North and was given part of the perimeter to guard for the night. Fred Hayhurst said:

None of us will ever forget the cold, it was bitter. When we weren't fighting the enemy, we were fighting the cold. When you were in action you forgot how cold it really was and within the Division there were numerous cold weather injuries. It was so bad that we have people in our association who don't pick their toes anymore, because they lost them to frostbite at Chosin.

The next morning 1st US Marine Division headquarters ordered that Lieutenant-Colonel Drysdale and his force fight their way to Hagaru at the southern tip of the Chosin reservoir. The group, which now totalled 922 men and 141 vehicles from 41 Independent Commando, G Company US Marine Corps, B Company 31st Infantry US Army and many elements of Divisional headquarters, was known as Task Force Drysdale. There was just time for the Heavy Weapons Group to break out a section of 81mm mortars and A4 Brownings before 41 Commando led the advance from Koto-ri at 0930hrs on 29 November 1950. Within 2 miles the Commando and G Company were up against serious resistance. The narrow road was banked by steep hills on either side and the CCF had poured forces in to ambush any movement along the road. It was estimated that more than 2,000 enemy troops were massed in the hills.

Early in the afternoon Task Force Drysdale was reinforced with seventeen tanks from D Company 1st US Marine Corps' tank battalion which had moved up that

A 3.5-inch rocket launcher team of 41 Independent Commando. The conditions the Marines faced in Korea were severe and the green berets found themselves fighting two enemies – the Chinese and the cold.

morning. Slow progress was resumed until at about 1615hrs the column was halted only 4 miles north of Koto-ri as it came under intense fire. Lieutenant-Colonel Drysdale asked Divisional headquarters whether he should resume the advance and because of the urgent need for reinforcements General Smith directed him to continue at all costs.

After a delay for the tanks to refuel, during which darkness fell and the CCF moved closer to the road, the advance continued. Drysdale wanted the tanks to spread out along the column to provide wider protection, but the tank commander insisted on keeping them together, leaving the soft-skinned vehicles unprotected. As they moved off and entered a part of the road on a tight bend they were hit again. This time the firepower was intense, grenades and small arms constantly targeting the convoy which had been separated into numerous groups and sustained dozens of casualties. Many of the drivers were hit by rifle fire. Among the wounded was Drysdale who had been shot in the arm and Marine Fred Hayhurst who was shot in the leg, but they would be the first to say they were the lucky ones – many others were killed.

In the dark and freezing conditions the CCF continued to pin down the column. Vehicles were now on fire, the road blocked by abandoned trucks and most of the unit still isolated into small groups. Some individuals were on their own, fighting as best they could. Major Aldridge kept part of the Commando together by walking up and down the length of the vehicles, despite the intense cold and the heavy gunfire, to ensure everyone was ready to continue into Hagaru.

The CCF ambush left one heavy weapons section, the assault engineers and elements of Commando headquarters with most of B Company and Divisional headquarters, who fought throughout the night, strung out in a number of defensive perimeters. Subsequently the heavy weapons section, led by Corporal Joseph Cruse, found its way to Hagaru, badly frostbitten. Twenty-five of the Commando headquarters personnel were led back to Koto-ri by Assault Engineer Officer Lieutenant Pat Ovens. Part of the column was trapped and running out of ammunition. Many men were taken prisoner, including twenty-six Royal Marines from 41 Independent Commando. The remainder of the column forced on under continuous fire in what Drysdale named 'Hellfire Valley'. About a mile from Hagaru the force was stopped by concentrated mortar and small-arms fire and yet again fought its way through. The column could now see bright lights in Hagaru and could not understand why the Americans had given the CCF such an easy target. In fact the US Marine Corps engineers were bravely working under floodlights to construct a 2,900-foot airstrip out of the frozen earth. The last vehicles to enter the 4-mile defensive perimeter at Hagaru were a 2½-ton truck and the heavy weapons group's 30cwt vehicle, both loaded with wounded and led by Heavy Weapons Officer Lieutenant Peter R. Thomas.

The journey through Hellfire Valley took its toll on the Commando as the intense fire came close to crippling it. At Hagaru Marine Hayhurst was taken by stretcher from one of the vehicles into a darkened room. No one was speaking and he presumed they were all asleep – he later discovered he had been put in the mortuary by mistake. Force Drysdale had sustained 321 casualties and lost 75 vehicles but, to quote from the official US Marine Corps history: 'To the slender garrison of Hagaru was added a tank company and some 300 seasoned infantry.'

Fewer than 100 of 41 Independent Commando got through. Sixty-one became battle casualties. 41 Commando was nominated Garrison Reserve under command of 3rd Battalion, 1st Marine Regiment. The first call came on the night of 30 November/1 December when B Troop, now led by Lieutenant G.F.D. Roberts (the Commando Adjutant), took part in a counterattack to regain G Company's left flank on East Hill. This dominating feature was critical to the defence of

Still wearing their life jackets, Marines of 41 Independent Commando climb a bank having just landed from the sea during one of the railway attacks.

the perimeter and the CCF had taken it with a view to launching an attack on the main force in Hagaru. The Marines of 41 Commando assaulted the position and fought fiercely with the Chinese before securing the objective. The following morning the snow was littered with bodies. The Chinese temporarily pulled back.

Most UN formations had disintegrated under the CCF attack. To the west the 8th Army was withdrawing and 10th Corps' commander placed all troops in the Chosin reservoir area under the operational control of 1st US Marine Division. A casualty rate of 75 per cent had been suffered by the three US Army battalions east of Chosin reservoir during five days of attacks. Only 385 able-bodied survivors eventually reached Hagaru across the ice-covered reservoir, to be re-equipped and reorganised as a provisional battalion.

In a high-level conference at Hagaru, 10th Corps' commander authorised Major-General Smith to destroy all equipment and fall back with all speed to Hungnam. Smith replied that his Division would fight its way out, bringing back its heavy equipment and that movement would be governed by his ability to evacuate his wounded. As 'withdrawal' was not in the US Marine Corps vocabulary this operation was to be called 'The Advance to the South'.

41 Commando made an abortive foray to recover nine 155mm howitzers which had been abandoned when their tractors ran out of diesel. These were later demolished – the largest loss of the Yudam-ni breakout.

While the men of the 5th and 7th Marines recovered in Hagaru, casualty evacuation and resupply continued apace. By nightfall on 5 December 4,313 men, including 25 Royal Marines, had been evacuated by air from the makeshift airstrip and 537 reinforcements had been flown in. The plan for the move from Hagaru to Koto-ri was that the 7th Marines would lead and 5th Marines with 41 Commando attached would bring up the rear. The operation was to be supported by US Navy and Marines aircraft from seven US Navy carriers.

The temperature was well below zero and the Chinese were still active as 41 Commando and the 5th Marines held the Hagaru perimeter, allowing the main Divisional force to advance out of the area. The move started at dawn on 7 December. It took 38 hours to transfer the 10,000 troops and over 1,000 vehicles the 10 miles to Koto-ri against fierce attacks from the seven CCF divisions now concentrated against US 1st Marine Division.

By dawn the following day the Chinese had withdrawn leaving more than 600 dead in the snow. Later 41 and the US Marine rearguard commenced their withdrawal/advance south, back through Hellfire Valley. Here Chinese forces had blocked the road and cut the rearguard force off from the main body. Constant fire fights and skirmishes, as well as the freezing conditions, made the journey a terrible experience.

En route some the unit's dead were recovered to be buried in a mass grave of 117 at Koto-ri on 8 December. They included US Marines and soldiers. At Koto-ri Lieutenant Oven's party of twenty-five was reunited with the Commando. There was a pause

By the end of the Chosin operation the Commandos had lost most of their specialist, such as machine gunners and radio operators. Some had cold-weather injuries, some had been wounded in fighting and others had sadly been lost or killed.

before the advance towards Hungnam could be resumed as steel trackway was airdropped to bridge a demolished culvert in the Funchilin Pass.

41 Commando had arrived in Koto-ri in a snowstorm in the afternoon of 8 December and was quickly given the task of holding the high ground overlooking the main supply route to guard against Chinese infiltration during the night. The unit set off with the 5th Marines column to march the final 23 miles to the Hungnam base camp bridgehead which was held by two US Army divisions. By the time 41 Commando and the 1st Marine Division reached Hamhung they had marched almost 70 miles. Apart from injuries sustained in the fighting, many men were now suffering from frostbite and exposure. The final few miles to Hamhung were covered in military vehicles.

By 11 December the whole of 1st Marine Division was clear. As Major-General Smith had promised, it had come out fighting, bringing its wounded and most of its equipment. In the process it had inflicted a major defeat on the CCF which had sustained an estimated 37,000 casualties from all causes, including the bitter sub-zero weather. Fred Hayhurst, who was flown out, said: 'All the UN forces were evacuated by sea from Hungnam to South Korea. It was the forgotten Dunkirk – thousands of troops were taken out by sea and more than 90,000 North Korean civilians.'

Those left in the unit travelled to South Korea, then to Japan to await reinforcements at Tokyo and Kure. 41 had lost 50 per cent of its manpower and

Left: A Marine prepares explosive charges during a raid on the railway. In the background a group of North Korean civilians are escorted to safety.

Below: The charges erupt as 41 Independent Commando's mission to destroy the railway takes effect. Having achieved their mission at Chosin the Commando was withdrawn from Korea on 23 December 1951 and disbanded 22 February 1952. It was later re-formed and disbanded again.

Baker Troop of 41 Commando marching through Kure to join the USS *Fort Marion* prior to a raid. The Green Berets were issued with US clothing and taught how to handle American weapons, although many still favoured their own British weapons.

specialist skills, such as heavy weapons personnel, assault engineers and signallers, had been hit hard. After UN forces recovered from the Chinese assault the land battle continued across the 38th Parallel. By April 1951, 41 Commando's strength was up to around 300 and the whole Commando mounted a daylight raid against the north-east coastal railway.

The Commando was now stationed on islands 60 miles behind enemy lines inside the communist-held Wonsan harbour from where it launched regular raids against shipping and shore installations. The Commandos first based themselves on Yodo island but others were taken during the six months of operations. Wonsan was vital in that it maintained a UN presence behind communist lines and forced the enemy to divert military resources from the main battle to reinforce coastal defences.

Having successfully achieved its mission, 41 Commando was withdrawn from Korea on 23 December 1951 and on 22 February 1952 the unit was disbanded at Stonehouse barracks, even though its prisoners were still held by the NKPA and Chinese until hostilities ended in 1953.

The campaign in Korea cost the lives of thirty-one of the Commando (three were Royal Navy personnel), while seventeen more spent several harsh years in prisoner camps before returning to Britain. For its outstanding service in support of the US 1st Marine Division during the Chosin reservoir action the Commando received a Presidential Unit Citation (PUC) and many British and US decorations for officers and men.

To this day there is great concern that those in 41 Commando who fought alongside the US Marines are not officially allowed to wear the ribbon awarded to them. The PUC award to 41 Commando was unique in that it was presented to a foreign unit. Fred Hayhurst said: 'The USMC lobbied the US government and their Navy department to have the rule changed and in 1957 when the PUC was awarded, the then Commandant General requested that Royal Marines who served in Korea should be allowed to wear the ribbon, but the UK government vetoed the request. In 1999 the Commandant General and the Royal Navy supported our request to be allowed to wear the ribbon, but the government refused to change the original decision.'

Perhaps the greatest accolade for the unit came from Major-General Smith of the US Marines who wrote to Lieutenant-Colonel Drysdale. He said:

As Commanding Officer of the First Marine Division, I desire to take this opportunity to acknowledge the high qualities of leadership, heroism, devotion to duty and self-sacrifice displayed by officers and men of 41 Independent Commando of the Royal Marines while serving with this division in North Korea.

I am familiar with the long and glorious history of the Royal Marines. This history records many outstanding feats of heroism, devotion to duty and self-sacrifice by units and individuals alike. The performance of the 41 Commandos during the drive from Koto-ri to Hagaru-ri, during the defence of Hagaru-ri, and during the advance from Hagaru-ri to the south will, in the perspective of history, take equal rank with the past exploits of the Royal Marines.

I can give you no higher compliment than to state that your conduct and that of your officers and men under your command was worthy of the highest traditions of the Marines.

Drysdale also praised his men. He said: '41 was undoubtably the best unit anyone could hope to command – they did everything I asked of them.'

For the men who served in 41 Commando at Chosin, the intense fighting, survival in the cold weather and the fact that they were such a small unit created a bond that has never been forgotten. Their association regularly meets up and in March 1991 the 'Chosin Few' who fought in the reservoir campaign presented the Chosin Trophy to the Corps and the Commandant-General decided it would be awarded to the top student on the senior command course.

The anniversary of Chosin is always celebrated by those who fought in Korea and the name itself is familiar to many Marine recruits at Lympstone. It was given to a special troop that catered for injured Marines who had the determination to pass the Commando course after their injuries had healed.

41 Commando lost more men in Korea than the whole of 3 Commando Brigade did in the Falklands. Those who died were: Marine Gerard Ahern, Marine Arthur Aldrich, Corporal Ronald Babb, Sergeant Charles Barnes, Corporal Jarvis Belsey, A/Sergeant Ronald Davies, Marine Ivan Garner, Marine John Graham, Lieutenant John Harwood, Marine Lewis Heard, Corporal Christopher Hill, Marine Stanley Hills, Marine Keith Hitchman, Marine William Jauncy, Marine Peter Jones, Surgeon-Lieutenant Douglas Knock, Marine Joseph McCourt, Marine Harry Melling, Marine Robert Needs, Marine Reuben Nicholls, Captain Ralph Parkinson-Cumine, Leading Sick Berth Attendant Dennis Raine, Marine Stanley Skelton, Corporal Ronald Southworth, Marine Eric Strain, Marine Dennis Stray, Petty Officer John Tate, Corporal Charles Trott, Marine William Walker, Marine Royston Wooldridge, and Marine Kenneth Wyeth.

PALESTINE

In 1948, 3 Commando Brigade Royal Marines moved from Hong Kong to the Mediterranean where it was tasked to cover the withdrawal of British forces from Palestine.

With the Second World War over, thousands of Jews had sought refuge in Palestine, but a British White Paper, drawn up in 1939, had limited Jewish immigration to 75,000, a figure that was soon reached. To the Jews, the decision by the British to impose a restriction on the number of people entering their 'homeland' was inhuman and could only lead to conflict. Soon extremist groups launched armed attacks against the security forces.

At the end of the Second World War the 'Commando role' had been exclusively passed to the Royal Marines and 3 Commando Brigade became 3 Commando Brigade Royal Marines. It included 45 Commando, which had served with the 1st Special Service Brigade, 42 Commando from 3rd Special Service Brigade, whose members had fought across Europe, and 44 Commando. The latter was renumbered '40', allowing the designation of the first ever Commando to be retained.

On 25 January 1948, an advance party of 40 Commando RM arrived in Israel from HMS *Cheviot* tasked to secure Haifa port. The remainder of the unit arrived in HMS *Phoebe* and the LST *Striker*. Once established, the unit mounted vehicle checkpoints between the Arna and the Jewish sector near an area called Hadassa. For the Marines it was an unbelievable situation. Just months earlier their actions had helped to liberate the Jewish prisoners of war; now they were being spat at and insulted by the same race.

Several terrorist groups, of which the Stern gang later became the most violent, began to ambush police patrols using the hit-and-run tactics of guerrilla warfare. To the Commander of the 1st Guards Para Brigade, Colonel John Nelson, the only way to resolve the constant problem of attacks was to mount an assault into Hadassa with 1 Guards Para and 42 Commando RM, who had arrived from Malta.

But the Palestine operation was fast coming to an end. The assault was cancelled and units began pulling out in May 1948; 42 Commando left on 12 May,

An immigrant ship arrives at Haifa quayside. Thousands of people arrived in Palestine after the Second World War. In 1948 the Commandos, along with other British forces, were directed to the country to cover the withdrawal of British troops, but conflict soon sparked.

45 Commando on the 24th and finally, on 27 June, 40 Commando RM, under the command of Lieutenant-Colonel 'Titch' Houghton was the last unit to leave.

THE MALAYAN EMERGENCY

The Malayan Emergency was the first postwar conflict in Asia between communism and the West. Chinese-backed guerrillas waged a military campaign against the British and their Malayan allies.

The British operation in Malaya was a war but it was called an 'emergency' to ensure that the London insurance market would continue to provide cover for vital business in the country, such as tea plantations and tin mines. If the insurance companies had pulled out, the economic structure of Malaya would have collapsed.

The Brigade returned to Malta after Palestine, although 40 Commando went to Cyprus first to guard illegal immigrants who had tried to get to Palestine. 42 Commando went to Malta via exercises in North Africa. By the middle of 1949 the Brigade was in Hong Kong, patrolling the border with China. Six months later the Commandos were back in action, this time in the Malayan jungle.

The focus of resistance to the Japanese occupation of Malaya during the Second World War had centred on the Malayan Communist Party (MCP). At the end of the war the British returned to Malaya and reimposed old-style colonial authority. Meanwhile, the newly created Malayan Races Liberation Army (MRLA) pressed for political and trade union reform and in 1948 vented its frustration against the British by launching a guerrilla war.

The MRLA, which was made up of ethnic Chinese, attracted massive support from Chinese squatters living in the jungle. The organisation waged a campaign of terror against local officials, attacked economic targets and attempted to establish 'liberated' areas. In the jungle MRLA units mounted attacks and became known to Marines who served there as 'CTs' (communist terrorists). The 'Min Yuen', undercover communist agents, lived among villagers and provided safe houses for the CTs. The 'Lie Ton Ten', the murder squads, butchered those accused of informing.

Commanded by Brigadier Campbell Hardy, 3 Commando Brigade RM arrived in Malaya in May 1950 and deployed to Perak, a small state the size of Devon and Cornwall, saturated with jungle-choked mountains. Rivers and villages were scattered across the region. From an operational point of view, Perak was a nightmare. The dense jungle often allowed MRLA ambush teams to melt away into the natural camouflage of the terrain. In addition, the nearby Thailand border offered a refuge to the CTs and guerrilla activity in the area was hard to control.

The Brigade commander deployed his three units across the patch; 40 Commando was based in the north around Kuala Kangsar while 42 Commando was deployed near Ipoh in Perak and 45 Commando at Tapah in the south. But conditions were difficult. The dense vegetation formed a constant canopy of cover. The Marines worked in subdued light and humid conditions during the day and the climate could turn very cold at night. After a couple of hours on patrol Marines would sometimes reach a jungle clearing and the sudden harsh light of the sun would temporarily blind them.

Because of the humidity everything was subject to moisture damage. Weapons rusted. In addition, there was the problem of wild pigs and monkeys which if startled could reveal the Marines' position to the enemy. The majority of men spent their entire time on patrol with their clothing soaked by the damp atmosphere of the jungle and no matter how well they tied their boots, the leeches always seemed to get in to attack their ankles.

Sergeant Ray Thompson, a DL (drill instructor) who later trained junior Marines at Deal, told his recruits that cleanliness was vital in the jungle. He said: 'Our clothing was wet and dirty and there was no sense in changing so we would stop to wash ourselves in the river and put the same clothes on again. It was important to try to wash every day and that was the time we checked for leeches. Sometimes the situation

The Marines of 3 Commando Brigade were deployed in the Perak area which included jungle-choked rivers and mountains. The Marines worked in subdued light and very humid conditions, which left equipment and clothing constantly damp.

didn't allow it, but the Marines did not suffer the medical problems that other units reported because we always gave priority to hygiene.'

The Marines employed Iban trackers from Borneo to act as their guides and jungle scouts. These tribesmen had an incredible knowledge of the terrain and many Marines were convinced the trackers could actually smell the communists. When the Marines killed communist guerrillas they had to return the bodies for identification and this could be heavy and slow work. The Ibans quickly resolved the logistics of this problem and took the heads off the enemy corpses.

During the period 1950–2 the Commando Brigade killed or captured 221 terrorists and received 40 gallantry awards, as well as 68 mentions in despatches, for actions in Malaya. But the conflict cost the lives of 33 Marines, many of whom were buried at Batu Gajah cemetery near Ipoh (known as God's Little Acre) or at Kamunting Road Cemetery in Taming.

FOUR

THE SUEZ OPERATION AND BEYOND

'I don't think anyone really sat and thought that we were the first to make a helicopter assault. We were too busy doing our job.'

Marine Cyril 'Ichabod' Penberthy

The Suez operation in 1956 was an Anglo-French mission, well planned and well executed by means of an airborne and amphibious assault, but its duration was short – British and French politicians buckled under the weight of international criticism and pulled their troops out.

After the Second World War British troops remained in Egypt, although forces prepared to withdraw as part of an agreement to remove troops from Cairo, Alexandria and the Nile Delta by March 1947. The rest of the units were to leave by 1949, although the agreement included a clause allowing the British to maintain a Canal Zone force in the event of any aggression from countries neighbouring Egypt. Continued unrest in the Middle East led to the retention of British forces in the Canal Zone and in 1949 tension erupted as the Egyptian Army was defeated by the Israelis. Egypt was in turmoil and by 1951 there was growing opposition to the British presence.

In October British troops were attacked by terrorists and rioting broke out at the British base in Ismailia. As the situation deteriorated British forces attacked the Egyptian police barracks in Ismailia in order to prevent further insurrection. More troops were deployed to the Canal Zone and the RAF drew up plans to neutralise the Egyptian air force and to support British troops in an advance on Cairo that never happened. The Canal Zone was sealed off from the rest of Egypt, adding further to the anti-British feeling.

A military coup was mounted in 1952, but it was short-lived and in 1953 General Mohammed Neguib's military council declared the country a republic with Neguib as President. Then just a year later he was deposed by Lieutenant Gamal Abdal-Nasser who became President in 1956 after an election in which it was compulsory to vote and Nasser was the only candidate. These events shattered Britain's long-term plans to influence policy in the Middle East and secure the establishment of a defence organisation in the region directed by the West.

In 1954, Britain and Egypt had agreed a treaty that included the withdrawal of British forces from the Canal Zone by June 1956. The political climate in 1954 was very unstable in the Middle East. The West feared Russia was gaining influence in the region after the Soviets offered assistance. In 1955 Britain and the US said they would fund the foreign exchange costs of Nasser's new dam project at Aswan on the Upper Nile. This support was to be made on the understanding that Egypt would back Western policy in the Middle East, but Nasser decided that Egypt should pursue a policy of non-alignment with either East or West and both offers were rejected.

Then, in July 1956, President Nasser nationalised the Suez Canal and refused free access to ships of all nations. Nasser carried out this action after the Western powers withdrew their offer to fund the Aswan Dam project. He then impounded the Suez Canal Company, which was jointly owned by Britain and France and generated $35 million a year. Nasser planned to use the company's funds to finance the dam. The West feared that the Soviets might still finance the project and gain influence in the region. In addition there was speculation that the Egyptians, who were already receiving arms from Eastern Europe, were about to join the Eastern Bloc.

Then the Israelis mounted a successful offensive against the Egyptians and pursued them across the Sinai Desert, where an Israeli parachute battalion dropped to cut the Egyptians off at the Mitla Pass. It was clear that the fighting would soon affect the Canal Zone. The British and French governments, as principal shareholders in the Suez Canal Company, issued ultimatums to both sides to draw back. The Israelis, who were in hot pursuit, agreed, but the Egyptians refused and consequently the British and French told the United Nations that if fighting took place around the canal, they would be forced to intervene.

Military commanders reviewed numerous options, including landing at Alexandria and occupying Cairo. Finally a decision was made to land at Port Said, but amphibious shipping was in short supply and it was more than twelve months since the units of 3 Commando Brigade had been able to mount an amphibious exercise. The postwar years had seen little investment in amphibious vessels and Suez gave a timely reminder to the government of the importance of maintaining an amphibious force. It also provided the opportunity for the Fleet Air Arm to demonstrate its new helicopter force: at Port Said the Commandos mounted the first helicopter-borne assault.

Much of the equipment and weaponry used by 3 Commando Brigade at Suez was of Second World War vintage. No. 4 rifles and Sten guns were issued, which the Marines of 40 Commando did not regard as a good start to the operation, particularly as they had been using the more modern 7.62mm FN rifle while on operations in Cyprus just prior to Suez.

The idea of mounting helicopter assaults from carriers offshore had been put forward to the Chiefs of the Defence Staff by Major-General Moulton in his effort to broaden the British amphibious capability, but the idea had not been received well. Now it was to be used in an operational role. On 31 October 1956, British and French air forces began attacks on Egyptian bases and virtually destroyed the country's air

ove: Whirlwind helicopters,
...ch mounted the first 'air
...ault' in military history
...en they airlifted
... Commando into Port Said,
...on the deck of HMS
...seus during Operation
...sketeer'. Parts of Cairo can
...seen burning in the distance
...he Anglo-French assault
...s launched.

...ht: Marines of 45
...mmando RM, who carried
... the helicopter assault,
...ade for a last inspection
...ore taking part in Operation
...sketeer'.

wing in forty-eight hours. The invasion plan was based on an amphibious assault, supported by relatively small numbers of British and French parachute troops. The Paras faced the same problem as the Marines – a lack of equipment, in their case aircraft. The seaborne landings were timed to begin on 6 November and were to coincide with the airborne drop, but at the last moment the parachute assault was brought forward by twenty-four hours. This meant that the joint British–French para-drop would not be able to call on naval gunfire support, but Royal Navy strike aircraft would be available for fire missions if required.

The airborne assault was spearheaded by 3rd Battalion the Parachute Regiment, who were based in Cyprus, while 45 Commando RM was to fly in aboard helicopters with 42 and 40 Commando and 2nd Battalion the Parachute Regiment, as well as supporting armour, landing by sea. The landing of 45 Commando in Operation 'Musketeer' has historical significance in that, as far as is known, it was the first 'hot' helicopter landing in the annals of war and without doubt influenced the future style of Commando operations, particularly in the development and concept of the Commando carrier. The tactical adoption of helicopters to ferry troops into battle was the brainchild of Vice-Admiral Sir Guy Sayer who was Flag Officer Home Fleet and, along with Major-General Moulton, had proposed the concept as a 'fast and effective method of deploying troops ashore'.

Early on 6 November a reconnaissance into smoky Port Said by Lieutenant-Colonel Tailyour's helicopter revealed that it would be a rather hazardous undertaking to land in the sports stadium originally selected as the touchdown point and it was decided to put 45 Commando ashore on open ground adjacent to the statue of Ferdinand de Lesseps, the builder of the canal. The task for 45 Commando during the initial stage of the operation was to contain any enemy opposition emanating from the poorer shanty quarter of the town while 40 and 42 Commandos swept south through the central business district alongside the canal.

Following final briefings the Commandos began to take up their positions in the assembled aircraft of the Joint Helicopter Unit (JHU). (The word 'experimental' had been dropped from the JHEU's title mainly for reasons of morale.) The JHU was commanded by an Army officer, Lieutenant-Colonel Scott, and was equipped with six Whirlwind Mk2s and six Sycamores. Both types of helicopter had been stripped of all excess equipment so that they could carry the maximum number of Commandos – five in the Whirlwind and three in the Sycamore. The operation was executed in conjunction with ten Whirlwinds of 845 Squadron.

Marine Cyril 'Ichabod' Penberthy was serving with 45 Commando and remembers the constant helicopter training and troop drills the unit underwent before Suez. He said: 'The introduction of helicopters was all new, but by the time we got to Suez it was a well-worked procedure. We knew exactly what to do and the assault went very well. I don't think anyone really sat and thought that we were the first to make a helicopter assault. We were too busy doing our job. I remember I sat in the doorway. We flew straight in and landed without any problem. Then we came under sniper fire.'

45 Commando had sailed from Malta aboard the carriers HMS *Ocean* and HMS *Theseus* (Whirlwinds of 845 aboard *Ocean* and the mixed JHU force of Whirlwinds and Sycamores aboard *Theseus*). The helicopters were to fly ashore in waves but there had been no time for a full rehearsal. The aircraft landed 425 Marines and 23 tons of stores.

One Marine was hit almost as soon as he touched down on the landing site, was dragged back on board the helicopter and flown to HMS *Ocean*. As the operation continued the aircraft picked up casualties and returned them to the waiting ships. One Whirlwind of 845 was so badly damaged by enemy fire that it ditched just short of the *Theseus* – the crew and the injured Marines it was carrying were all rescued.

Marine 'Tex' Cooper, who served with Baker Troop of 45 Commando during the helicopter assault at Suez, recalled in the *Globe and Laurel*:

After cleaning our weapons (chopper landings in Egypt are very sandy and dusty affairs) and more heavily laden with equipment and ammunition than at any time during training, B Troop set off, immediately following Tac HQ. Pausing at the intersection where we had to turn inland in order to seal off the shanty town, we were halted, thankfully. For some minutes we observed the work of the Fleet Air Arm planes which were rocketing various targets in the town centre. Regrettably recognition 'silks' [white or yellow panels to indicate the location of the landing site to pilots] had not been laid out – tragedy resulted. A roving plane took our column to be a strong force of the enemy and brought his cannon to bear with terrifying accuracy so that we suffered our worst and most uncomfortable seconds.

Three Whirlwinds make their approach in to the LS (landing site) as the assault is launched. The unit, 45 Commando, had carried out limited exercises with helicopters before Suez but there had been no time for rehearsals. The helicopters landed 425 Marines and 23 tons of stores.

The landing by 45 Commando at Port Said, painted by William Lane and reproduced with kind permission of the Royal Marines Museum. The de Lesseps statue can be seen in the background.

The CO was hit in the elbow, his signaller (who later died) in the guts and members of 7 Section, immediately behind them, were close enough to receive severe leg injuries. Corporal (later Major) 'Sticks' Mead, grazed on the inside of his thigh, and 'Lofty' Sharplin, with a minor wound, were among the lucky ones. More unfortunate were Johnny Gotobed and 'Tuffer' Smith with hospitalisation wounds; but most unlucky of all were 'Bomber' Clark and 'Errol' Ireland whose leg injuries made amputation necessary.

Both 42 and 40 Commandos were to come ashore on beaches either side of the Casino Pier at Port Said soon after first light; 40 Commando would land to the left and 42 to the right. The French seaborne assault was to take place at Port Faud, across the canal from Port Said. The British airborne troops from 3 Para were to drop at El Gamil and the French at Port Faud – both landing ahead of the seaborne assault. The two Royal Marine Commandos landing by sea were to be supported by armour from the Centurions of 6th Royal Tank Regiment, which was under command of the

Commandos. After landing and securing the beachhead the Commandos were to advance into Port Said where each unit was assigned a sector of responsibility.

The vast armada had left Malta on 31 October and, taking its speed from the slowest of the amphibious ships, spent the best part of a week sailing east towards Port Said and the entrance to the Suez Canal. Numerous briefings were carried out on board the landing ships during that week, but it was only on the night before the operation that troop officers received aerial photographs of their initial objectives, mostly 'obliques' taken by aircraft of the Fleet Air Arm. The photographs showed that beyond the five rows of wooden huts that stretched along the beach, there were more buildings which could slow the Commandos down if they were in the hands of Egyptian snipers. This new intelligence resulted in a hasty reorganisation of plans and a reappraisal of operational timings.

Marine Tom 'Jan' Webber landed at Suez with 42 Commando. For Jan and his colleagues, several of whom had served in the Far East and had been captured and spent three years working on the Burma railway, Suez was to be a doddle. However, that didn't stop the pre-assault nerves. He said: 'We were all full of apprehension. We didn't know what to expect. It was just like the feeling you get before any operation. As it was, the landing was unopposed, the Paras gave flank protection although a French aircraft did shoot up one of our vehicles.'

On the evening of 5 November Marines taking in the fresh air on the deck of the tank landing ship HMS *Suvla* could hear the dull throb of aircraft engines in the distance, presumably flying in support of the 3rd Battalion the Parachute Regiment, who had been dropped on Gamil airfield, some 6 miles to the west of Port Said, earlier that day.

The Marines who had seen action before, either during the Second World War or in the jungles of Malaya, were a great value to 42 Commando. However, there were also many national servicemen in the unit and this was their first experience of action. Later that night the order was passed to go down to the tank deck to embark in Buffaloes – tracked amphibious vehicles (known as LVTs).

At first light on 6 November thirty-two RAF Venoms led by Squadron Leader Ellis, each armed with eight squash-head rockets, took off from Cyprus and flew in to attack a number of identified Egyptian military targets, particularly in the west mole breakwater where two gun emplacements had been located by aerial reconnaissance. Then the Fleet Air Arm's fighter bombers (Sea Hawks and Sea Venoms) went into action with a 10-minute strike on the beach. This was followed by a 45-minute bombardment by 4.5-inch naval gunfire from ships offshore which had not been able to pre-position themselves in time to support the air drop. By now the minesweeper force had ensured the approaches were clear and ready for the assault force.

Each Buffalo (LVT) could carry up to thirty men, swim at about 5 knots, and then run up the beach on its tracks. At 0410hrs the bow doors of HMS *Suvla* opened and the vehicles slowly churned their way out, motors thundering in the enclosed space of the tank deck of the mother ship. The start of the naval gunfire support was the signal for the run-in to begin. A last-minute decision by the British government had limited the size of guns to be used for the bombardment to no larger than 6 inches. The French battleship *Richelieu* with her 15-inch guns and the British cruiser HMS *Jamaica* with her 8-inch armament turned dejectedly away in the distance.

As the Royal Marine Commandos approached the shore they could still see naval shells bursting ahead. A couple of Fleet Air Arm Sea Hawks swooped down from the cloudless sky and strafed the beach. Captain Derek Oakley, a distinguished Corps historian who served at Suez, recalls an amusing incident, now on record at the Royal Marines Museum. He said:

> Lieutenant Hudson, an impeccable but very tough Royal Marines officer who had risen through the ranks, gathered his sections around him. His first objective was a large, oriental building with a huge, solid oak door. It was securely locked. Although there appeared to be no enemy opposition at this stage, he took every possible precaution and called up the Assault Engineers with an explosive 'pole' charge.
>
> They lit the fuse and when they had retired to a safe distance, a tremendous explosion rent the air and the massive door disintegrated in a cloud of smoke and dust. I watched this with subdued amusement from across the road.
>
> As the smoke died away, I saw a small dilapidated Egyptian, obviously a caretaker, emerge from a ditch beside the road waving the key!

Port Said after the landings showing a LST (Landing Ship Tank) with its bow doors open on the main beach with troops and vehicles lined up on the right-hand side of the picture.

By 0535hrs C Squadron, 6th Royal Tank Regiment, with their Centurions, had now joined 42 Commando and the LVTs were being refuelled and mustered in the lee of the seafront houses as C and X Troops advanced to secure blocks of houses further inland. Many of the men took this opportunity to make a quick wet (Marine expression for cup of tea). Captain Oakley said:

Calling an 'O' Group [orders group], I was glad to hear that we had suffered no casualties and that the men were in good heart. But bad news was in store; an uncontrolled air strike mistook some of our supporting anti-tank gunners from the Somerset Light Infantry for enemy and strafed them with disastrous results.

The CO, Lieutenant-Colonel Peter Norcock, called us together and briefed us for the next phase of the battle – a dash through the town in our LVTs, supported by tanks, to secure the Nile Cold Storage Depot and the Port Said power station on the southern outskirts of the town.

It was then that the familiar, comforting face of the Commandant General Royal Marines, Lieutenant-General Campbell Hardy, appeared as he strolled by offering friendly advice and encouragement to all. His visit to the operational area so early after H-hour had been tabooed by the Admiralty, but he had nevertheless landed with 45 Commando by helicopter, and to us he was a most reassuring sight. He spoke to many of the Marines, his steely blue eyes shining brightly.

At 0630 we climbed back into our LVTs, this time leaving the rear ramps partly lowered for a quick exit if necessary. The dust which had choked our throats had now been cleared by the refreshing tea, ammunition had been redistributed and we were ready to go. I was well aware that this ride through the town would not be easy, as the Egyptian Army might well have taken up sniping positions on the high flat-roofed buildings.

While I travelled in the cockpit with the driver and his mate, the Marines sat in the well of the LVT with their backs to the sides, Lieutenant Westwood and Sergeant-Major Casey, with a Bren gunner, sat in the rear with their feet dangling on the ramp.

The plan was that we should move with a Centurion leading, followed by my LVT, another tank, an LVT and so on. A and X Troops followed with CO's Rover, the Vickers medium machine guns and some Assault Engineers. The land speed of the LVT, about 15mph, governed our rate of progress.

Lieutenant Peter Hetherington, a Royal Tank Regiment national service officer, was in the leading tank. We had practised infantry/tank cooperation on numerous exercises in Malta during the autumn, so we understood and trusted one another implicitly.

With a roar of engines this long, snake-like column moved off along the sea front, turning inland at the end of the block down one of the widest streets in Port Said, the Rue Mohammed Ali.

The time was still only 0645 and, as we rumbled into enemy territory, the adrenalin once again started to flow and nerves became tense. Turning into the wide street, my leading tank seemed to gain on me, making me feel a bit neglected. I felt a tug on my trouser leg and looked down.

My driver was trying to say something to me. I cupped my ear and with a remark that relieved all my tensions he asked, 'Sir, do they drive on the right or the left in this country?'

A burst of machine-gun fire hit the vehicle, causing it to swerve momentarily. A scream and a moan came from one of the Marines sitting in the well. I was sure that the fire had not come in from the top of a building onto their unprotected heads and I could not understand it.

Corporal Jim Peerless groaned and said, 'I've been hit', and as he turned over blood oozed from his buttocks. It was only then that it dawned on me what must have happened. When we had left Malta, such was the secrecy surrounding this particular operation, we had thought we were just off on another of the interminable exercises into Malta's Mellieha Bay.

Each LVT had the facility for armoured plating to be lowered into the side skins of the craft, but this task took several hours of hard work with a crane and was unpopular with the crew. The awful truth that the sides of the vehicle were not bulletproof came as a severe shock to morale.

The deserted street looked so peaceful in the morning light, but this was war and danger lurked up every side street. I anxiously peered ahead for our objective, the power station and the area to the south of it where we were to act as stops, when the air was broken by a shout of 'Grenades'.

I looked up and caught a glimpse of an Egyptian soldier who had obviously just thrown a grenade from some seven storeys above. His aim was impeccable and he had judged the speed of the vehicle well. But luck was on our side. Instead of exploding in our midst, it landed on the feet of my subaltern, David Westwood, in the rear of the LVT. He twitched as the grenade hit him, and it rolled out into the road behind us.

When the explosion came, splinters of grenade caught the Sergeant-Major in the head. Our Royal Navy sick berth attendant bandaged him quickly and efficiently, but Casey was not amused that he could no longer wear his green beret because of the dressing.

I could now see the Cold Storage Depot building in the distance, and beyond that our target. As we approached, I warned the Marines to be ready to disembark, but to my horror my leading tank had not recognised the buildings.

The Centurion rolled relentlessly on. I was in a quandary over what to do; peel off to our stop position without the protection of my tank, or follow him in case he had seen some enemy and was skirting them? I tried in vain to call him up on the radio.

In Malta it had worked perfectly, but now we were in action, communications failed. I took the decision to trail him further south and B Troop followed me. A further 150 yards down the road and only just beyond our area, Lieutenant Hetherington's tank calmly turned left through the main gates of an Egyptian Army camp.

I shuddered to think what might lie ahead. But to my immense relief the camp was deserted, though signs of recent occupation were all around. My LVT came to a halt and I told the driver to take cover behind a brick hut. The remainder of my troop, with their accompanying tanks, fanned out into defensive positions. Engines were switched off and suddenly there was an uncanny silence. No sound . . . no movement.

I waited, anxiously assessing the situation and pondering on what to do next, knowing that I had gone a little beyond my objective. My signalman called up Commando headquarters and explained our situation. I was relieved to hear that A and X Troops had taken their objectives against some spirited resistance, but a few snipers were still causing annoyance. But that was not helping me.

Hetherington remained securely locked inside his tank and I waited for him to appear to help sort out the situation. I tried, again in vain, to contact him on the radio. My training had taught me that the second line of communication with a tank was through its telephone encased on the rear of the hull. I tentatively picked it up and whirred the handle. Nothing. I whirred it again. Still nothing. I waited. It was now 10 minutes since our arrival at the camp and a sense of urgency gripped me.

I told my signalman that I would try and contact the tank through the turret. I climbed gingerly up onto the hull and, as I was about to knock on the hatch, its main gun fired, throwing me backwards onto the ground in a cloud of dust and sand. I picked myself up and dusted down, more indignant than angry.

After a reasonable pause I tried again and this time my knock was answered when Peter Hetherington raised the 'lid' about an inch and a half and said, 'Sorry old boy, I think I've made a mistake.' The understatement of the year! 'I saw something moving in the prison over there and had a pot shot.'

A quick conference and 'O' Group were called as I had planned to go back to the Cold Storage Depot. Meanwhile, Leslie Hudson had called up rear headquarters for a casevac [casualty evacuation] helicopter for the Sergeant-Major, Corporal Peerless and Marine Chaffer, who had also been wounded. Casey removed his field dressing, put his green beret back on, and refused to go, saying that he was quite alright. It is sad to relate that he was killed in Cyprus six months later.

There had been no enemy to the south and I informed the CO of this. By the time we had withdrawn to the Cold Storage Depot building, our task completed, we heard with some dismay that a temporary ceasefire had been negotiated. We felt, and knew, that we were only halfway through our task. Once more a decision taken far away in London had prevailed. We could not even turn a deaf ear and finish the job.

There was a distinct feeling of deflation. Leaving A and X Troops in position, I took my troop back down the Rue Mohammed Ali, still being made uncomfortably aware that the snipers had not heard of the ceasefire.

The operation over, the Marines celebrate with a photograph of an Egyptian flag. But it was to be a short-lived victory. Days later the Commandos and the French were pulled out after international condemnation of the operation and the call for United Nations forces to replace the Anglo-French troops.

We reached the sea front where we fed and watered ourselves in the comfort of some of the buildings which had not been our first objective. We were, however, inwardly proud that we had won the day and that our professionalism had been rewarded.

The ceasefire, announced at 2100hrs to be effective from midnight, was received on 6 November. The Egyptian episode lasted only a few days. On 14 November the Marines boarded the *Empire Fowey* which had disgorged the Royal Scots the previous day. The adventure was over. The total Royal Marine casualties were ten killed and fifty wounded.

CYPRUS: INTERNAL SECURITY DUTY

Trouble flared in Cyprus in the mid-1950s and as 42 Commando RM returned home to the UK after Suez, both 40 and 45 Commandos were redirected to the island ready to mount internal security duties as the continued unrest escalated. Within months they would be fighting terrorists who were campaigning for British withdrawal from the island.

Cyprus had been leased to Britain by the Ottoman Empire in the late nineteenth century, then in 1914 Turkey allied herself with the Germans and the British annexed the island. In 1915 Britain offered Cyprus to Greece if it would join the war against the Turks, but the Greeks refused. British rule was recognised by the Treaty of Lausanne in 1923 and the island became a crown colony in 1925.

The Turkish and Greek communities shared the same areas but the Turks were in the minority. Greek Cypriots had called for union or *enosis* with Greece in 1931 but this prospect was unacceptable to Turkey which had no wish to see its people ruled by the Greeks. Britain ignored its demands. As calls for union intensified, Turkey threatened to invade in 1954.

Both Turkey and Greece were members of NATO. Britain was still running the island and the sensitive situation threatened to get worse. Then, because Britain clearly had no plans to accept Greek Cypriot demands for *enosis*, a number of extremists formed a terrorist organisation to seek independence. Called EOKA – Ethniki Organosis Kuprion Agoniston or National Organisation of Cypriot Fighters – the group was commanded by a former Greek colonel named Georgeios Grivas. In 1956 EOKA won considerable support when, following Suez, it became clear that many British military assets would transfer to Cyprus. Anti-British sentiment was heightened by the move which included the transfer of the Commander-in-Chief Near East's headquarters. Initially, EOKA organised riots and strikes. Then it raided a British base at Famagusta, acquired a large quantity of weapons and ammunition, and the number of shootings increased.

EOKA enjoyed hard-line support in the villages around Kyrenia and Troodos. 45 Commando RM was deployed initially to Kyrenia where, in three months, it came to dominate the region and cut EOKA's freedom of movement. Later the Commando moved to the Troodos mountains, working in snow at 6,000 feet above sea level.

40 Commando RM deployed to Polhemdia Camp on the outskirts of Limassol and while the majority of casualties in the fighting were Greeks or Turks as the two communities attacked each other, the Marines also came under regular fire.

In 1959 the Zurich agreement was signed, creating the independent Republic of Cyprus. The agreement renounced union with Greece and partitioned the island into separate Greek and Turkish states. At the same time British Sovereign Base Areas (SBAs) were established in Akrotiri, Limassol and Larnaca. Then in 1974, Turkish paratroopers invaded and both 40 and 41 Commandos were flown to the island again to reinforce the British garrison. The invasion resulted in the

Above: A 45 Commando patrol searches for EOKA hideouts in 1956. The Commandos were often involved in searches for weapons and terrorists in what was called Operation 'Turkey-T'

Below: Marines of 45 Commando at Akenthau (1956) are pictured during a search operation in a remote farmhouse. The patrol appears to be armed with Lee Enfield rifles, a revolver and a sub-machine gun (Sten).

partition of the island but left the SBAs untouched. During the Gulf War Cyprus played a key role as a forward operating base and is still strategically important to the UK.

ADEN AND SOUTH ARABIA: CONFLICT WITH NATIONALIST ARABS

The small British protectorate of Aden on the southern tip of Saudi Arabia first saw conflict in 1963 when the people of Radfan, north of Aden, came increasingly under the influence of the nationalist Arab movements surrounding the tiny state.

Situated more than 60 miles north of Aden, the Quteibi, Ibdali and Bakri tribes traditionally supplemented their income by looting travellers on the Dhala road which connected Aden to the state of Yemen. In the mid-'60s, with the support of extremists from an organisation called the National Liberation Front (NLF), they were armed and willing to join the struggle to force the British to withdraw from the colony.

45 Commando RM arrived in Aden on St George's Day, 23 April 1960, having seen action at Suez in 1956 followed by two operational tours in Cyprus. The Commando went to Little Aden to relieve an Army battalion and was tasked to guard the BP oil refinery next to the camp; 40 also detached two troops to Dhala on the frontier to guard against potential insurgents crossing into Aden from the Yemen.

Just a year after deploying to Aden, the unit was sent to Kuwait in response to a threatened invasion by Iraq. After three weeks 45 Commando, working alongside 42 Commando and other units, had restored order. It then returned to Aden. Next, in January 1964, the unit embarked in the aircraft carrier HMS *Centaur* and sailed 1,500 miles south to Tanganyika in Africa where the army had revolted. The Commando quickly gained control and as the politicians negotiated the unit again returned to Aden to resume the key role of guarding the oil refinery at Little Aden. But opposition to the British presence in the protectorate was growing and finally exploded into violence in 1963 when a bomb attack was made on the British High Commissioner.

Aden centred around the harbour. Steamer Point was at the entrance to the breakwater and the three main areas within the peninsula were Crater, Ma'alla and Khormasksar. Steamer Point was the site of Government House and was a favourite with families who wanted to view the Royal Navy warships and carriers that regularly visited Aden. Crater was, as the name suggested, situated within an area of volcanic rock. This was one of the poorest parts of Aden and it would later become one of the most active areas of support for the terrorists. Khormasksar was the home of Aden's international airport and the RAF; it was residential and offered a clean environment, but was to become packed with Service families as trouble in Crater forced the military to evacuate them to safer areas. Ma'alla was the focus for the business community and the region's biggest shopping centre. Its busy dual carriageway, which ran through the centre of the area, was fittingly called 'Ma'alla Straights'. A fourth area, called Sheikh Othman, could be accessed via a small roundabout at the end of a causeway linking Aden to Little Aden. It was on the route that the British Army used for convoys to

Anti-clockwise from top left: Marines of 45 Commando yomp across the rocky wasteland of Radfan, laden with ammunition and supplies; 45 were based in Little Aden, but spent a lot of time on operations in the Radfan.

Marines of 45 Commando climb aboard a Royal Navy Wessex helicopter which was part of the flight assigned to HMS *Albion,* as indicated by the letter 'A' on its tail. As in so many missions mounted by the Commandos since Suez, helicopters played a critical role in the success of operations in Radfan and Aden.

The back streets of Crater, named after the remains of a volcanic eruption. Marines can be seen on the right of the picture, supported by armoured vehicles as the security situation deteriorated.

A Land Rover of 45 Commando pictured in the Ma'alla suburb of Aden. The vehicle's bumper is fitted with a steel bar which ensured that any wire strung across the road did not decapitate the driver and commander of the Land Rover.

An RAF Bristol Belvedere helicopter lifts off from the main base at Radfan. Marines spent a lot of time on patrol in the rugged hills that surrounded the airbase; it was here that supplies and reinforcements would be flown in from Big Aden.

Dhala. Regular market days at Sheikh Othman were now replaced with daily shootings.

Rioting and terrorist attacks increased and by late 1964 British military families in Crater had been evacuated after the violence soared in the area and homes were attacked with rocket launchers. By now children of British servicemen were being taken to school in military vehicles fitted with security nets as protection against stones or even grenade and rocket attacks. They were escorted by armoured Scout cars. It was exciting but dangerous.

Most of the action initially took place up on the frontier east of the Dhala road or in the stark mountain country of the Radfan, 6,000 feet above sea level, where tribesmen regularly ambushed convoys heading for the region. Units that deployed to Dhala and the Radfan area called it 'going up country'. As the conflict raged 'up country', tension increased in Aden and Little Aden. The terrorists intensified their campaign. At Khormasksar the trouble continued, with regular shootings against the British military and a grenade attack on families using the open-air cinema at Waterloo Lines. Finally, many families were moved to Little Aden, but then the terrorists mounted more attacks on the married quarters there, blowing up the swimming pool and forcing families and soldiers to live in camps surrounded by barbed wire and security. At their camp in Little Aden 45 Commando appeared to the author, whose father was based in Aden with the military, to run everywhere. The only access to one of the best beaches in the area was to drive through the Commandos' camp and to a young boy the Marines always seemed to be involved in physical training – even in the full heat. As the violence increased a decision was made to send families home.

By late 1966 the Marines of 45 Commando were regularly mounting patrols in Crater and Ma'alla from their base in Little Aden as well as constantly deploying to Dhala – a 9-mile convoy journey from Little Aden across the desert and into the mountains. The commanding officer of 45 Commando RM, Lieutenant-Colonel T. Stevens, who had won an MC at Normandy, believed that night patrols into enemy-held territory would give the Commandos the edge as the tribesmen were not night fighters. As part of a major plan to cut the tribesmen off from routes to the Yemen 45 Commando was ordered to capture the high ground on the north side of the Danaba Basin.

The Commandos were joined by B Company, 3rd Battalion the Parachute Regiment who came under command of 45 for the operation. Stevens' intention was to seize two features, codenamed 'Rice Bowl' and 'Sand Fly'. The initial plan called for a night-time drop by B Company on a key feature codenamed 'Cap Badge'. But the jump was cancelled after an SAS DZ (drop zone) party was spotted by tribesmen and the entire plan had to be changed. The overall force commander, Brigadier Hargroves, radioed Colonel Stevens to halt on 'Sand Fly' and 'Coca Cola' – an additional feature listed in the operational plan.

In darkness Tac HQ, Xray and Yankee Companies scaled the 1,500-foot feature called 'Coca Cola' and by dawn they could see the Danaba Basin and 'Cap Badge', 9,000 feet high and to the east. Several days later the Commando, plus B Company 3 Para, marched by night to secure 'Cap Badge'. It was an eventful journey in which

A gun GPMG gunner of 45 Commando RM takes aim at an enemy position in Radfan as a troop officer directs an air strike by RAF Hunter aircraft. The terrain in Radfan was harsh and bare, leaving little scope for protection against the harsh sun or cover from the tribesmen.

B Company found themselves trapped in daylight on low ground dominated by the village of El Naqil. The Paras came under constant sniper and machine-gun fire from the tribesmen. Meanwhile, Zulu company, 45 Commando, was flown forward in rear of the tribesmen and climbed down 'Cap Badge' to attack the tribesmen from behind. The Paras who had marched for eleven hours and fought a ten-hour battle renamed El Naqil 'Pegasus Village'. The Commando and B Company 3 Para spent another three days patrolling and discovered that the tribesmen had abandoned the Danaba Basin, before they returned to base.

There were many more operations in Radfan and along the Dhala road, as well as an incident at Sheikh Othman and in Big Aden. Crater in particular had become a focal point for terrorist activity and 45 Commando played a major role in rounding up terrorists here. When the Argylls marched into Crater to restore order it was Royal Marine Commandos who provided the cordon. At the time the Corps wore 'stay bright' cap badges and according to a former NCO it was after a Marine was shot by a sniper in Crater that the decision was made to introduce anodised ones. 'As I remember, the unit believed his stay bright cap badge had been spotted by a sniper in the glaring sunshine. Later we received the anodised cap badges which the Corps now wears all the time unless Lovats, one of our best uniforms, are being worn', said the NCO who later served with the SBS.

Almost every operation generates the opportunity to improve tactics and it was after Aden that the commanding officer of 45 Commando, Lieutenant-Colonel Owen (later

Major-General), reviewed the procedure of camouflaging vehicles. In Aden desert-coloured matt paint had been used on vehicles at Radfan. Lieutenant-Colonel Owen and his recce troop commander, Lieutenant Terry Knott, discovered that emulsion paint could be used on vehicles in the UK for exercises and washed off for inspections. Later the Colonel received permission to paint all the unit's vehicles matt green and the policy was subsequently adopted by units across the British Army.

By May 1967 45 Commando had completed thirteen operational tours in Radfan, but these were soon to end because in 1966 the British government had announced its intention to hand over sovereignty to the Federation of South Arabia.

It was in May 1967 in Aden that a young Royal Marine recce troop officer demonstrated outstanding courage and was awarded the Military Cross. The rebels had attacked a Royal Engineer convoy in Radfan and 45 Commando's recce troop was airlifted to the area as a quick reaction force. An airstrike was called in on the enemy position but the terrorists were present in great numbers. Lieutenant Terry Knott and his Marines landed from their Wessex and immediately came under heavy fire. The troop commander was almost shot dead by a rebel at point-blank range.

The rebels then withdrew into a cave and Knott threw in a grenade, only to see it emerge as the terrorist threw it out again. In order to prevent his men being pinned down in the cave Knott then drew his pistol and charged in, leading from the front in an outstanding display of courage. The terrorists were in such strength that additional forces, including a 105mm gun, were moved into the wadi to rout them. Lieutenant Knott's citation adds that his coolness and judgement under continuous heavy fire inspired his troop: 'His determination effected the relief of the wounded sappers, all of whom recovered.'

The withdrawal from Aden was originally planned for 1968 but was brought forward to 29 November 1967. 45 Commando and 1st Battalion the Parachute Regiment held a line north of Sheikh Othman in order to keep the airport out of the range of terrorist small-arms fire. One by one the units flew out. 45 Commando left at midnight on 28 November aboard a fleet of thirteen RAF Hercules C-130s. The following day 42 Commando left by helicopter and landed on HMS *Albion* which was offshore; it was the last unit to leave Aden. The carrier HMS *Bulwark* was also offshore with 40 Commando on board, just in case any departing troops became trapped and needed support.

Twelve Royal Marines are buried at Ma'alla cemetery and the grave of Marine Dunn lies at the British military cemetery in Silent Valley, Little Aden, just a mile or so from 45 Commando's former camp. In 1998 Major-General Andrew Keeling returned for a remembrance service and placed poppies on the graves.

BRUNEI AND MALAYA: BACK IN THE JUNGLE

In 1957, Malaya was granted independence from Britain but it was necessary to maintain British military support there in order to hunt down several thousand communist terrorists who still roamed the jungle. Then in 1962 the North Kalimantan National Army launched a revolt in Brunei aimed at seizing power from the Sultan and

A Royal Navy Wessex hovers above a patrol of Alpha Company (The Saints) 40 Commando RM after it has just dropped them at the company headquarters base in the Danua area of Brunei.

preventing the accession of Brunei to a Federation of Malaysia. The rebels moved on key positions in Brunei and in parts of Sarawak and Northern Borneo. At Limbang and Seria the insurgents seized British hostages. Seria was retaken on 10 December and on the same day L Company of 42 Commando RM, who had been in Singapore in the run up to Christmas, were put on standby to move to Brunei. Two days later they were in Brunei along with Commando headquarters.

The mission to release the hostages was to be led by Captain Jeremy Moore (later to head the British land component in the Falklands War). In Brunei Captain Moore with the assistance of Lieutenant-Commander Black, the senior Royal Navy officer in Brunei, located two flat-bottomed lighters that could be manned by crew from the minesweepers HMS *Fiskerton* and HMS *Chawton*.

The force made its way up the Brunei River to Limbang where the fourteen British hostages were being held at a police station. The plan was to arrive at the town by first light. As the force was just 300 yards from the target the intelligence sergeant called over a loudhailer, in Malay, for the rebels to surrender. They replied with machine-gun fire and other weapons. The Marines opened up with mounted Vickers machine guns and landed from both craft. In the firefight two Marines were killed. More fighting was to follow and by the time the battle finished on the following day L Company had

A Wessex of 845 Naval Air Squadron based aboard the converted Commando carrier HMS *Albion* drops Marines and Gurkhas during operations in Brunei and Malaya.

lost a total of five men and had seven wounded. All the hostages were rescued, Captain Moore received a bar to his Military Cross and Corporals Lester and Rawlinson received the Military Medal.

Limbang, along with actions by the Queen's Own Highlanders at Seria and the Green Jackets at Miri, broke the back of the rebellion although it took until 1963 to clear all the terrorists. The remainder or 42 Commando arrived in Brunei in late December and mounted patrols. It was followed by 3 Commando Brigade headquarters and 40 Commando. In spring 1963 the whole Brigade returned to Singapore, although it would soon be back in the jungles of Malaya.

The Indonesian conflict was to keep Commandos in the jungle for the next three years as they mounted operations throughout Borneo and Malaya to counter raids by rebels.

Although several British infantry battalions served in Borneo between 1962 and 1966, the brunt of the campaign was undoubtedly borne by the eight Gurkha battalions and 40 and 42 Commandos. Between December 1962 and September 1966 there was always one Commando in Borneo, and on several occasions both were there. The Gurkhas lost 43 killed and 87 wounded and the two Commando units lost 16 killed and 20 wounded. 40 Commando, the last Royal Marine unit to serve in Borneo, arrived in May and left in September 1966. The Corps had been among the first in and the last out.

FIVE

THE FALKLANDS CONFLICT

'Gentlemen, this will be no picnic.'

Brigadier Julian Thompson, 1982

On 2 April 1982 Argentinian troops invaded the Falklands, a small British dependency in the South Atlantic. A long-running claim by the South American country to sovereignty over the islands had finally erupted after General Leopoldo Galtieri was appointed President and announced that his administration would undertake to recover 'the Malvinas', by military force if necessary.

In March 1981 Roberto Viola, a former army commander, became Argentine President but the military junta failed to give him its full support and by October his days seemed numbered. A reshuffle of the junta, which normally took place every two years, was called for and by December Galtieri and his supporters had effectively secured power. Late that month Viola retired from the presidency on grounds of ill health and Galtieri took office with the significant support of his old friend Admiral Jorge Anaya, a hard-line member of the junta. Anaya was keen to see the recovery of the Falklands and Galtieri saw this as an opportunity to raise the country's morale and, more importantly, encourage support for himself. The two men are believed to have struck a deal to get the islands back in Argentine hands within two years. Unsurprisingly, Anaya's naval forces were to head the invasion. By early 1982 the new President and his junta had opted to take the Falklands quickly and plans had been drawn up for an invasion between July and October. The Argentine press leaked Galtieri's secret and the 'possibility' of an invasion was revealed when the newspaper *La Presna* wrote that the government was to submit a number of conditions to the British, adding that the paper believed if the negotiations failed Buenos Aires would take the islands by force.

It is unclear what action, if any, the British Foreign Office took in respect of this media report, which it could have discounted as post-election bravado by Galtieri, particularly as in the past there had been many claims of sovereignty by Argentina and plenty of military hot air about a potential invasion. However, as the Argentine military developed its plan for invasion in spring 1982 a number of events followed that should, and may, have been identified by British intelligence.

Royal Marines who had served in previous detachments of Naval Party 8901, the Falkland Islands Royal Marine unit, were well aware of Argentina's long-running

Smoke hangs over a deserted road during the Argentine attack on the Falklands. This main road leads to Government House where the thrust of the attack was mounted against Governor Rex Hunt and the Marines of the NP 8901 detachment.

claim and over the years there had been several 'significant incidents' that had inflamed the political situation, as well as 'intelligence indicators' that an invasion or landing force might take place.

The annual 'sabre-rattling' from Buenos Aires and several events in the decades prior to 1982 had continued to remind the islanders and the UK government of Argentina's intent. In September 1966 a group of Peron supporters calling themselves the New Argentina Movement hijacked a Dakota and flew to Port Stanley, landing at the racecourse – the airstrip (later, airport) did not exist then – and detained two British officials at gunpoint. However, the Royal Marines from the resident detachment quickly arrested them and they were later flown back to Argentina. A year later negotiations over the Falklands took place in New York between British and Argentine politicians and reached the conclusion that the UK government would only consider a concession on sovereignty if it were clear that the Falkland islanders themselves regarded such an agreement as satisfactory. Then in 1968, after a study and further talks on sovereignty headed by Lord Chalfont, the Foreign Office minister Michael Stewart announced that 'no transfer could be made against the wishes of the islanders'. The Tory opposition spokesman Sir Alec Douglas-Home supported the announcement and added that the Conservatives would strike 'sovereignty from the agenda' when they returned to office.

Throughout the 1960s and '70s talks continued and it emerged in 1982 that the Argentine Navy had drawn up plans in the early 1970s to recover the Falklands by means of a naval task force. This plan, developed by Admiral Emilo Massera, was never executed, possibly because of the threat posed to the Argentine surface fleet by the presence of British submarines in the region.

By 1976, relations between the two countries were at an all-time low. Lord Shackleton visited the Falklands with a fact-finding team tasked to prepare a study on the future of the islands. He was refused permission to fly via Argentina and instead sailed to the South Atlantic. The Argentine junta believed a British scientific research vessel, which was in the South Atlantic on routine work, was carrying the peer and ordered its naval vessel the *Admiral Storni* to fire a shot across the ship's bows. The UK reacted with fury and despatched the frigate HMS *Chichester* to the region as gunboat diplomacy took centre stage.

Late in 1976 relations between London and Buenos Aires deteriorated still further when more than fifty Argentine technicians landed at Southern Thule in the South Sandwich Islands. Information about the occupation was suppressed for almost a year until the Callaghan government finally revealed the situation to the House of Commons in May 1978.

The British government had announced in 1975 that the ice patrol ship HMS *Endurance* was to be withdrawn from the South Atlantic and, while the decision was later revoked, it had clearly sent a message to Argentina that Britain was reducing her military commitment and her responsibility in the region. Then in 1977, British intelligence indicated that it believed that the Argentines could be planning to mount a further landing after Southern Thule and the government tasked the Ministry of Defence to respond. The Royal Navy deployed the 'Leander'-class frigate HMS *Phoebe*, the Type 21 frigate HMS *Alacrity*, the support ships RFA *Resource* and RFA *Olwen*, as well as the nuclear submarine HMS *Dreadnought*. Codenamed Operation 'Journeyman' the mission was planned to provide a significant naval presence in the South Atlantic. It was classified as top secret; the crew were sworn to secrecy and the incident was only revealed to the Commons in March 1982 at the height of the tension between the UK and Argentina.

By mid-1981 the very mention of the word 'Falklands' was enough to prompt tired yawns from most British politicians. This reaction was perhaps not surprising as the dispute over the islands had dragged on for decades with no conclusion in sight. But Britain seems to have assessed wrongly in 1981 that the subject of sovereignty had slipped off the political agenda in Argentina. Throughout that year General Galtieri received numerous visits from US envoys who discussed ending the arms embargo with Argentina. Then in November 1981 Galtieri visited Washington and met with Ronald Reagan's national security adviser Richard Allen. Galtieri is believed to have been encouraged to retain command of the army if he took power. By early 1982 Galtieri, the new president, and his old colleague Admiral Anaya, as well as his planning staff, had opted to invade the Falklands between July and October. However, their strategy was thrown into confusion in March when Argentine scrap dealer Constantino Davidoff applied for permission to implement a contract which he had signed with the UK in 1978 giving him an option to buy redundant machinery at the old whaling station in Leith harbour on South Georgia. The contract stated he must dismantle and remove the scrap to Argentina. Permission was granted and while he denied collusion with the junta, it was the Argentine Navy ship *Bahia Buen Suceso* that transported him and his workers, along with a military landing force who raised the Argentine flag. Britain immediately demanded the removal of the flag and military personnel and on 23 March at least twelve workers left aboard the naval vessel.

The UK government diverted HMS *Endurance* to the area. Then on 24 March an Argentine survey ship called the *Bahia Paraiso* entered Leith harbour with orders to protect the remaining workers, this time landing a full-size naval infantry detachment under Captain Alfredo Astiz. With HMS *Endurance* in the area tension mounted and the chances of an international incident soared. The Argentines reviewed their invasion plans. Then in late March Galtieri directed two Argentine warships to reinforce the *Bahia Paraiso*. At this point the Royal Navy despatched three nuclear submarines as Argentina prepared for an immediate invasion.

The Argentines decided to mount an amphibious landing on 1 April but bad weather delayed their plans by twenty-four hours. Falkland islander John Smith remembers 1 April 1982 very well. He said: 'There was an announcement on local radio that the governor was to make an important announcement. Then we listened as Governor Hunt said there was mounting evidence that an Argentine invasion was imminent. Everyone was stunned, the Falkland Islands Defence Force were ordered to report to

Argentine troops pour into Port Stanley, marching down Moody Brook Road after the initial Buzo Tactico attack on the nearby Royal Marine barracks.

the drill hall. Then Mike Smallwood, the radio announcer, said "don't panic folks we will now continue with record requests. The show must go on."'

Just days earlier the new incoming Royal Marine Commando detachment aboard the research ship *John Biscoe* had been buzzed at low level by an Argentine C-130. The incident was reported but there was little they could do apart from salute in true 'Royal' response by lowering their trousers and mooning at the aircraft.

Corporal George 'Geordie' Gill, one of the longest-serving members of the Royal Marines had already served in several Falkland Island NP8901 detachments and in 1982 he was preparing to return to the UK with Major Gary Noote and other members of the outgoing team. (Naval Party 8901 is the official Ministry of Defence name assigned to the Royal Marine detachment in the Falklands. The Corps operates two NP detachments; the second is on Diego Garcia.) Gill, a sniper who had served with numerous recce troops, remembers the week before the invasion as though it were yesterday. 'There had been a lot of signals. Then on the Tuesday before the landings a group of Argentine oil workers arrived in Stanley on holiday. They had short hair and a military bearing and we were convinced they were Argies. They were rounded up and detained by the Falkland Islands Defence Force just before the invasion', said Gill.

The radio station in Stanley was the key source of information for the islanders and throughout the night updates were constantly broadcast regarding the potential invasion. At 0430hrs Governor Rex Hunt reported that an invasion at dawn was inevitable. At 0540hrs he reported that Argentine landing craft were entering the Narrows.

By now the Royal Marines based in Stanley with NP8901 had evacuated their barracks at Moody Brook and dispersed in small groups to various locations outside Stanley. The Marines planned to ambush the invaders before they got into Stanley to slow down their advance. If things got really bad the Marines at Government House were ready to escape to the hills with the Governor. But events took a different turn.

Shortly after 0600hrs the Argentine special forces unit, the Buzo Tactico, swept through the Royal Marine barracks and quickly made for Government House. As they advanced additional Argentine units who were moving through Stanley came under intense attack from various groups of Marines who had pre-positioned themselves to ambush the invaders.

Governor Sir Rex Hunt who, in the face of overwhelming opposition from several thousand Argentine troops, ordered the Marines to stop firing. Every year since the Falklands Conflict Sir Rex has attended a special reunion with the men who served with NP8901.

George Gill, who had married in the Falklands and had two daughters, takes up the story:

We heard the first explosions at around 0555hrs and they were on our position about five or ten minutes later. They came very close, possibly about 30 metres before the firefight with us started.

Suddenly six of them [Buzo Tactico] came over the back wall at Government House where three of the lads were waiting and they dropped three of them straight away. Three others ran away in the morning darkness. They were about 10 feet away from each other and it was a case of just pull the trigger.

Two of us searched the rooms and we could hear them upstairs in the maid's accommodation so we sprayed the ceiling and heard them shout something in Spanish. We found all three of them and took them prisoner.

It is difficult for anyone who was not there to imagine the thoughts that were going through the minds of the Marines at Government House on that morning in 1982. They faced an overwhelming force which was equipped with massive firepower and could easily overrun their position. Gill said:

Quite honestly we were threaders [Royal Marine term for fed up]. We just wanted to get on with it. We were prepared for the fact that by midday we could be dead. It wasn't something we accepted in any sense, but when you compared the size of their force to us it was a real possibility.

We had no intention of giving up. Quite the opposite – we wanted to fight to the last man. They had torn our flag down and I personally had two daughters just down the road. I wasn't ready to give up.

Their first wave was probably about 200 strong and consisted of their special forces. It was pitch black and we couldn't see a thing, but we fired every time we saw a target. The fighting was very close. You are talking eyeball to eyeball at just 100–200 yards.

George Gill, with beer in hand, was frustrated at being ordered to stop firing during the Argentine assault on Government House; he was not ready to give up, but knew the small Royal Marine unit could never win; all they could do, and did, was damage the Argentines and slow down their advance for a short time.

As the Buzo Tactico attempted to storm Government House the Argentine 2nd Marines Battalion landed from the *Cabo San Antonio* and drove into Stanley in their amtracs (armoured amphibious tracked personnel carriers) to link up and reinforce the first wave of troops. The leading elements of the 2nd Argentine Marines headed for Government House. Then on the edge of town they came under fire from a team of eight Marines commanded by Lieutenant Bill Trollope. The Marines blasted the amtrac at the head of the column with a 84mm Carl Gustav round, then banged two 66mm LAW missiles into it and for a short time the Argentine armour and the advance was halted.

Lieutenant Trollope's Marines engaged the Argentines with small arms, before withdrawing into the town without loss or injury. This one attack is believed to have killed more than thirty-two Argentine Marines. In a separate incident another party of Marines crippled an Argentine landing craft, hitting it with an 84mm Carl Gustav round as it entered the harbour.

An experienced sniper, Corporal Gill was armed with an L42 and along with his colleagues waited at Government House for the Argentines to come within range of their sights. He said:

No one said anything. As I have already mentioned we were determined to put up a strong fight. We dropped a number of Argentines as they approached and I had a couple in my sights and made sure they were taken out of the game.

It was initially estimated that we had killed five and injured seventeen, but we only counted the bodies that we saw drop in front of us. We know there were many others killed who were not accounted for. By 0900hrs they had landed the rest of their forces, about 3,000 in total, including armoured personnel carriers which were now heading for Government House.

The small force of Marines at Government House was now fighting against an opposition which heavily outnumbered them in men, equipment and armour, yet they had crippled the initial advance, albeit for a short time, had taken Argentine prisoners and had forced the Argentines to bring in their second wave of armour before making a final assault. Islander John Smith said: 'Just after 0900hrs the Governor speaking on the radio said that Government House was under increasingly heavy fire. There was a huge force of armoured vehicles massing near Government House.'

The Governor's decision to call a truce was not what the Marines wanted, but if Major Mike Norman had not ordered them to stop firing they would without question all have been killed, the Governor included. Corporal Gill was frustrated at the order, but knew they could not afford for the Governor to be killed. He recalls:

At 0930hrs the Governor Rex Hunt made the decision to stop firing. He told us that the situation was hopeless. We were devastated. We could never have won, but we were damaging them. Suddenly it was all over.

We were kept in the paddock, several of the lads were very angry and were snarling at the Argentines, then in the afternoon we were shipped off in a C-130

The remains of the Argentine Puma helicopter that Lt Keith Mills and his Marines, who had taken to the hills of South Georgia, brought down as they harassed the enemy. The Marines also attacked an enemy warship, firing the Carl Gustav anti-tank weapon at it.

to an Argentine air base on the mainland. We were then put onto a Boeing 707 and flown, we thought to Buenos Aires, where we had been told we would be paraded through the streets.

We were all tired but several of the lads made it clear they would rather die than be paraded like goons through the streets of the capital and prepared themselves mentally for a confrontation. When we got off the plane there were crowds cheering us and we just snarled back, unaware that we were not in Argentina.

We had been flown to Uruguay and the people were in fact cheering us with their support. Later we flew back to the UK and the Commandant-General, Sir Steuart Pringle, was there to meet us. He told us what a good job we had done and added that we were all due some leave.

Many of us weren't interested in leave and went to the CG and told him that we wanted to get back south as soon as possible and he personally guaranteed that we would go back. After being re-equipped at Eastney we flew to Ascension and had to wait for the Task Force, where I joined 40 Commando's Recce Troop.

The determined stand put up by the Royal Marine detachment in Port Stanley has never been fully appreciated by the media, although there were press men there to witness the events. In fact great resentment built up between the Marines and the press after it became clear that at the media's request the Argentines ordered the Marines to lie down so the photographers could get their picture.

The Royal Marines who had sailed to South Georgia were now in action. Having been landed by HMS *Endurance* the twenty-two Marines, commanded by Lieutenant

Opposite: Brigadier Julian Thompson and his planning team discuss the military options before departing to retake the Falklands. From left to right, Major Southby-Tailyour, Lieutenant-Colonel Holroyd-Smith, Captain Rowe, Major Wells-Cole, Major Chester and Brigadier Thompson.

Keith Mills, harassed the Argentines and inflicted as much damage on the enemy as they could. Like the Commandos in Stanley, their heaviest weapons were the 84mm Carl Gustav, a shoulder-held anti-tank weapon weighing 36lb, and the smaller and lighter 66mm LAW – a fire-and-forget weapon that could only be used once.

An Argentine Puma helicopter from the landing ship *Bahia Paraiso* overflew the Marine detachment and landed. Lieutenant Mills went forward to talk to the crewman, who opened fire on him. The remaining Marines opened up and 'malletted' the helicopter. While it managed to get airborne it quickly crashed, the crew either killed from 7.62mm fire or on impact.

When an Argentine frigate arrived offshore and called on the detachment to surrender Lieutenant Mills and his team opened fire, hitting the vessel several times. The frigate, which withdrew out of range of the Marines' weapons, then began to pound the detachment with its 100mm gun, and with no options for escape and almost no ammuntion left Lieutenant Mills and his men were forced to surrender.

The small teams of Royal Marines operating in Stanley and South Georgia had destroyed an amtrac, a landing craft, a Puma helicopter and killed and wounded at least 137 Argentines. Civilian Graham Bound witnessed the entire invasion and when the opportunity arose took photographs, some of which recorded the dead Argentines in the streets of Stanley. Bound, who at the time of the invasion worked for the local paper *Penguin News*, said it was very difficult to estimate how many Argentines were killed, but the Marines certainly put up a very good fight. He added: 'The night of the invasion is something I will never forget. It was very scary. You just didn't know what was going to happen to you.'

Don Bonner, the Governor's driver in Stanley, who was held captive at Government House during the conflict, was horrified at the barbarous treatment that Argentine officers meted out to their men. He said: 'The Argentines executed their own blokes. Many of them were just young lads who were shot because they were homesick and wanted to go.'

When the Falklands were invaded in 1982, Britain's only brigade available for operational deployment was 3 Commando – a formation specially trained in amphibious operations and cold-weather warfare. At the time the Brigade was under the command of Brigadier Julian Thompson, who had led 40 Commando RM and was regarded as a quiet but tough officer who employed guile rather than strength in his planning estimates.

Landing craft from the assault ship HMS *Fearless* 'cross deck'
Commandos to other warships in preparation for the landings at
San Carlos, which took place in total darkness on 21 May 1982.
On that first day the frigate HMS *Ardent* was sunk and sixteen Argenti
aircraft shot down by the British Task Force.

Left: Marine Mark Spencer applies camouflage cream to the face of hi
colleague just hours before the landings. The men who both served w
the Reconnaissance Troop of 40 Commando were one of several snipe
teams and were armed with the L42 rifle.

The headquarters of the Brigade was at Stonehouse barracks in Plymouth and it was routinely on seven days' notice to move – it was now put on seventy-two hours' notice for operations and all formations within the force were suddenly busy packing and checking equipment. In an interview he gave to the author in 1987, five years after the campaign, Major-General Thompson said: 'I was determined that no one in my brigade would be under any illusion, but that we would have to fight to win.'

The Brigade was, and still is, based on three front-line Commando units – 45, 42 and 40 – which were supported by a Commando-trained Royal Engineers unit and a Green Beret gunner regiment. In addition, the Brigade had its own integral logistics regiment which allowed the force to sustain itself for a period of sixty days. However, units of 3 Commando were scattered across the globe when the 'recall' signal was ordered. Elements of Brigade headquarters were in Denmark on a recce for a future exercise, 45 was about to go on Easter leave with one company training in Brunei, 42 was already on Easter leave after returning from Norway and 40 had just returned from a range course.

Sergeant 'Lenny' Leonard, a mountain leader (ML) and troop sergeant in 42 Commando, was about to start an intensive phase of DIY on his new house when the balloon went up. But within hours he was packing his kit and returning to Bickleigh barracks. Just days later he would be heading south aboard the *Canberra*. Others serving on training teams at the Commando Training Centre and on attachment to Army units fought a paperwork battle to make sure they sailed with the Task Force – some were fortunate, others had to stay behind.

Staff officers in 3 Commando Brigade headquarters worked around the clock to collate and produce the directory of orders that would inform every unit in the Brigade of how their formation would travel south. It sounds tedious but this number-crunching work is always vital to ensure that sufficient ship space is allocated to those with heavy requirements, such as 29 Commando Regiment RA with their 105mm light guns. At the same time detailed tables of ammunition loads, ration reserves and stores must be collated and made available in case they are needed to be cross-decked (relocated to another ship) to support units once a decision had been made about who is landing where.

Amazingly there was very little intelligence available about the Argentines and this caused a serious headache for the Brigade intelligence officer Major Viv Rowe, a tall Welshman who had served in Oman and previously commanded 40 Commando's Recce Troop under Brigadier Thompson, then a lieutenant-colonel. He now found himself thumbing through the pages of various Jane's defence manuals.

3 Commando Brigade was to be augmented by two battalions from the Parachute Regiment. The Marines had worked with these excellent soldiers on many previous occasions, including operations in Palestine, Suez, Cyprus, Aden and Northern Ireland. 3 Para was to travel aboard the *Canberra* and 2 Para aboard the ferry *Norland* (2 Para later came under command of 5 Infantry Brigade).

On 5 April a Royal Navy carrier group sailed from Portsmouth. On the 9th the *Canberra* sailed with 3 Commando Brigade and 3 Para aboard. By the end of April a

Assault Engineers from 45 Commando RM had to pick and prod their way through a minefield using their bayonets. Here they show a sample of their find. The Argentines had screwed anti-personnel mines into anti-tank explosives; usually the larger anti-tank device would only explode when several tons depressed it. But the Argentines were aware that the Brigade was a 'light force' without tanks and adapted the weapons' pressure plates. Initially, the Argentines laid 12,000 mines.

Task Force of warships and civilian vessels requisitioned by the Ministry of Defence had sailed for Ascension Island and the 8,000-mile trip to the Falklands. The Task Force included 2 carriers, 23 destroyers and frigates, 6 submarines, 2 assault ships and 7 landing ships, as well as 12 RFA support ships and more than fifty requisitioned ships. The force was immense and as vessels trickled out of Portsmouth and Plymouth the crowds turned out to wish them good luck.

For those on the *Canberra* weapons training and helicopter drills were the order of the day. As Ascension Island got closer and it was clear that the force was to be ordered south, more attention was given to the terrain of the Falklands. Every day was packed with briefings and lectures about Argentine forces, equipment was checked and weapons zeroed.

As it sailed south the Task Force heard that an advance force had recaptured South Georgia on 25 April in an operation codenamed 'Paraquet'. The force, which included M Company of 42 Commando, the SAS and SBS, had to endure severe weather but their early success lifted morale.

A maritime exclusion zone had been announced by the British on 12 April and at the end of April a total exclusion zone was implemented. By 1 May SAS, SBS and

Royal Navy Sea King helicopters of 846 Squadron airlift the headquarters unit of 3 Commando Brigade to Mount Kent. Helicopters gave the landing force the extra mobility required to leapfrog limited troops across the island. But additional Sea King and Chinook airframes were lost when an Exocet missile hit the *Atlantic Conveyor*.

artillery forward observation parties landed on the Falklands. On the same day an RAF Vulcan bombed Port Stanley runway. The pressure continued with Sea Harrier raids and on 2 May the Argentine warship the *General Belgrano* was sunk by the submarine HMS *Conqueror*. Then suddenly as final plans were made for the landing force, HMS *Sheffield* was sunk by an Exocet missile and two Harriers crashed in fog.

On 7 May the Task Force assembled at Ascension. The exclusion zone around the Falklands was extended to 12 miles off the Argentine coast. On 9 May special forces attacked the trawler *Narwhal*, then on 14 May the SAS assaulted Pebble Island. Political options were now running out of time and on 18 May 1982 the junta rejected British proposals to avoid conflict – the UK government had made a final offer for the withdrawal of Argentine forces from the Falklands. The decision was now made that the Task Force would land on 21 May at San Carlos, a small settlement 50 miles from Stanley. It offered good landing beaches but the Task Force ships would be vulnerable to air attack, as, critically, the Royal Navy had not been able to win the air war. Pucara ground-attack fighters based on the Falklands and other Super Entendard fighters on the mainland threatened the fleet.

On 10 May the Royal Navy's biggest amphibious force since the Suez operation weighed anchor and slipped silently away from Ascension Island towards the South

Atlantic. Each vessel in the Task Force was allocated a time to leave and a position to maintain within the force. Aboard the assault ship HMS *Fearless* Brigadier Julian Thompson gave his formal orders for the landings to the commanders and key staff officers within the Brigade. This secret briefing covered all aspects of the operation as well as the options available if things went badly wrong. There was a lot of information to consider. In addition, the weather was against them, they only had a short time to achieve their objective and the lead units would have to carry all their equipment with them. As the briefing was called to a close, Thompson, drawing on the words of the Duke of Wellington, told his officers: 'Gentlemen, this will be no picnic.'

The Task Force now included more than 100 warships and support vessels. Many vessels had been requisitioned by the Ministry of Defence and were known as STUFT ships (ships taken up from trade). The troops of 3 Commando Brigade, known as the embarked force, were accommodated aboard warships, naval support ships and STUFT vessels.

As 45 Commando continued south, the weather had been growing steadily worse and final preparations for the landing began in earnest. Memories faded of the hilarious equator-crossing ceremony in which Lieutenant-Colonel Andrew Whitehead and most of his officers had been unceremoniously lathered, shaved and dumped in a huge canvas bath.

The Task Force had no airborne early warning systems because the dedicated naval fixed-wing AEW planes had been withdrawn from service. Now the carriers had to rely on poor weather preventing the Argentine air force getting airborne, but this respite was short-lived and as the force got closer to the islands, the air threat increased.

Final adjustments to the tactical loading were carried out at sea and Zulu Company moved across to HMS *Intrepid*. On 20 May 45 Commando received their orders, giving D-Day as 21 May, H-hour as 0630 (GMT) and authorising the breakdown and issue of first-line ammunition. Aboard HMS *Fearless* the landing force was preparing for action. Colin Pearson, who served as a sailor aboard the warship, remembers the period prior to the assault. He said:

We now had over 1,500 men and their equipment on board. To say the ship was busy was an understatement. Our normal complement is around 350 with a maximum of 550 when we have the embarked forces on board for the exercises in Norway. This amount of men and equipment affected everyone on board.

The galley was working overtime to feed everyone. They were living in any spare floor area. We even had them in our mess. They slept on the floor with all their gear. Guns and all. We had live ammunition rolling about the floor and getting everywhere.

Even when they left we found it under lockers, fridges, behind valves and any other little hole it could get into. Every time I went on watch I would have to turf one of these guys off my bed when I came back. They were actually a pain in the arse but it was an inconvenience we were all prepared to live with. If they could find a comfortable space in a mess as small as ours they were welcome to it.

The evening of 20 May we were told the landings were going ahead on the morning of 21 May. I didn't know then that it would be a day I would never forget, and that it was the beginning of a very short and intense period of my life. I'm like a lot of people, I forget birthdays, anniversaries, but 21 May is a day which I will never forget.

I was on watch during the actual transit so I had the opportunity to walk all around the ship whilst carrying out my tasks. All the Marines were ready and primed. They were waiting in the passageways, some sleeping, others just sitting staring into space. Very few were actually talking and none were laughing and joking.

We had some senior officers walking around the passageways trying to boost their morale but it appeared to me that each and every Marine had to deal with what was coming in his own way. No outside influence seemed to break their concentration. Normally there were some comments when walking round doing my work – Marines ribbing sailors, sailors ribbing Marines – but on the night of the 20th there was no such banter. They all had ammunition hanging from every pocket, the guys carrying the GPMG's [general-purpose machine guns] looked especially mean, draped in bandoleers of 7.62 ammunition, faces blacked out for action and ready to go. All I could think was I'm glad they are on my side. They looked like a mean force and I pitied the poor bastards who were about to be shot to shit by them.

It was about 3 a.m. when we actually began the transit into Falkland Sound. We were all closed up at action stations. The whole ship's company were ready and prepared for any trouble that may be ahead. The skipper said that we had had some good intelligence so the beachhead should be clear. He was not so sure about mines but that was a risk we would have to take. One of the frigates had transited the straits before us and she did not encounter any problems.

Just before we closed up for action stations I was on the upper deck having a last bit of fresh air. I could actually see the SAS finishing off an observation post on an area called Fanning Head. If these guys hadn't been spotted they could have reported on every move we made. It looked like 5 November all over again and it was difficult to believe that what I was seeing were actual bullets meant to kill whoever got in the way. This was definitely going to be a strange day.

As the Task Force prepared to land, the Falkland islanders monitored the BBC's World Service for progress on the arrival of British troops. Some islanders in the Port San Carlos settlement started to become aware of activity which they correctly thought was British advance units.

Fred Ford is one of the unsung heroes of the Falklands campaign who has never really been recognised for his outstanding courage and bravery during and after the landings. Exceptionally modest, Ford, a member of the Falklands Island Defence Force, lived at Port San Carlos and was one of the key guides who directed the Commandos across the island. He said:

We knew that special forces were around the settlement area weeks before the main landings. I had gravel around the house and on a couple of nights I heard someone moving around outside. I later learnt it was an SAS team trying to make contact with me.

Days before the landings we heard a helicopter fly low over the settlement and I knew it was a British one. Then on the night before the landings the bombardment started at Fanning Head. We watched the landings and a massive amount of troops seemed to come ashore in a short space of time. They were so welcome. It was great to see them and it was a sight that nobody here will ever forget.

Ford, who had immense knowledge of the inlets and coastal routes around the islands, received a telephone call from Major Ewen Southby-Tailyour. Ford said: 'He asked me if I could possibly help and of course I was delighted to do anything I could.'

In the early hours of 21 May, the men of 40 Commando and 2 Para landed under the Verde and Sussex Mountains by San Carlos settlement, both going ashore in darkness at 0440hrs. Almost an hour later 45 Commando were landed at Ajax Bay and 3 Para a mile west of Port San Carlos. Brigadier Thompson expected a counterattack, possibly from troops at Goose Green, and before his force could break out from the bridgehead Thompson needed to secure Goose Green where intelligence reports had confirmed that at least 400 Argentines were based. If the position was ignored, the Argentines would be behind the British force as it advanced to Port Stanley and could threaten an attack on the bridgehead or a counterattack on the main force.

Thompson had worked with the Parachute Regiment before, both on operations and at staff college, and welcomed their involvement. But he was concerned that the units should operate within the Brigade as 'one force'. There was no place for rivalry. Not favouring his own units, he gave the first task to the Paras and ordered the 2nd Battalion to Goose

Sergeant Bill Eades, a drill instructor who headed a Royal Marine detachment aboard the frigate HMS *Sirius* earlier in his career, leads men of 45 Commando to Teal Inlet. All are carrying bergans – back packs in excess of 80lb which contained food, clothing and ammunition.

Green. Both 45 and 42 Commando, along with 3 Para, were given missions and moved out of San Carlos, but Thompson's old unit, 40 Commando, was ordered to remain in reserve at San Carlos in case the Argentines attempted a counterattack with airborne troops.

The men of 2 Para were to mount the first and bloodiest action of the land war when they marched from Sussex Mountain for the assault on Darwin and Goose Green. But before the Paras could even get to the objective an unbelievable lapse of security resulted in the battalion's mission being broadcast on the BBC's World Service. As well as revealing that 2 Para were heading for Darwin the World Service also reported that 3 Para and 45 Commando RM were advancing on Teal Inlet and Douglas. The commanding officer of 2 Para, Lieutenant-Colonel 'H' Jones, and the force commander, Brigadier Thompson, were furious. There had clearly been a gross breach of security which was blamed on the MoD press desk back in London. The radio broadcast resulted in an extra 400 Argentine troops being flown into Goose Green. It was an act that caused deep anger and resentment of the media. The battalion felt that they had been betrayed by the BBC and to this day the 'media wound' has never healed for those who took part in the battle.

As the initial landings took place tragedy struck when two Gazelles flying in from the Task Group were shot down by the Argentines. Both aircraft were from the Royal Marines' own air squadron and went down less than a mile from the troops who had landed. The first was hit by enemy fire as it escorted a Sea King. The crew, Sergeant Andrew Evans and Sergeant Edward Candlish, shut down the engine and made a perfect landing on water. However, as they swam ashore they came under fire from Argentine forces and Sergeant Evans, who had already received injuries, was killed. Fred Ford and other islanders rushed to help: 'I was very close to the area when one of them came down

The yomp across the island; 45 Commando make their way across the rugged terrain of the Falklands. A tracked BV 202 vehicle, which the Marines used in Norway, heads the column of troops.

Mortar Troop of 42 Commando bound for Mount Kent loads aboard a Royal Navy Wessex helicopter. The mortars were regularly flown forward or to the flanks to support the advance.

in water. The crew suddenly bobbed up on the surface and the Argentines started firing at them. It was sickening. I went in and helped pull out Sergeant Evans, but sadly he died.'

During follow-up operations a second Gazelle flown by Lieutenant Ken France and Lance Corporal Pat Griffin was also hit and both men were killed. The three Royal Marines aircrew killed on D-day were buried at sea from the *Canberra* on 22 May. A third Gazelle flown by Captain Robin Makeig-Jones, a Royal Artillery officer serving with 3 Brigade Air Squadron, was also hit by enemy fire on D-Day. Captain Makeig-Jones had been directed to locate enemy troops who had fired at a Sea King helicopter. He said:

On a second attempt to find them, I surprised them and they opened up with small arms including machine guns. They were in deep shadow and the sun was in my eyes. I was doing a dirty dash between cover when they opened up. The tail rotor was hit and a round came up through the cockpit from beneath because I was tilted at quite an angle.

If my observer had been sitting in his normal seat beside me, I think he would have lost a leg. The bullet passed about 2 feet from where I was sitting. I saw tracer before we were hit, so I was in an evasive manoeuvre by the time the aircraft was being hit. Everything was working all right, although the vibration had increased. I was able to fly into dead ground and then back to our ship.

I told brigade where the enemy were and they were taken out by the Paras. When we were hit I knew what I had to do. I was not scared then, but afterwards I was when I realised how close things had been. At the time I wasn't aware that we had lost two other helicopters from the squadron.

Later at Goose Green another Gazelle would be hit with the loss of Royal Marine pilot Lieutenant Richard Nunn.

At Ajax Bay under the command of Lieutenant-Colonel Whitehead, 45 Commando carrying full bergans and extra ammunition were ordered to yomp across East Falkland and then launch a night attack on the Argentines defending the Two Sisters feature. At Ajax Bay the air defence detachment attached to 45 Commando recorded numerous successes as Argentine aircraft swooped in low and fast to attack the Task Force ships. Marine Wally Walton of Air Defence Troop is credited with destroying a Mirage jet. Marine Walton fired four missiles, making his 'kill' with the fourth. Marine Alan Steven also shot down a Mirage using the Blowpipe system and Corporal Derek Obbard brought down a Skyhawk at Ajax the day after the landings.

Lieutenant-Colonel Whitehead had joined the Corps in 1961 and was a very experienced officer, having already seen extensive service in the Far East and Borneo. As commanding officer of 45 Commando he was mentioned in despatches in 1981 following a tour of duty in Northern Ireland. He recalls in an account held at the Royal Marines Museum:

We landed at Ajax Bay, on the south side of the beachhead, at 0945 hours GMT, that is 0545 hours local time. [The Task Force operated on GMT not local time.] That would give 45 Commando one and a quarter precious hours of darkness in which to secure its objective, the old mutton factory and the ridge of hills 1,000 metres beyond it.

We were to land in four LCUs, the large landing craft crewed by Royal Marines based in *Fearless* and *Intrepid*, and were to be the second unit ashore. However, the unit ahead of us was delayed for over an hour in getting ashore, and communications with Brigade Headquarters chose that precise moment to break down, as did one of the landing craft.

So we endured an agonising wait, standing on the deck of *Stromness* listening to the steady crump of naval gunfire falling upon the hills around us and the distant crackle of rifle fire as the SBS dealt with a small pocket of resistance on Fanning Head in the northern sector of the beachhead.

It was light enough to see when I finally crammed 45 into the three remaining landing craft and we began our run up San Carlos Water towards the beach at Ajax Bay. It was now extremely quiet. I felt very naked and exposed as I travelled in one of the landing craft with X-Ray and Yankee Companies. This was the most vulnerable period of the amphibious operation, the time when the first Marines had to jump onto hostile soil and begin to move inland to their objectives.

The ramps went down and the leading sections of X-Ray Company and Yankee moved up the shallow beach. It was deserted, and in a matter of only a few

The Falklands weather was severe during the advance and regular snow storms and freezing conditions caused additional problems to the advancing Brigade. Here Brigade headquarters makes a crash move from Mount Kent in driving snow.

minutes X-Ray Company had passed through the mutton factory, reported it clear, and started up the steep rocky slope in a southwesterly direction towards Mount Campito, the highest point of our objective.

Yankee was also pouring ashore, spreading out and moving westwards up the hill. Some 15 minutes later came Zulu, completing the clearance of the beach area and swinging south to prepare for the arrival of our gunner support later in the morning.

It had been an uneventful landing, and by noon 45 Commando had 'disappeared' like chameleons into the hillside, the Marines quickly digging themselves into the soft peaty soil or building sangars of rock where the ground was too hard for a shovel to penetrate.

Across the water I could see the Marines of 40 Commando preparing their positions and below me a battery of artillery was being flown in. Rapier air defence missiles were being positioned by helicopter on the hills around the beachhead, and even a few vehicles, groaning with radio sets and ammunition, were struggling across the difficult terrain from the beach.

It was not until well into the afternoon of D-day that the relative quiet of this scene was shattered by the arrival of Argentinian Air Force. Flying at masthead height, weaving and twisting among the mountains which surrounded the beachhead, the Argentinian Skyhawk pilots displayed incredible skill and courage.

Their targets were the ships unloading in San Carlos Water and we watched – in helpless fascination – the extraordinary spectacle being played out below us, as the Royal Navy flung everything it had into the sky against the aerial invaders.

The Argentinian Air Force paid a terrible price for each assault, and by the end of D-day something like sixteen aircraft had been shot down, either by the Navy's Harriers, ship-borne air defence, or our own Rapier and Blowpipe missiles ashore.

On 27 May we were moved by landing craft to Port San Carlos and moved up the high ground through 42 Commando's positions. The Commando yomped all day, paused for a meal, then marched on through the night. It was raining and windy and the ground was wet and spongy.

The unit continued, with recce deployed ahead and on the flanks with elements of surveillance troop, and secured Douglas settlement on 28 May. That night five Royal Marines were killed in an Argentine bombing raid at Ajax Bay. The unit's next objective was Mount Kent, which was to be secured first by 42 Commando who would be lifted by helicopter to their start line.

From Kent the Commando spent the next week collating intelligence about enemy positions and strengths on Two Sisters. By 10 June, 45 Commando had received its orders to take the twin peaks of Two Sisters. The plan tasked X Company to attack the western Sister at 0100hrs, followed two hours later by Y and Z Companies from the north-west to attack the eastern peak.

As darkness fell the Commando made its last preparations and moved off at 2300hrs with Recce Troop leading, followed by Y company, TAC HQ and Z Company – they were just 5 kilometres from the enemy positions. X Company's attack was delayed, which put back the attack on the eastern peak.

The leading elements of 45 Commando were within 450 metres of the enemy when suddenly the sound of X Company launching their attack startled the enemy on the eastern peak who realised they were also about to be attacked. The Commando moved forward using its own artillery and mortar support while X Company cleared positions with Milan.

It had been a bitter fight. The Argentines were re-equipped with .5 machine guns and attempted to pin the Marines down, but several men in 45 Commando were decorated for their bravery in clearing enemy positions. Later Lieutenant-Colonel Whitehead commented:

We lost four dead and ten wounded. It could have been much worse, but as I looked back down over the direction from which we had assaulted, the enormity of our success came home to me for the position was theoretically impregnable.

On the bloodied Two Sisters Mountain Sergeant George Hunt's action saved many Marines from injury or death, despite the fact that he was seriously wounded himself. Hunt, then a corporal, was the point man in the first section of Zulu Company in 45's assault. The Argentines were heavily dug in and the Marines had planned to get as close to their positions as possible before launching a surprise attack. As he led his men through a minefield, marking the way for others, he fell into a bog and was soaked

A Royal Marine of Air Defence Troop pictured at Goose Green. It was here that a Marine stood up with his Blowpipe missile on his shoulder in full view of the enemy and fired at an Aeromacchi, scoring a direct hit. The Argentine air force had dropped napalm on the Paras and engineers later discovered additional canisters.

Below: The overall force commander Major-General Jeremy Moore, centre left, salutes both Royal Marines, Paratroopers and Army Commandos killed the early days of the conflict and buried in a temporary grave.

from head to foot. He recalls: 'We had no spare kit on us and all I could think was that I would be freezing cold. The fact that I might be killed didn't enter my head.' With bayonets fixed the Marines advanced still closer to the enemy, stopping every few yards to scan the Argentine positions through night-sights.

Suddenly a diversion attack began. Shaken by the close battle the Argentines started firing down the mountain. Now within sight of the enemy Hunt noted the Argentine positions and radioed them back to companies following on behind in the main Commando attack. The steep, rocky terrain of Two Sisters gave the advantage to the Argentines, and as the battle began Hunt launched a section attack on a machine-gun post. A section nearby was hit and two Marines were killed instantly. As Hunt and his men went forward he was blinded by the flash of an explosion. His left arm was shattered, but despite the pain he got up and led his men in an assault, using his damaged limb to support his rifle as he returned fire. For the next two hours he fought with total disregard for his own safety and only stopped for treatment when the battle was over and Two Sisters was completely controlled by 45 Commando.

After the Falklands Hunt trained as a helicopter pilot serving at Yeovilton with the Commando Air Squadron. He said:

> There was a lot of heavy fire. I can remember the drone of the Browning machine gun beating at us all the time. But you don't have time to think. The young guys in my section were brilliant. They worked really hard and it paid off in the end.
>
> I remember a flash and the shrapnel ripped into my arm, but the training took over and I simply moved forward using the skills I had learnt in training. When the Argentines realised we were not going to stop until we had Two Sisters they started to run away – there were a lot of dead bodies.

Hunt was awarded the Military Medal for his outstanding action.

Finally, 45 Commando moved towards Sapper Hill before getting the signal to move into Stanley. After the conflict, the men returned home aboard the *Stromness* and the *Canberra*. The names of those who died in the Falklands during 45's operations are carved in stone at the entrance to 45 Commando Group's base at Arbroath in Scotland. Sergeant David 'Yorkie' Malone who was serving with 45's Zulu Company remembers the landings very well. He said:

Sergeant George Hunt served with 45 Commando and was seriously injured during the battle for Two Sisters but continued to fight and was awarded the Military Medal for his actions.

It was very business-like, well organised and professional. Shortly after we went ashore a flock of upland geese landed near us. A lot of the lads were townies and wondered what the hell they were.

We had a dry landing and I must admit there was a lot to take in. We were ashore. Later we moved off for Two Sisters. It was freezing and you could hear the ice crunching under your feet. We were obviously trying to be quiet and the noise was causing me some concern.

As we went into the assault we called down artillery which was dropping 200 yards in front as our advance formed. It was a textbook operation. Everything was very well planned and everyone was involved right down to the section commanders who gave their own orders.

As 2 Para mounted their bloody assault on Goose Green, Marines from Air Defence Troop, armed with Blowpipe missiles, joined them. As the battle raged two Aeromacchis came in low to attack the Paras with napalm. Marine Rick Strange stood up and took aim, recording a direct hit. He was so elated that his colleagues had to pull him to the ground. He said: 'As the Paras advanced over open ground they came under heavy fire and wounded were falling everywhere. Two Aeromacchis jets came in low to attack and one dropped napalm on Para positions. I was under fire throughout the attack on the aircraft, but I was just doing my job. There was mortar and small arms fire all round. I saw the missile hit the aircraft. It then carried on for about 200 metres and exploded in a great big ball of flame and hit the deck. I felt elation, I was jumping up and down, then I was dragged down before I got shot.'

Sappers from 59 Independent Commando Squadron Royal Engineers also supported 2 Para at Goose Green. The Green Berets engineers lost Corporal Michael Melia. It was also at Goose Green that four aircraft from 3 Brigade Air Squadron constantly ferried ammunition forward in support of 2 Para and evacuated casualties. They were often under fire. After Lieutenant-Colonel 'H' Jones was hit, a helicopter flown by Royal Marine Lieutenant Richard Nunn flew in to casevac the 2 Para commander, despite the intense enemy fire and Pucara aircraft known to be in the area. As the aircraft flew forward to pick up the Colonel it was shot down by an Argentine Pucara and Lieutenant

A Royal Engineer from 59 Independent Commando Squadron peels back the soil around an Argentine anti-tank mine. Sappers from 59 supported the Paras at Goose Green and one of their team, Corporal Michael Melia, was killed.

Lieutenant-Colonel Nick Vaux, the commanding officer of 42 Commando, chats with his Marines of Lima Company after the battle for Harriet. During the fight he picked up an Argentine FAL rifle.

Nunn was killed. He was posthumously awarded the DFC and his body temporarily buried with the men of 2 Para killed in the battle.

As Goose Green raged, 42 Commando was 'stood to' ready to reinforce 2 Para, but they were not called in. Instead 42 was tasked to fly forward to Mount Kent. K Company led the advance to Kent with the rest of the Commando flying in the following night. In wet and freezing conditions the unit prepared for its main objective – Mount Harriet.

Lieutenant-Colonel Nick Vaux, the commanding officer of 42 Commando was another very experienced officer. He had joined the Corps in 1954. During his officer training he took part in the first heliborne assault at Suez in 1956 and served numerous tours in Northern Ireland. Before they departed for the South Atlantic Vaux addressed his men on the parade square at the unit's Dartmoor camp. This was the last time the Commando formed up together in the UK before landing in the Falklands and as the parade concluded he gave the order '42 Commando to the South Atlantic. Quick march.' The national media quickly picked up on his quote, which was widely reported and still used years later – Vaux had put himself in the history books.

The battle for Mount Harriet was never going to be an easy task. The Colonel had codenamed the main feature of Harriet 'Zoya', after his eldest daughter. The feature rose approximately 300 metres and covered the ground leading into Stanley. A second feature called Wall Mountain, from which 42 could observe Harriet, was codenamed 'Tara' after the CO's second daughter. Some of the approaches to Harriet had been mined and heavy machine guns covered the forward slopes, so a frontal assault was

Marines from 40 Commando search Argentine prisoners on West Falkland. The workload in guarding and processing prisoners was immense and in the final days of the conflict became logistical nightmare for commanders.

A Marine from 40 Comman
maintains guard over three
Argentine Special Forces
soldiers who were captured
around San Carlos where th
had been directing enemy a
attacks on the Task Force. T
men of 40 Commando
remained at San Carlos as a
rear protection force in case
the Argentines attempted ar
airborne counterattack to th
rear of the advancing
Commandos and
Paratroopers.

ruled out. After a reconnaissance patrol was sent out to evaluate routes the commanding officer decided to attack from the south-east, almost to the rear of Harriet. This posed the danger of running into more minefields and being compromised by the moonlight during the yomp to the start line, but Lieutenant-Colonel Vaux had secured permission to use artillery and mortar fire in a diversionary plan and the Commando made it to the point from which the assault would begin. Vaux had opted to make maximum use of the Commando's Milan and 66 LAW to clear Argentine positions and it proved an effective policy.

At 0200hrs the attack was launched by K Company and by 1000hrs Harriet had been secured. It was a hard and long-fought battle in which the unit lost only one Marine – possibly because of the use of Milan and 66 LAW to clear enemy positions. As Vaux stood on Harriet, hundreds of Argentine prisoners were rounded up by the Commando. The assault had been an outstanding success.

A significant battle of the Falklands War which deserves special mention was the action taken by the Mountain and Arctic Warfare (MAW) Cadre who routed the Argentine special forces unit 602 Commando Company at Top Malo. At Top Malo, an isolated farm some 20 kilometres north-west of Bluff Cove, nineteen men of the MAW Cadre surprised the enemy with a rocket attack and a classic right-flanking assault. The attack on 31 May was headed by Captain Rod Boswell, a no-nonsense officer who had dedicated his career to the mountain leader branch of the Corps with tremendous enthusiasm and motivation. He had previously commanded 40 Commando's recce troop in Northern Ireland and was well respected for his ability to get things done – whatever the task.

A Cadre observation post had spotted sixteen Argentines of a specialist unit at Top Malo. Boswell's first thought was to call in an air strike but 42 Commando was about to start a highly dangerous low-level airlift by helicopter across enemy-held ground and the available Harriers were needed for air cover. Other units were resting after events at Goose Green – 45 and 3 Para had just yomped across the islands, 40 was in the rear to deal with any Argentine counterattack. The presence of an Argentine special forces unit presented a serious threat to 3 Para and 45 Commando and Boswell therefore decided the Cadre would have to mount an assault.

Because of a communications breakdown the whole Cadre could not be contacted and that night Boswell gave orders to nineteen of its members – almost the same number of men as they intended to attack. The plan called for the entire team to be airlifted before first light and dropped just over a mile south-west of the target. The force would then divide into a seven-man fire section and a twelve-man assault group. As they approached the farm it was apparent that only one building, a white-washed stone outbuilding, could contain any force. The others looked dilapidated and deserted.

The fire group was armed with L42 sniper rifles, Armalites and SLRs as well as three M79 grenade launchers and eight 66 LAW rocket launchers. On Boswell's signal – he would fire a green flare – the fire group was to open up with the LAWs and then pepper the building with automatic fire. At this point, operating in pairs, the assault group was to skirmish forward.

Boswell, with the assault group, ordered his men to fix bayonets and then fired the flare. The fire group quickly destroyed the target house, but the Argentines stormed out, firing back and very quickly two Marines, Sergeant Terry Doyle in the assault group and Sergeant Rocky Stone of the fire group, had been shot and injured. Then Corporal Steve Groves was shot in the chest.

The assault group had almost charged down on to Top Malo, blazing firepower from the hip and with Boswell leading. Boswell then came face to face with an Argentine who fired his FN. Untouched, Boswell fired back with the Armalite, but it took him four rounds to floor the Argentine. Five Argentines were killed and seven wounded with the rest taken prisoner. It had been a bloody fight and those who took part are immensely proud of the operation, although at the time it received very little recognition.

The MAW Cadre also played a key role in preventing a major 'blue on blue' when a lone Chinook was spotted carrying elements of 2 Para towards Fitzroy where British gunners had orders to destroy any helicopters in the area. The swift action of a Cadre corporal behind binoculars in a forward OP without doubt saved eighty-two members of 2 Para.

Later, when the entire brigade located itself in and around Stanley, many Marines could not believe the manner in which the Argentines had savaged the town. Everything

The lead element of 45 Commando makes a tired but triumphant entrance into Port Stanley after the Argentine surrender. They had walked from San Carlos, an epic 'yomp', which had illustrated the benefits of Commando training and the high standard of fitness maintained by the Marines.

Above: Marine Alan Gibson's patience wears thin as he attempts to deal with some of the thousands of Argentine prisoners who surrendered. Their weapons had to be taken off them; they were then searched and given a meal and somewhere to sleep. Many had lost their equipment and others had injuries that had not been treated.

Left: Back in Southampton Water aboard the Canberra *Brigadier Thompson meets the Commandant General Sir Steuart Pringle who flew aboard along with Prince Charles to congratulate the Brigade on a remarkable achievement.*

had been smashed, set on fire and destroyed. Corporal Geoff Page-Bailey said: 'Stanley was a mess. There was a lot of abandoned big guns. The Royal Marines barracks was completely levelled and there were piles of guns and abandoned kit. The majority of the Argentines just wanted a good meal, they appeared to be hungry and totally demoralised. The majority of the prisoners just wanted to get home. Many were very young and when they arrived aboard *Canberra* they were scared and smelly and looked like exactly what they were – a beaten army.' Page-Bailey had been directed to the *Canberra* to assist in the documentation of prisoners of war being shipped back to Argentina. He said: 'We had to ask them if they had fleas or anything else and offer them a tin of soup. It seemed a very strange list of questions and you could only feel sorry for them, they were broken men.' But Page-Bailey recalls a lighter moment: 'Several of their officers had been educated in the UK and spoke excellent English. One of them approached me and asked how his country had fared in the World Cup. I told him they had lost 3–2

Former members of NP8901, which was re-formed as J Company and attached to 42 Commando Group, outside Government House to replace the flag they had seen torn down by Argentine soldiers two months earlier.

and he replied in a perfect Oxford accent "It hasn't really been our week, has it?"'

Merchant Navy officer Phil Hancock said: 'I am proud to have been associated with the Marines, even if only for a short time. The toughest, most professional people I have ever met. The Argentinians didn't have a chance when competing on even terms.'

During the war naval Commando photographer Peter Holdgate took what has become one the most memorable pictures of modern warfare. It showed Corporal Peter Robinson yomping across the Falklands with 45 Commando, the Union Jack flying from the aerial of his Clansman radio. After the war a 12 feet high sculpture of a yomping Marine was commissioned by the Royal Marines Museum. The statue, by Philip Jackson, was erected at the entrance to the museum at Eastney barracks in Southsea, Hampshire.

The Falklands sparked a shake-up in military doctrine and saw a review of almost every aspect of equipment, from boots to weapons. The lessons learned from the war were also to shape the future of new formations and demonstrated to the world, particularly the Soviet Union, that Britain was still prepared to stand up to aggressors.

Inset: The Falklands image shot by Peter Holdgate, which became famous after the conflict. It shows Peter Robinson, a radio operator, who along with Mortar Troop of 40 Commando, was attached to 45 Commando. *Main picture*: Robinson can be seen looking at the ground because at the time the unit was passing through a minefield and the Marines were watching their every step. The photograph was taken at 1030hrs just as a snow storm had ended. The Marines were heading for Teal Inlet having left Two Sisters and Sapper Hill.

SIX

OPERATIONS IN ULSTER

'The IRA are cowards, but that's why they are terrorists not soldiers.'

Marine 45 Commando RM, 1973

When the first Royal Marine Commandos deployed to Northern Ireland in September 1969, few could have predicted that they would be the advance party for the Corps' longest operational campaign and bear witness to some of the most sickening terrorist violence of the twentieth century. Furthermore, no one could have forecast that more than three decades later Green Berets of 3 Commando Brigade would still be serving in the Province as peace initiatives seemed to come and go while bitterness and deep-seated religious rivalry continued to split the communities. British troops were rushed to the Province on an emergency tour in 1969 to defuse confrontation between Protestant and Catholic communities with the aim of creating a climate of security. The aim was not realised; instead, the operation developed into the military's longest active-service campaign.

At this point through the fog of a thousand myths and the propaganda of the Republican press machine, it is important to remember the mission of the British Army units and the Royal Marines who first deployed to Ulster – to protect the Catholic community. In five days of relentless riots that raged from Londonderry to Belfast 7 people were killed and 750 injured. More than 1,500 Catholic families had been burnt out of their homes; just 315 Protestants lost theirs.

Trouble had flared throughout the 1960s as Protestant extremists hit back at Nationalists following the failure of an Irish Republican Army (IRA) campaign that took place between 1956 and 1962. The campaign cost the lives of six members of the Royal Ulster Constabulary (RUC) and eleven B Specials. In retaliation the Protestant Ulster Volunteer Force (UVF) shot dead a Catholic on 27 April 1966. Another victim was shot in June.

A period of calm returned for about two years, but then in 1968 there was more civil unrest when a Northern Ireland civil rights march, formed by Catholics from across the social classes, paraded through Londonderry on 5 October 1968. The demonstration had been banned by the Home Affairs Minister and when it went ahead police units moved in with batons; seventy-five people were injured.

Marines of 41 Commando face rioters during one of their early deployments to the Province. The canvas roof of their Bedford truck has been reshaped into an apex so that petrol bombs will slide off. As the conflict progressed canvas-roofed vehicles were replaced by armour-protected Land Rovers and personnel carriers.

Throughout 1969 tension increased as the situation deteriorated. The Army's senior officer, Lieutenant-General Sir Ian Freeland, had only 2,500 troops based in Ulster and had made contingency plans to deploy them to guard government buildings. By July the government had approved the use of CS gas by the Royal Ulster Constabulary and on 12 August it was deployed for the first time in the UK as riots flared in the Bogside area of Londonderry.

On 13 August 400 troops from the Prince of Wales's Own Regiment of Yorkshire were sent to HMS *Eagle*, a naval shore base in Londonderry. The following day, Thursday the 14th, they were deployed to the Bogside after an exhausted 3,200-strong RUC requested military assistance. Then in the city on the night of the 15th 10 civilians were killed, 145 were injured and 4 policemen were wounded in gun battles. The troops had been sent in by the Labour Prime Minister Harold Wilson at the request of the Northern Ireland government who sought military assistance following months of sectarian violence.

The Green Berets of 41 Commando arrived in Belfast as part of Operation 'Banner' in September 1969. Their task was to protect the Catholic community from extremist Protestant attacks and the Marines were welcomed with smiling faces, clapping and offers of tea and cakes whenever they entered a Republican estate.

Sergeant David 'Yorkie' Malone arrived in Ulster with 41 Commando in 1969 as a young Marine and at one point his company commander was Paddy Ashdown, later leader of the Liberal Democrats. Malone recalls:

> The situation changed very quickly and the riots could be really fierce and often we would be stood in the middle facing everything from both communities.
>
> The hatred was unbelievable; I think all of us found it a bit of an eye-opener. But we had some funny times, like the occasion the assault engineers searched a roof space on a council estate and found a lead running through the lofts of every house. It turned out that every property in the street was running its electric on the bill of one person.

During its two-month emergency tour 41 Commando suffered seven casualties. Across the Province there had been more than 70 shootings, as well as 10 bombs, and an RUC officer and 10 civilians killed. Two Republican terrorists had died and 14 weapons were recovered. Although 41 Commando had only witnessed a small fragment of this, it had been a busy tour.

In June 1970 45 Commando RM arrived in Belfast. The men adopted tactics last used in Aden and stripped their Land Rovers down – canvas roofs and doors removed – to give them greater visibility and the flexibility to deploy from the vehicle at speed in pursuit of suspects. The principle was obviously a wise one because within months a wide range of other units followed suit. However, stripped-down Land Rovers were only practical until the Marines faced a crowd of brick-throwing Republican rioters.

Shortly after its arrival 45 Commando was tasked, with the 1st Battalion the King's Own Scottish Borderers and the 1st Battalion the Royal Scots, to keep protesting Nationalists away from marching Orangemen. The Commando was responsible for a district of Belfast that included the Crumlin Road with the Republican Ardoyne to the north and the Protestant Shankhill to the south. On 26 June eight Orange lodge bands marched, totalling some 500 people in the parade with a further 2,500 following behind and by early evening a crowd of more than 200 Nationalist youths had begun stoning elements of Support Company who had used a 3-tonner and a Land Rover to block a side street where the mob was advancing.

Among the small force of Marines was John Naughton, a young lad who had not been out of training long, and was now in the thick of a riot. Everything from housebricks to ball-bearings, bottles, marbles, coins and cans was thrown at the Green Berets and almost every man received some sort of injury. The troop officer, a young lieutenant, was hit straight in the face with a brick. While his wounds were being dressed the troop sergeant took command.

A much larger crowd of approximately 2,000 Nationalists was held back by the main force of the Commando while the RUC prevented 3,500 Orangemen from attacking the Catholics. Throughout the night the rioting continued but at dawn the crowds disappeared home. Later that morning confrontation sparked across Belfast with hospitals reporting more than 200 injured. 45 Commando's patch was quiet until mid-afternoon when another Orange march sparked an IRA sniper attack in the Ardoyne in which a Protestant civilian was killed.

The Commando's medic, Petty Officer Freddie Maclaughlin, gave first aid to a civilian as a firefight continued around him. As he carried the civilian into an ambulance, which was clearly marked with red crosses, he was shot in the face. He was later awarded the George Medal for his courage.

By early evening the trouble had been quelled by the Commando, but later that summer's night alcohol fuelled the rioters' bravado and they were back on the streets. A stolen bus was driven into a pub and within minutes an angry crowd of more than 150 had gathered. Just one troop of Marines ploughed in to restore order, donning respirators and using tear gas to push the crowd back while at the same time sending in snatch squads to arrest seven of the ringleaders. Then a gunman fired several rounds, possibly from an Armalite, one of which cut through Marine Terry Glover's riot shield, struck his belt and lodged itself in the cleaning kit box for his SLR. The rioting continued throughout the night with cars set on fire and houses torched, but the following day normality returned and the Butler Street riots were over – at least as far as 45 was concerned. Throughout the 72-hour period the Commando had stayed on the street, taking turns to grab a few hours' sleep.

The Commando adopted a policy of dominating its tactical area of responsibility (TAOR) in an effort to deny the terrorists freedom of movement and used maximum aggression where it was needed, while at the same time mounting a heart-and-minds campaign in the local community. A retired officer who served in Belfast as a troop commander said: 'There was no point in being nice to those we knew were the players – they simply took it as a sign of weakness. When we were called into a riot we went in hard and fast. You had to. It was the only way to achieve success.'

By mid-1971 mobs were out on the streets every night, stoning soldiers, torching buildings, hi-jacking buses and generally destroying the infrastructure and economic fabric of Ulster. This high level of public disorder, combined with increased terrorist attacks against the security forces, resulted in the government introducing internment on Monday 9 August. In support of the internment a massive operation was mounted to round up the 'alleged known players'. In the early hours of the 9th, battalions across Northern Ireland were given allocated areas in which they were to 'lift' suspects. The operation was codenamed 'Demetrius'.

At this time 45 Commando RM was on standby as the MoD's 'Spearhead' battalion, ready to deploy on operations anywhere in the world. (The Spearhead is a readiness role in which all Army and Royal Marine Commando units take part in turn.) Now as the security situation deteriorated 45 Commando was flown back to Northern Ireland to assist in 'Demetrius' and arrived on 10 August for a three-week stint. Reaction to internment was fierce and crowds gathered to protest throughout the Nationalist areas. Barricades were erected and as 45 moved in to clear them, petrol bombs rained down.

Royal Marine Commandos question a man during a deployment by 42 Commando in the late 1970s. All patrols regularly stopped and questioned local people who were not suspects but were checked in the battle to safeguard the public against terrorist attacks.

Later that year 45 Commando RM returned, this time for a four-month tour of Belfast, arriving on 17 October. Just a week later 42 Commando RM also arrived in the Province and deployed in Armagh and Dungannon. Both units sustained casualties but no fatal injuries. Between 1970 and 1974, 45 Commando was to serve five tours in Ulster, one of them a short emergency Spearhead operation.

Former Marine Peter Winsmore, who served in Ulster during the early '70s, spoke of his first time on the ground:

My section commander was an old sweat and before we got on the ground he told us not to take any shit, 'Just stay calm lads', he told us, 'and if you hit a problem get my attention and I will come across and deal with it.'

It was a weird sensation being on the streets for the first time, trying to watch where you were walking while at the same time looking at every spot you thought could be used by a sniper. I don't mind telling you I was delighted when that first patrol was over and we returned to base.

On 24 March 1972 Westminster dissolved the Stormont parliament and took direct control of Northern Ireland. It was a controversial decision which Republicans refused to accept and resulted in 'no-go' zones being established in many hardline Republican areas as they attempted to establish their own communities in protest at the British government's action.

In June 40 Commando RM arrived for its first tour in Ulster and was to witness some of worst days of violence in the Province. Protestant marches reached their peak and the creation of Catholic 'no-go' areas forced a major military operation. By the middle of 1972 'no-go' zones had spread across West Belfast and Londonderry. The violence increased as gunmen sought refuge from the security forces in the Nationalist estates where they thought they would be free from capture. After Bloody Friday, 21 July, when bombs shattered Belfast and left nine people dead, a plan was drawn up to clear the 'no-go' areas and restore law and order in the Province. Codenamed 'Motorman', the operation took place in July 1972 and was the largest to be mounted by the British Army since Operation 'Musketeer', the air and sea assault on Suez in 1956. It involved 21,000 troops from 27 different units and included 4 Centurion tanks, which were fitted with bulldozer blades to clear the barricades. These tanks were known as AVREs (Armoured Vehicle Royal Engineers) and were deployed from landing craft on the River Foyle. Hundreds of armoured vehicles supported the operation which began at 0400hrs on 31 July. 45, 40 and 42 Commandos took part in the Belfast phase of 'Motorman'. 42 moved into Ligoneil and 40 into the New Lodge. The operation attracted massive television coverage as Saladin and Saracen armoured personnel carriers drove through the streets of Republican estates, the convoy smashing down the Nationalists' checkpoints. The 'no-go' barriers were destroyed in the first six hours of the operation which took twenty-four hours to complete; constant vigilance was required in the days that followed. 'Motorman' was an outstanding success. During the operation 2 terrorists were killed, 30 arrests were made, and 32 weapons, 1,000 rounds of ammunition and 27 bombs were recovered. But despite the success, the IRA was allowed to regroup and return to the streets.

In the summer of 1972 40 Commando deployed to North Belfast in an area which included the hard-line Republican community of Unity Flats and the New Lodge. The Commando was led by Lieutenant-Colonel John Mottram, a robust officer who led from the front and was respected by all his men. This was perhaps one of the hardest tours faced by a Commando. Almost every day there were gun battles and two months into the operation Lieutenant-Colonel Mottram was given the additional responsibility of commanding 1 Royal Scots and two companies of 42 Commando as well as his own unit for 'Motorman'.

It was during this tour that the first Royal Marine Commando to be killed on active service in Ulster lost his life: he was Marine Lennard Allen. Later during the same tour a second Marine from 40 Commando RM, Marine Anthony David, was killed. A further seventeen Marines were injured, some of them seriously. (The first soldier to be killed in Ulster was Gunner Robert Curtis who was shot by an IRA gunman as he patrolled the New Lodge on 6 February 1971.)

As the years passed many Marines and senior officers became frustrated with the situation in the Province. A retired officer who served with 42 and 45 Commando on numerous tours summed up his feelings about Ulster with disgust. He said:

Royal Marines of 45 Commando pictured during an early tour in the 1970s. They are armed with SLR rifles, later replaced by the SA80 assault rifle. The rifle sling was clipped around the right wrist to prevent the weapon being grabbed by a terrorist.

'The problem is the IRA were at war with us, but we were not allowed to be at war with them. There was never any resolve to move ahead. The mission was always containment.'

In the true style of the Corps the Commandos were, as in previous campaigns, keen to introduce new tactics to make their job more efficient. Assault engineers formed special search parties because they had all the necessary kit and in 1974 Marines of 45 Commando introduced the first Eagle flights across the notorious bandit area on the border. Heliborne sections of Marines flew across designated areas, landing at regular intervals to mount vehicle checkpoints. This gave 45 Commando the advantage of surprise in their pursuit of terrorists. Other units adopted the procedure and it became a successful tactic until the IRA obtained surface-to-air missiles.

At the height of the car bomb threat, disposal teams were stretched to the limits dealing with suspect devices across the Province. The Marines adopted their own tactics for tackling suspect cars – the Carl Gustav 84mm anti-tank weapon. However, as Sergeant Yorkie Malone recalls, some young Marines needed extra tuition in operating the weapon. Inside one of the security force bases in West Belfast an instructor got his team together and went off to do some 'dry drill training' in one of the spare rooms within the old mill they were staying in. All training rounds are, of course, marked 'drill' but a low calibre live round was used on the range for training. As the trainee team went through their paces the inevitable happened. The live round, which for training purposes included a .22 round, was fired and despite its small calibre caused chaos. But the most embarrassing fact was to emerge later when the daily operational sitrep (situation report) was signalled to each unit serving in the Province. Listed at the bottom of the signal were the contact reports (reports of shooting incidents) for the previous twenty-four hours. The unit concerned took a lot of stick after their 'Negligent Discharge' of an 84mm Carl Gustav appeared on the sitrep. Many who read it reacted with disbelief and immediately telephoned the unit for confirmation.

Geoff Page-Bailey, a Marine in 40 Commando RM during a tour in 1973, recalls his first trip over the water. He said:

We were all on an LSL which had sailed from Liverpool. When the ferry pulled into Belfast we carefully looked over the side. I suppose we were expecting to be shot at as we arrived. But everything was quiet and all we could see was a massive line of military trucks ready to take us into our location. We boarded the wagons and I said cheerio to a few mates who were heading for a different location to me. My company was off to an RUC base in West Belfast.

We took over from 42 Commando and our main patch was the Unity Flats and New Lodge. Looking back, I was very lucky, I was in a section of old sweats who had just come back from Singapore. They had done it all, read the book and seen the film and probably starred in both.

But as I was just a bit of skin [Marine expression for very young lad] these older blokes looked after me and made sure that I quickly became very street wise. I think the fact that we had so much experience within the ranks was a great benefit to the Corps in the mid-'70s.

Marine George Gill, known to everyone in the Corps, joined the Marines in September 1963 and served his first tour with 45 Commando in the early '70s before going on to clock up a total of ten tours in Northern Ireland – one of them a twelve-month 'resident battalion' deployment. He said:

It was all bricks and bottles. Then as time went on the shootings increased and the Corps started to take casualties, like everyone else. To counter this the commanding officer of 40 Commando, Colonel John Mottram, decided to deploy our snipers.

A Land Rover patrol of 40 Commando pictured in April 1975. The Marines now stripped their vehicles of roofs and doors to allow soldiers to see more and escape if they were shot at. All drivers were attached from the Royal Corps of Transport (later RLC) who were based in Belfast for two years at a time and knew the area well. They wore their own cap badge on a green beret during their attachment.

They were a great success and by the end of the tour had recorded something like twelve confirmed kills. The deployment of snipers was such a success that the Army quickly adopted our tactics and started their own course at Warminster.

The Commando Spirit made a significant contribution to the Corps' endeavour in Ulster. For instance units never deployed thinking they might lose someone. The attitude was, as always, positive – achieve, challenge and win.

In 1974 two Royal Marines from 45 Commando RM were killed during the unit's tour in South Armagh. The men, Corporal Dennis Leach, aged twenty-four, and Marine Michael Southern, nineteen, died when they were blown up by a radio-controlled IRA bomb which had been buried near their position at Drummuckavall. At Condor in Arbroath, the home of 45 Commando, two roads on the married quarters estate were named after them – Leach Close and Southern Close. On 13 August 1999 a remembrance service was held by the Royal Scots who at the time of the anniversary were manning a permanent observation post (OP) near where the Marines were killed.

One event that must have astonished the locals of West Belfast and will always be remembered by 40 Commando took place at Glassmullen camp in May 1975 when Marine Jim Martin, later Regimental Sergeant-Major Martin, broke his leg. Once it was plastered, he painted it green and was back out on the street, sitting on the tailgate of a Land Rover, rifle in hand – he wasn't going to miss anything.

In 1976, 40 Commando RM deployed to South Armagh. Terrorist attacks in the border region had soared and it had been some time since a unit sent to the area had not sustained a fatal casualty. 40 Commando would lose no one. The unit had spent most of the summer in East Anglia, training for rural operations and exercising the various skills of OP work, surveillance, patrolling and helicopter deployment. It was an intense period of training and as the men honed their skills, the UK baked in record-breaking sunshine. At the time the Commando was commanded by Lieutenant-Colonel Julian Thompson, a tough, no-nonsense officer who had the respect of every man in the unit. He was not a great admirer of ceremonial occasions and appeared to relish the opportunity to get in the field and do what he most enjoyed, soldiering.

RSM Brian Bellas, the unit's senior NCO, was also admired by the unit, even if they never told him. Bellas, a tall, fit man, seemed to have the ability to know everything that was going on in the unit without ever asking. He would never accept excuses: if you failed to do something, the best policy was to admit it.

Prior to the South Armagh trip 40 Commando's Recce Troop had been ordered to grow their hair long, but not tell anyone why. In the words of the troop commander: 'If anyone has a problem, tell them to see me.' When some of the younger members of the troop passed the RSM their salute was greeted with a look of horror. Bellas, always immaculate, demanded an explanation and the lads replied, 'Sorry sir. We can't tell you.' Within minutes the RSM had discovered for himself that the troop would be working undercover with other units and as such had been 'officially' ordered to grow their hair! (The night before the unit returned to mainland UK he told one member of the troop: 'I want to see all that cut off by tomorrow, goldie locks. It's time you started looking like Marines again.')

During his pre-tour recce the commanding officer, Lieutenant-Colonel Thompson, was personally briefed by the commander of 3 Brigade, the Army brigade headquarters, with responsibility for the area including the South Armagh patch. Three points were made plain to him during the briefing:

1. The Commando was to make sure that sectarian killings in the area were kept to a minimum – none if possible.
2. The Brigade commander would not look kindly on Thompson if any trains on the Dublin–Belfast railway, which passed through the Commando's TAOR, were hijacked by the IRA. This had happened frequently in the past, although the tactics employed by 3 Para, 40 Commando's immediate predecessor, had brought it to a stop.
3. If any of 40 Commando's patrols were caught south of the border, the CO would be on the next boat home.

The commander of 3 Brigade was very clear about his aims and the tough brief could almost be described as 'an interview without coffee'. Without doubt the commander's concerns had been fuelled by a series of incidents on the border. Just prior to 40 Commando's arrival, an SAS patrol had been temporarily detained by the Gardi in the Republic.

Speaking some years after the tour Thompson, now Major-General, said:

As an antidote to the wave of sectarian killings some months earlier, an SAS squadron was based at Bessbrook and operated in the South Armagh patch. Although not under command of 40 Commando, the squadron commander liaised closely with me and cooperation was excellent.

I decided that the key to carrying out the first two tasks laid down by the brigade commander was good intelligence and dominating the ground. Our predecessor, 3 Para, had achieved this by good patrolling and excellent OP work, especially by their patrols company.

So I decided to expand the Recce Troops to over fifty strong, consisting of three sections, each commanded by a very experienced sergeant: Sergeant John Matheson, a platoons weapons instructor sniper, Sergeant John Moate, on loan from the SBS, and Sergeant Bill Wright, a mountain leader.

The Recce Troop covert OP network was the framework around which the rifle companies were to operate. Thanks to their skill and professionalism, the Commando's Recce Troop quickly gained the confidence of the resident SAS Squadron, who 'subcontracted' some of their OP tasks out to them.

The patrols mounted by Charlie Company overlooking the railway, known as the 'The Railway Children' after the film of that name, would ensure that no trains were hi-jacked.

The brigade commander's final point regarding any of the unit's patrols being caught south of the border was to be 'self-regulating' by all company commanders. The sensitive nature of this issue could not have been made clearer and any officer or troops sergeant whose section strayed across the border faced career asassination.

On 17 August 1976 40 Commando RM arrived at Belfast harbour on an LSL and drove to Bessbrook in a convoy of 4-tonners escorted by Land Rovers of 3 Para. From Bessbrook companies were flown forward to their various locations, including Crossmaglen and Forkhill, with the gunners of 145 Commando Battery and elements of Support Company located at Newry RUC station.

The Commando's first incident occurred within one minute of their taking over the area with a report of an incendiary bomb in a shop at Warrenpoint. The Battery and 40 Commando's mortar troop were co-located at Newry RUC station. Their quick reaction force and bomb disposal team quickly dealt with the incident – the first of many.

Bessbrook helibase, described during the 1980s as the smallest and busiest helicopter operation in Europe. Aircraft operated around the clock, flying routine patrols into the countryside of South Armagh and mounting constant surveillance of potential terrorist activity. Here an RAF Wessex lifts off with a patrol from 40 Commando aboard while a Lynx waits to land in the background.

Newry became a busy patch with regular hijackings and shootings. In one of these incidents 'Bungy' Williams was shot in the back of the thigh. He was evacuated by Scout helicopter to hospital and when his mates realised he was going to recover they preferred to say that he had been shot in the backside rather than the thigh.

Alpha Company, commanded by Major Colin Howgill, had a very difficult task. It was based in Crossmaglen, the heartland of the Nationalist community which has seen more British soldiers killed by the IRA than any other area of Northern Ireland. The IRA made great use of IEDs (improvised explosive devices) because they provided maximum impact and maximum chance of escape for the Active Service Unit (ASU) involved. Crossmaglen had seen IEDs on roads, culverts and farm gates. In fact, just before the Commando's arrival the IRA had packed a bike with explosives and detonated it just off the main square in Crossmaglen as a patrol from 3 Para passed. Private James Borucki was killed. Later, a sangar was erected on the corner of the square and named in his memory. Borucki Sangar remained a key observation tower in Crossmaglen until 30 July 2000 when work started to dismantle it as part of the Good Friday peace agreement.

Recce Troop commander Captain Rod Boswell opted, with the CO's approval, to maintain a number of the operations established by the Patrols Company of

A member of 40 Commando's Recce Troop uses a powerful pair of binoculars during a surveillance operation in South Armagh in 1976. Covert monitoring became the most important skill in the battle against the IRA and other groups and by the 1980s the Army's surveillance grip on the Province made it very difficult for terrorists to operate with the freedom that they had in the 1970s.

3 Para, one of which was a permanent overt OP overlooking Jonesborough – a small village on the border. The OP was situated on high ground and provided constant 'eyes and ears' on the border while at the same time acting as a deterrent to the IRA and providing reassurance to the local community. The overt observation post, known as OP Phoenix, was based on a labyrinth of underground sangars and a command area. These were covered by sandbagged sangars which overlooked the approach flanks just in case the position was attacked. They included general purpose machine guns in the sustained fire role.

Further out from the location were more overt sandbagged sangars with manikins in uniform. These clearly confused the IRA who never really established how many troops manned the OP. The whole idea of Phoenix was to make the community aware of the military presence. It was an innovative concept which without doubt reduced terrorist activity in Jonesborough. Major-General Thompson said:

> It was a successful tour. The Commando made 174 arrests, seized more than half a ton of explosives and recovered 17 weapons. Some 37 bombs were found and dealt with, over two per week in a seventeen-week tour.
>
> In return the IRA inflicted 13 casualties on 40 Commando, but none were killed; the first unit to complete a South Armagh tour with no dead for years.

There were 69 shootings, of which 24 were against the security forces. There were no civilians killed.

The most serious attacks were against A Company in Crossmaglen, both by mortars. On both occasions the IRA used the Mark 8 and Mark 9 mortar bombs for the first time against the base. For clearing some of the unexploded Mark 8s from the base Staff Sergeant Bruce RAOC [Royal Army Ordnance Corps], the ATO [Ammunition Technical Officer], was awarded the George Medal.

After the second mortar attack, the CQMS [Company Quartermaster Sergeant] of A Company C/Sgt Jones was awarded a bar to his MBE for his tremendous example to his company during and after both mortar attacks. The Mark 9 was so large that in the words of the ATO, it 'made all types of mortar bomb used in the Province previously look ridiculous'.

The covert observation tasks mounted by 40 Commando covered the unit's entire TAOR with particular emphasis on Crossmaglen where the Marines dominated the ground and used OPs to collate intelligence and if necessary provide support to patrols on the ground. An example of these was an operation on the Cullaville road in which three Marines from Recce Troop were inserted into the roof space of an old property with the specific task of monitoring the road. In particular they were to look for several key players who, it was suggested, might be carrying out their own recce on Crossmaglen for an IRA attack.

The three joined a routine patrol with A Company out of Crossmaglen and entered the property in the early hours of the morning, having peeled off from the patrol. The OP was initially to last for a minimum of six days and kit for the trio included one sleeping bag, which would be shared. A tile in the corner of the roof was drilled through and a small portion removed to provide a good field of vision towards the area of interest. On the first night one of the team, Steve Lord – who has sadly since died – thought he heard intruders. Weapons ready, the trio waited as the noise got closer. Then two huge rats scurried through an upstairs doorway.

The rats were to prove a menace. They would climb on top of the sleeping bag of the off-watch member of the team, presumably because it was warm, and dance around. Often the weight of the rat would wake the Marine who thought his colleagues were calling him for his watch.

No hot food could be consumed for obvious reasons and the only luxury was the occasional flask of black tea which was dropped off in a 'dead letter box' (DLB) by other patrols in the area. Waste food was bagged, along with the natural human products, and collected in the DLB. A DLB was a pre-arranged rendezvous point where supplies were left. These supplies could include food, new radio codes and photographs to update the intelligence of the operation. The DLB would usually be at least half a mile from the site of the observation post. DLBs were rarely discovered by the IRA because they were cleverly disguised.

By day three the rats had become such a problem that the team used a little poison to control the situation. They took great delight in sending out a bag of twenty-five dead brown rats with a special note to the A Company patrol who lifted it saying, 'Many thanks for the excellent food. Please accept this as a gesture of our thanks, enjoy!'

The OP lasted several weeks and proved the value of good log-keeping. Two individuals who had been identified in the Cullaville area were spotted by patrols and were believed to have been assessing the potential for an attack on a Marine patrol in the square at Crossmaglen. They were stopped and questioned by a patrol and their identification checked when they approached a vehicle checkpoint at Forkhill. No IRA attack was mounted. However, the success of the Royal Marine Commandos against the IRA in Ulster in closing down terrorist border operations, arresting key players and constantly dominating the ground on which they were deployed, thus preventing the IRA's freedom of movement, made the Corps, along with the Parachute Regiment, a prime target of the Republican movement.

In 1978 the first military helicopter to be hit and forced down was flown by Navy pilot Lieutenant Nick Richardson whose Army Lynx (identification X-ray Zulu 664)

A mobile patrol of 42 Commando drives through a Loyalist patch of West Belfast during August 1989, the twentieth anniversary of the current troubles. Land Rovers were now fitted with extensive armour protection and the Marines in the back of the vehicle stood up, looking though an open hatch and were known by their colleagues as the 'top cover'.

was working in support of 42 Commando RM on the border. Then on 27 August 1979, during 40 Commando's year at Ballykelly in Londonderry, the IRA brutally murdered the Life Colonel Commandant and Admiral of the Fleet, Earl Mountbatten of Burma, as he was holidaying with his family at Mullaghmore. On the same day the Provos killed more than twenty soldiers at Warrenpoint when they trapped a Para and Queen's Own Highlanders patrol in a bomb attack on the main road to Newry at the Castle of the Narrowwater.

Before the Commandos deployed to Ulster in 1976 the IRA propaganda machine announced that it would kill ten Marines. Despite mounting two attempts in separate mortar attacks, it failed. Then on 17 October 1981 the IRA attempted to murder the Commandant-General of the Corps, Lieutenant-General Sir Steuart Pringle Bt KCB. In a car bomb outside his home the Commandant-General suffered serious injuries and lost a leg, but his cheerful spirit and determination was an inspiration to the Corps and by early 1982 he was back at work in his Whitehall office.

In 1989 the IRA was still looking for a major attack on the Corps and on 22 September it struck at the Royal Marine barracks at Deal in Kent, killing eleven band musicians in one of the most sickening attacks the organisation has ever carried out.

The deployment to Northern Ireland has been the Corps' longest operational campaign. Here a Marine is pictured in South Armagh, otherwise known by the security forces as 'bandit country'.

Above: A car is stopped at a routine checkpoint in Belfast by Royal Marines. This was a very effective way of curbing the terrorists' freedom of movement in the city and in the remote areas o[f the] border. *Below*: A patrol of 45 Commando pictured during a dawn patrol on the border. Patrols in this part of the Province relied on helicopter support to drop them off in remote areas [far] from their base. This was mainly due to the geography of South Armagh and the border area but was also prompted by the fact that roads could be mined with culvert bombs. Helico[pters] were also subject to attack and for several years the IRA attempted to shoot down aircraft full of troops.

While Northern Ireland remains the longest campaign for the Royal Marines and all other British military units operating there, it is perhaps the only one where progress has been limited by political indecision and more recently 'political correctness'. Marines taking part in today's pre-Ulster training no longer hear the word 'riot' being used by instructors. Instead they speak of a 'street disturbance'. While the Gulf War, Bosnia and Kosovo generated horrors that no doubt left many soldiers with terrible memories, Ulster remains the forgotten psychological war. An eighteen-year-old Marine who served at Crossmaglen, the border town where more British soldiers have died than in any other area of Ulster, remembers the fear of going on the street, even after the excellent training he had received at Lympstone to prepare him. He said:

> None of us said anything at the time, but I think we were all scared. We had just arrived and didn't know the ground very well and the stories we had heard definitely had an effect on us. The problem was no one back at home was interested.
>
> When the guys came back from the Falklands and the Gulf the country turned out to welcome them home, but Northern Ireland is almost like a dirty word. I was at Reading railway station one day sat in the buffet and this Irish bloke started singing rebel songs.
>
> Everyone to a man just put their papers up in front of their faces and ignored him, but he spotted me and obviously thought I was in the Army and proceeded to lecture me about the IRA and how they would wipe the floor with the Brits. Then he started pushing my arm across the buffet table and I had enough. It was almost like being on one of those NITAT [Northern Ireland Training and Tactics] patrols where you lose the plot and score hundreds of points for getting all your procedures wrong. As he grabbed my arm I lifted him up and punched him all round the buffet before throwing him onto to the station platform.
>
> I wasn't proud of what I did, but I had been pushed as far as I could go. The bloke was in a bit of a mess and

A Corporal from 42 Commando pictured in West Belfast during 1989. By now equipment had been significantly improved and as the security threat was 'high' helmets were worn. The standard protective 'flak' jacket had been replaced with a sophisticated INIBA (Improved Northern Ireland Body Armour) vest which was worn under the combat jacket.

...copters are the key means of travel for military operations in the rural areas of the borders. RAF, Navy and Army helicopters operated from Bessbrook's heliport, deploying small units into ...ote areas and on occasions flying company groups to mount major search operations.

...he aftermath of a riot a child plays among the remains of burning rubbish in July 1999 ...a mural on a wall voices the opinion of the local Loyalist residents. Northern Ireland has ...n the British Army's and the Corps' longest operational campaign and while troop ...mbers reduce the potential tranquillity of peace does not seem any nearer.

Warrant Officer Bob Ewing (later promoted to RSM) pictured during 42 Commando's deployment to West Belfast in 1989. This was a particularly tense period as it included the twentieth anniversary of the conflict.

...osite: The future of the Province hangs in the balance. By 2000 the Royal Marines had completed almost forty tours of duty in Northern Ireland and the marching season of 1999 and ...00 overshadowed the peace process as petrol bombs and riots erupted. Here a section of 42 Commando takes the blast from petrol bombs.

seconds later the police arrived and were all set to arrest me as everyone in the buffet remained tight-lipped, apart from two old ladies who witnessed the entire event and stepped forward in my defence.

By 2000 the Royal Marines had recorded thirty-nine tours of duty over almost fourteen years worth of duty. Fourteen Marines had lost their lives in Ulster and ninety-four had been injured, many of them seriously. As the Royal Marines and the British Army enter the twenty-first century many of the old security force bases are being demolished. Glassmullen in West Belfast, Whiterock, and North Howard Street were among the first and as troop numbers reduced on the streets the potential for peace looked very good.

But for many Marines the political and military changes that have taken place in Northern Ireland do not guarantee peace and there is a cynical acceptance that the Corps will be deployed in Ulster for some years to come. One young officer summed up the situation in an article in the *Globe and Laurel*, the Royal Marines' journal. He said: 'We learn from history that we don't learn from history.'

In summer 2000 tension flared across the Province as the Parades Commission refused to allow Loyalists to march down the Garvaghie Road in the heartland of a Nationalist estate to Drumcree church. (The commission is an independent body designed to work apart from the RUC and build confidence in the community as part of the ongoing peace process.) 40 Commando recorded the Corps' fortieth tour of duty when it was deployed to Northern Ireland as a Brigade reserve for the period of the marching season and in particular the Drumcree march. On 5 July 2000 there were more incidents across the Province than in the whole of the previous year. Molotov cocktails, shots, fireworks and acid bombs were thrown at the security forces. The RUC used water cannon for the first time in thirty years.

In the same month an extremist Nationalist group called the Real IRA, whose members refuse to accept the Good Friday agreement, claimed responsibility for bomb attacks on Hammersmith Bridge in London and on the capital's rail network. Then in late July the last of the Republican and Loyalist prisoners held at the Maze were released as part of the peace agreement. The men included some of the IRA's former players. As the prisoners (eighty-six in total) walked free, a huge arms shipment bound for rebel Republican terrorists intent on wrecking the Northern Ireland peace talks was seized in Croatia. The haul, which was intercepted at the port of Split, included anti-tank rockets, weapons and ammunition.

The final word on Northern Ireland must go to those on the front line. A young Marine who deployed in 2000 on his first tour of duty said: 'The main areas seemed normal to me, but there is little harmony in the hardline Republican and Protestant estates. The hate is what sticks in my mind. Both communities seem miles apart and yet we have released their top players back into the community.'

SEVEN

EARNING THE GREEN BERET

'The hardest challenge of my life. I never thought the training would end.'

Marine Billy Peters

Britain's Commandos earned a reputation during the Second World War for establishing one of the most physically demanding training courses within the military system. The Green Berets of the twenty-first century maintain this pedigree of excellence with a selection process that is the longest of any infantry unit in Europe.

Situated on the banks of the River Exe at Lympstone in Devon, the Commando Training Centre Royal Marines is home to a thirty-week course that demands 100 per cent and more from each individual if they are to earn the privilege of wearing the green beret. Recruits face a programme of physical training which gradually increases in tempo to prepare them for a series of Commando tests.

The primary function of Lympstone is to train regular and reserve new entry personnel for service within the units of 3 Commando Brigade. It is unique within the British armed forces in that all young officer, recruit and non-commissioned officer training, as well as much specialist training, takes place at the same centre. Today's potential Royal Marine Commandos enjoy some of the best facilities in the armed forces. Lympstone has its own modern gymnasium, swimming pool and complex of outdoor assault courses. The Commando Training Centre is truly a mecca of military physical fitness.

The origins of today's training centre can be traced back to 1939, when the Royal Marine Corps expanded. This resulted in a camp being built at Lympstone for training reservists. It was initially called the Royal Marines Reserve Depot. By November that year staff had begun to form training teams at the new camp, formerly part of the estate of Sir Francis Drake, and by late January 1940 the first of many thousands of Royal Marines arrived at the depot. These were HO ('Hostilities Only') Marines, not Commandos, and during 1940 the recruits trained at Lympstone while regular troops destined for sea service trained at their naval divisions. The base, then known as Exton Camp, was also the temporary home of the 7th and 8th Royal Marine Battalions as well as a naval unit which was accommodated under canvas.

In the early days at Lympstone recruits cross the river at Postbridge as they take part in the 30-miler. The test is still a key feature of Commando training in the twenty-first century and involves a four-man team map reading their way across Dartmoor, sometimes in snow, fog or driving rain.

On 5 September 1941 the camp was renamed Depot Royal Marines Lympstone and at its peak was training 800 men a month for war service. During this period a second camp at nearby Dalditch in Budleigh Salterton was home to the Royal Marines Infantry Training Centre (RMITC), which was responsible for the second phase of training. In 1943 the course was extended from six to eight weeks and in 1944 expanded further to eighteen weeks.

At the end of the war, the Commando role, first established by the Army, was passed exclusively to the Royal Marines and No. 3 Commando Brigade became 3 Commando Brigade Royal Marines. The Commando School at Achnacarry in Scotland closed, with its responsibilities transferring to the Royal Marines Training Group at Towyn in Wales.

Records for 1946 show that 3,000 officers and men were living in 74 wooden huts at Lympstone, with an average 1,000 recruits in training at any one time. Dalditch was closed and Lympstone was renamed the Infantry Training Centre. It began to expand its role when both the officer and NCO schools were transferred to the base.

Opposite: Sergeant John Simpson sees recruits through the water tunnel on the endurance course. These recruits of 76 Troop completed their training in early 1973. Having finished the course recruits must then run 5 miles back to Lympstone, soaking wet and freezing cold. To avoid rubbing injuries to the back, recruits were advised to 'tailor' their equipment and put their poncho roll on top of their webbing pouches as the rookie in the front of the picture has done.

During the 1960s the majority of the Corps' specialist infantry training, command and communication courses, and virtually all other aspects of Commando training held at Bickleigh Camp, near Plymouth, were relocated to Lympstone. A major building programme began and the first of the new accommodation blocks was opened on 12 July 1963.

In 1970 the camp was finally renamed the Commando Training Centre Royal Marines (CTCRM). Four years later the move to put all elements of training and continuation courses under one roof was completed when the first phase of the Junior Royal Marine course, which until then had been held at Deal in Kent, transferred to CTCRM. The centralisation of all specialist training resulted in all levels of command courses being located at CTCRM, along with the sniper (PW3) course, which has become so highly regarded that special forces now attend it.

Throughout the 1970s work continued to shape Lympstone into a centre of military excellence. A swimming pool and gymnasium complex, cottage hospital, indoor range, lecture complex and even its own railway station were built. In 1976 the trees that held the 30-foot high Tarzan course were retired and replaced with a safer metal-framed-structure. Lympstone also includes an assault course and an aerial confidence test, which are key aspects of the selection procedure.

For many new recruits the transition from civilian life to the disciplined routine of

Commando selection can be a 'culture shock' and the psychological expectation of what lies ahead of them only adds to the mental pressure. Many forget that this course, like any physical challenge, can be completed with the correct training and presence of mind.

Today, arriving at the camp's own railway station, called Lympstone Commando, new arrivals are escorted to an induction centre where, after completing paperwork and other administrative tasks, they are given a tour of the camp. They then have an attestation in which they swear allegiance to the Queen and officially sign on the dotted line as Royal Marine recruits.

The first few days are absorbed with routine matters, haircuts, kit issue and gentle PT as well as an introduction to the role of the Commandos and a presentation from their training team. It is initially all very cosy, then the course begins – fast, furious and full of fitness periods.

Mike Johnson remembers his first few days at Lympstone. He said:

The physical demands of the course are immense. It is not designed to be easy and without exception all recruits will hit the pain barrier at some stage.

I didn't know what had hit me. We were marched away for haircuts and were issued with a uniform which looked like it had been left over from the war. It is difficult to describe but you are permanently wound up, preparing for the next day, making sure all your kit is ready and thinking about the days ahead. Unless you have actually been there and done it I am not sure that you can appreciate it. The physical training is a major culture shock. I never knew I could run so far and I think on reflection it was the prospect of running with all the kit that really worried me.

The first phase for recruits in Portsmouth Company includes induction and individual training. This induction phase lasts two weeks and is the process by which a recruit makes the transition from civilian to service life. Individual training covers a wide spectrum of skills, such as the use of weapons, field craft, physical training and map reading. During the initial fifteen weeks the focus is on physically preparing recruits for the more arduous and challenging training ahead of them.

Throughout the course it is common for recruits to sustain injuries. Generally, these are of a minor nature and can be treated relatively simply while the recruit remains with his troop, although his participation in some training activities will be limited. For more serious injuries or illness, a recruit will be transferred to Hunter Troop, the medical rehabilitation and remedial organisation. The aim here is to keep the recruits who want to stay in the system and get them back to fitness.

The recruits work under a regime that demands self-motivation to become a member of the Corps. Those who continually do not meet the standard in routine training, fail runs and give a lacklustre performance will be invited to leave.

Many of the tactics and disciplines taught to recruits at the CTCRM may be viewed as 'politically incorrect' in the twenty-first century, but the sometimes brutal nature of the Commandos' training is vital in order to maintain the Brigade's ability to deliver an 'aggressive punch' to any enemy when required.

In the early weeks of training recruits find themselves on Dartmoor in what is essentially a survival exercise. Carrying all their newly issued equipment and rifle the young trainees will yomp (march) across the moor and in the late afternoon make themselves a shelter. The exercise format changes regularly but often the training team tells the recruits that food is on the way. Sure enough a lorry arrives with a number of 'hay boxes' (insulation carriers usually used for hot food). The recruits line up for their meal thinking it must be Christmas because instead of a couple of containers for the whole group, there is one allocated per section. They are told to open the container and when they do, a live chicken jumps out – dinner! In the previous week the recruits will have been taught how to cook food in the field, in earth ovens and over open fires. Now they have to put the knowledge to good use.

The recruits who arrive at Lympstone, either as Marines or potential officers, are from a wide variety of backgrounds, skills and professions but they all have one thing in common – the willingness to give up everything for the adventure of becoming a Royal Marine Commando. Lieutenant Jeff Moulton (later Major) who served on

New recruits arrive at the camp's own railway station, Lympstone Commando, then it's off for an introduction, swear allegiance to the Queen and, for those who need it, a haircut.

The first weeks are spent developing fitness in training sho before recruits start running in boots, carrying equipment and rifl

The trained Commando, ready for action. After successfully completing training the recruits are put through a final exercise in which all the skills they have been taught, from weapon handling to fieldcraft, beach-raiding tactics and helicopter drills, as well as map reading and radio procedure, will be tested in a kind of military 'finishing school'.

Recruits can expect 'surprise' kit inspections at any time. Here in the middle of an exercise on Woodbury Common instructors decided to check at 0600hrs that the trainees were carrying all they should have been and that everything was clean.

e assault course must be completed within a set time and each recruit must cross the water tank and carry out a 'regain' in which he drops his legs, then pulls himself back up onto the rope
nd continues across. At some point every man will end up in the tank.

various training teams at the Commando Training Centre recalls a fully qualified dentist who gave up his civilian career to become a Royal Marine officer. Another Moulton remembers was a Sergeant serving with the Royal Tank Regiment who decided to join the Corps. He was married, had a successful career in the Army and stood to lose everything if he failed, but he was determined to join.

Those who opt to become Marines must be totally committed and focused on the challenge ahead of them. Many who arrive very fit but slightly unsure of their own ability can have success snatched from them as the physical aspect of the Commando course increases in tempo.

This is a Junior Marine's story:

I arrived at Deal on a cold and wet September afternoon in September 1972, having caught the train from London. I hadn't got a clue what to expect, although I had read just about every leaflet I could about the Marines. The train was full of lads and we all looked each other up and down. When we arrived at Deal it was obvious we were heading for the same place as we hung around outside the station.

A Navy blue coach pitched up with Royal Marines in big white letters stamped across the side. A small tough looking corporal walked across to us with a clipboard and ticked our names off as we climbed aboard the vehicle. A few minutes drive and we were in Deal barracks. It looked old and very unfriendly and I think quite a few people were having second thoughts if the look on their faces was an indicator.

The 9-miler. This exhausted troop is nearing the end of its run as it enters the notorious 'Heartbreak Lane', the final leg of the run back to camp. All are carrying packs, fighting order and rifles. Instructors allowed them to carry their helmets, as the heat on this day was intense.

We were ushered into a massive dormitory full of bunk beds. Each one had a name on it in alphabetical order and a basic set of uniform and a woolly hat known as a cap comforter. There was also a postcard on the bunk that we were told to send home to make sure our families knew we had arrived safely. This huge room contained almost eighty recruits and by now it was early evening.

Suddenly a sergeant marched into the room. It was a moment most us will never forget. He was Irish, Sergeant Thompson, and our first impressions were that he was a hard bastard, although within days everyone admired him. He had been there, done it, seen it, read the book and seen the movie and had the medals to prove it. He called everyone into one area of the room and went through the basics of what was called induction. Later that evening we swore allegiance to the Queen and signed the dotted line.

We were shown how to wear our uniforms and the following day we were gently broken in with two visits to the gym and a visit to the 30-foot ropes on the edge of the playing field and told that by the end of the month we would be climbing these.

Within days we were running around Deal like gazelles and within weeks we were running along the shingle beach between the camp and Kingsdown ranges wearing full kit and carrying our rifle. At the ropes we discovered the physical training instructor wanted to know what strength we had in our arms. We had to climb without using our feet.

He was a hard Geordie and just like all the instructors he was manic about cleanliness and perfection. We would arrive at the gym and before we would do anything he would inspect our white canvas training shoes, checking the laces had been scrubbed the night before.

Anyone who had a slight trace of dirt was ordered to one side and told that if he wanted to join the Corps he had better shape up or be prepared to ship out. The offender was made to run around the fields twice – a distance of about a mile.

The ethos at Deal emphasised generating the best recruits and sometimes the mentality made you question the instructor's approach. I can recall one day we were in full Lovats [green dress uniform] and had taken all night to prepare our boots and belts but for whatever reason the instructor was not happy with our turn out. We marched up and down and then he halted us and ordered us to run around the parade square, then still in full Lovats he made us climb the perimeter wall that surrounded Deal barracks – which destroyed our polished toe caps. When we lined up again he told us that we had learnt two important facts today: one never turn up for drill unless our kit was perfect as in his view we were letting the Corps down and secondly by running around the parade square and climbing the wall we had learnt that the Corps must always remain flexible for different jobs. Many of us failed to appreciate his teaching style.

Deal was a harsh place where those who failed were quickly invited to leave and those who made mistakes were given tough treatment. On one occasion a room mate who had brothers in the Corps was picked up on a locker inspection which took place regularly sometimes unannounced.

These inspections required that all shirts were ironed to the size of the *Globe and Laurel* the Corps journal and that everything was in place. In this case things weren't up to scratch and the instructor decided to tip most of the locker out of the window, then told the recruit to pick up his mattress and follow him. He spent the next 20 minutes running around the parade ground with the mattress on his head while we picked up his kit which had been tossed out of the window from the top floor of a four-storey building.

The instructors were not the screaming bullying type but they had the attitude that the Marines was their Corps and if we wanted to join then we had to reach their standards. Fail and you said goodbye to your military career. I am sure such a policy would not be accepted today, but I believe it worked well.

Our main instructor had served in the jungle and aboard ships and was always stressing the importance of cleanliness. He had a real dislike of Army personnel whom he called pongos and regarded them as dirty and would always claim that the Germans didn't have a problem finding the 8th Army in North Africa because of the smell and mess they left in the desert.

Then we were off to Loch Ewe in Scotland for mountain training. The camp we stayed at was being used by the Argylls and I think they thought we were mad. Our instructors would start the day at 0500 with a 5 mile run to the novice climbing area making sure we passed the Army accommodation. Some mornings the Argylls would stick their heads out to see what was going on and our training team would instruct us to shout 'morning percy pongo'.

It was so cold we would wait in the huts until the last minute then run out for inspection. We were only too grateful to run. It was the only way to keep warm. Then as we almost reached our physical peak we transferred to Lympstone and the unknown. We were now in the serious phase. We had made it to CTC, but the rumours and stories about how hard the training was forced some people to quit before we arrived at the base. A new training team was on hand to meet us and the next day we were being introduced to the assault course.

Throughout the next sixteen weeks we were made to believe that we were the best troops in the British armed forces and we were. From abseiling over cliffs and out of helicopters, to mounting night raids and constantly running with full kit around the lanes near the camp, we were like a pack of elite racehorses.

I remember we had to take part in a one minute boxing round with the smaller blokes being pitched against the monsters. We were in the gym at the same time as another troop and they [the instructors] pitched us against each other. I ended up fighting a huge bloke who quickly put me on the deck.

There is a final exercise, either before or after the Commando tests, in which almost every aspect of the training is integrated. It starts with an amphibious raid, then a long yomp across Dartmoor and a survival phase before receiving an air drop of supplies from an RAF Hercules. Plans are then drawn up and the troop mounts a second attack by helicopter.

A Royal Marine instructor lectures recruits about cleaning and looking after their SA80 assault rifles. Throughout training they will wear blue berets with a red backing behind the Royal Marine cap badge.

I guess my long standing memory of the course will be those early days at Deal, up all night cleaning kit, ironing shirts and always being tired. At CTC the pressure increased and the daily race around the Tarzan assault course is an image I will always remember.

Being presented with the green beret is a major achievement for anyone who passes the course, but it is the confidence that the course instils in you that I also look back on with great pride. I passed the course. It wasn't easy, but as the Marines teach you nothing in life is.

Today, all training takes place at CTCRM and as the course progresses recruits move to Commando Training Wing (CTW) which is responsible for the training of recruits who wish to become Royal Marines, as well as Army and Naval personnel who volunteer to serve with 3 Commando Brigade. In addition the wing undertakes the training of Royal Marine Reservists and Territorial Army volunteers who serve with the Royal Marines Command.

Under the direction of CTW recruits transfer into Chatham Company. This marks the second phase of Commando training and the start of a more intensive military skills course. It involves teamwork, the Commando Course and the King's Squad pass-out.

At one time recruits faced the mud run in which, wearing full equipment and rifle, they would run across the mudflats of the River Exe at low tide and if they didn't perform to the expected standard press-ups in the mud would follow. Such aspects of training have now been assigned to the history books.

During team training the recruits work together in fire teams (four men), section (eight men) and troop (twenty-eight men) organisations. At this early point the training teams identify potential leaders who will be made section leaders and awarded a red diamond badge to wear on their left sleeve. As training progresses these diamond candidates will be closely monitored by the training team and their ability considered when the King's Badge is awarded to the best all-round recruit in the troop, if any is considered worthy.

The troop will learn to handle and fire all the infantry weapons available to a Commando unit from the Milan anti-tank missile system to the general-purpose machine gun, as well as receiving instruction in the use of grenades and mortars. This is an intense period of learning during which men must also develop physical stamina. Recruits learn tactical skills, to work as a team and are taught how to operate in all phases of war. Their expertise is tested in a series of exercises which involve the use of both blank and live ammunition. Throughout their training, instructors from Infantry Support Wing will assist in nuclear, biological and chemical warfare training and platoon weapons instruction as well as drill.

During this period the physical part of the course intensifies in a carefully planned programme designed to prepare the recruit for the Commando Tests. At the same time instructors introduce small tests to make sure the recruits, no matter how exhausted, still have the mental capacity to make decisions. They will be given a map-reading task or a test known as 'Kim's Game' where they are shown a collection of items and then six hours later are asked if they can remember what they saw.

In a typical year's programme the target for Commando Training Wing will be to process 23 troops of 55 recruits, five all-arms Commando courses of 75 students, four phase 1 and five phase 2 reserve courses each of 50 students, as well as two TA Commando courses. This adds up to a possible training total in excess of 2,000 students. The schedule is daunting, but it is achieved by precise programming and detailed planning carried out by dedicated instructors. The instructors, who all have recent operational experience with the Brigade, are carefully chosen and stay with a troop throughout its thirty weeks of training.

But ultra fitness and courage are not enough to pass the course. Recruits must give everything in mind and body or face defeat, often in Heartbreak Lane, the infamous landmark which forms the finishing mile of most runs. The psychological impact of being so near yet so far after a gruelling speed march is too much for some and over the decades the tiny country lane has claimed thousands of recruits who have failed to meet the punishing time limit on the tests. At the end of all runs recruits are halted near the playing fields and their physical condition checked before they cross the road bridge and march back into camp. The exception to this is the endurance course where individual recruits keep running straight over the bridge and on to the rifle range.

The intensity of the exercises and the Commando Tests is such that the recruits require all the determination and motivation they can muster to overcome the fatigue of the final exercise. The King's Squad is perhaps the easiest week of training. Several days are spent preparing for the pass-out parade, the green beret presentation and the King's Squad parade.

The final part of the course is designed to examine the recruits in all aspects of the training they have received. The exercise is particularly realistic, incorporating a raid from the sea, an abseil and an assault. It is spread over several days and recruits cover distances up to 70 miles to get to their objectives. They carry full kit and throughout the exercise they get very little sleep. At the end they are utterly exhausted and it is at this point that they need all their determination to overcome fatigue. A day after arriving back at Lympstone the recruits face the ultimate selection – the Commando Tests:

The endurance course: Starting early in the morning trainees must complete a 1½ mile course across rough terrain, which includes a host of obstacles – for example, culverts, deep pools and an underwater tunnel – then run 4 miles back to Lympstone. At the camp they fire their weapon on the range. They must achieve six out of ten shots on target, otherwise they will have to do it again.

Time: recruits 72 minutes, officers 70 minutes

The Tarzan and assault courses: The Tarzan course is an aerial confidence test which starts with a death slide and includes numerous obstacles high up in the trees. It culminates with trainees climbing a 30 foot wall. The assault course incorporates a dozen or more obstacles ending with a series of underground concrete tunnels. The Tarzan and the assault courses must be completed one after the other.

Time: recruits 13 minutes, officers 12 minutes

The 9-mile speed march: Carrying full fighting order, rifle and helmet, recruits and officers must run as a troop, then complete a troop attack at the end of the run.

Time: recruits and officers 90 minutes

The 30-mile load carry: Carrying full fighting order, safety equipment and weapons, both recruits and officers must complete a 30-mile yomp across Dartmoor. Starting early in the morning they will be split into teams and are required to navigate their way across the moor.

Time: recruits 8 hours, officers 7 hours

Battle swimming test: Wearing full kit and rifle the recruits must swim 50 metres.

Having completed the tests the troop then moves into the King's Squad phase of training in which they are the senior recruits at Lympstone. This period will be spent preparing for the pass-out parade and in most cases feeling very proud that in just a few days they will become Royal Marine Commandos.

Throughout training instructors will have assessed the troop and the 'diamonds' appointed earlier in the course will be selected for the King's Badge. The recipient can usually expect faster promotion. The King's Badge has a long history. On 7 March 1918, George V visited the Depot Royal Marines at Deal in Kent. On this occasion he inspected Royal Marine recruit squads and took the salute of the 4th Battalion at a march past. Six weeks later the 4th Battalion stormed ashore onto the mole in the raid on Zeebrugge and won great fame and two Victoria Crosses. To mark his visit, the King directed that the senior recruit squad in Royal Marines training would in future be known as the King's Squad. He also directed that his royal cypher, surrounded by a laurel wreath, would be known as the King's Badge, and would be awarded to the best all-round recruit in the King's Squad, provided that he was worthy of the honour. The badge was to be carried on the left shoulder and worn in every rank. Queen Elizabeth II approved that the custom and privilege of the King's Squad remain unaltered. The King's Badge is not given to a member in every squad. It is only given if a recruit measures up to the very exacting standards required.

A Commando Medal is also presented and awarded to any officer or man who shows throughout training that he possesses the following qualities to an outstanding degree: leadership, unselfishness, cheerfulness under adversity, courage and determination, high professional standards. These qualities define the Commando Spirit.

Potential officers who join the Royal Marines face a much tougher selection process than general recruits. Although the physical course is the same, they must complete it in faster times. Each officer course is fifty-three weeks long and is structured to develop the required attributes and skill levels. The initial ten weeks of training mirror those undertaken by the recruits and include fitness training, personal administration and basic military skills. Corps history and regimental traditions are also covered. Then in the second phase of the course the young officers or YOs learn about tactics at troop level. They are introduced to military doctrine and operational procedures.

The YOs are also instructed in the art of receiving and giving NATO orders, as well as combat estimates and the development of their leadership attributes through command appointments at section and troop level. At the end of this phase they undergo amphibious training at Royal Marines Poole. This includes an introduction to amphibious operations, the capabilities of landing and raiding craft that relate to troop and company manoeuvres.

They then face the Commando course. The objective is to meet the universal Commando standard and earn the right to wear the green beret. The tests are almost exactly the same in content as for RM recruits, but the qualifying times allowed for completion are reduced. Most of the course is spent on physically and mentally demanding field exercises. The final phase of officer training embraces more tactics training to company level. The

academic pressure is increased and potential officers are put in the command spotlight, given tasks to complete and navigation tests. Every young officer under training is assessed throughout the course.

The high quality of training for today's Royal Marines is paramount in maintaining the permanent readiness of the Royal Navy's amphibious role and its function as a core component of the Joint Rapid Reaction Force (JRRF). Together the Royal Navy's assault ships and the Commando Brigade represent a highly mobile, self-sustained and versatile organisation, with a strategic power projection capability that is unique among the British armed forces.

The training, advice and specialist support provided by

A young recruit during a training exercise.

A King's Squad passes out at Lympstone wearing blues and white caps. This is the big day on which they will arrive on the parade ground as the senior recruits within Lympstone and leave the ceremony as qualified Commandos. Later they will be awarded their green berets. The tradition in which the Adjutant parades on horseback was ended on 22 December 1994 when 674 and 675 Troops passed out, as shown.

Lympstone to the Commando Brigade and beyond is the adhesive that bonds the whole Royal Marines Command. It succeeds by ensuring complete interaction between the five training wings which, along with the headquarters, work together to produce Royal Marine Commandos, capable specialists and commanders.

On leaving Lympstone a newly qualified Marine or officer can be sent to an operational unit. He might go to Bosnia, Ulster or to be part of a Spearhead force sent to provide humanitarian relief. The in-depth training he receives at Lympstone will always remain with him as a bedrock of his character, even after he has left the Corps. A small but powerful Corps, the Royal Marines have served in some capacity in every military operation since the Second World War and deployed on active service every year, except 1968, when the world's terrorists took a holiday. From Palestine, Cyprus, Suez, Borneo and Aden, to Ulster, the Falklands, through to the Gulf War, northern Iraq, Bosnia and Kosovo, Royal Marines have excelled as a direct result of the high-quality training provided by CTCRM.

Like all areas of the armed forces in the twenty-first century the Commandos are suffering a manpower crisis and while senior commanders need to see more recruits passing out of Lympstone, they do not want to compromise on any of the Commando Tests. It is a difficult task and many senior NCOs believe the Corps is ready to cut training standards in

Opposite: Recruits on their final exercise. The format can vary but it usually involves operations by air, land and sea and can take up to five days with very little sleep for the trainee Marines.

Trained and ready to go on operations, many newly qualified Commandos are drafted into a Commando unit which is about to deploy on operations or join a unit 'on station'.

order to maintain manning levels. The fact is that in the late 1990s and early twenty-first century the Royal Marines are forced to recruit from a changing society. People no longer expect to have a job for life and the culture of spending three to six years with an employer before moving on has affected the military: retaining personnel has become a problem. A lifestyle in which training shoes are worn all the time has left youngsters with soft feet, unable to withstand combat boots during their initial period of training. At the same time the prevalence of fast-food, the absence of milk in schools, the general lack of sport in the national curriculum and the availability of computer technology have left society with a generation of intelligent but physically weak young men. In 1972 the average failure rate at CTCRM was 50–60 per cent in each troop; in 1999 that failure rate was the same, indicating that altering some aspects of training may be the way ahead if the vital numbers game is to be won. Equally, the selection of instructors will no doubt become more important to CTCRM in the future as staff try to take on board the 'limitations' of today's recruits. They must present training in the same robust manner, but perhaps adapt the selection tests.

The demand for prudent financial housekeeping in the mid-1990s hit all areas of military spending and resulted in the retirement of the horse at Lympstone. It had been a standing tradition that a senior officer headed the King's Squad on horseback. But on 22 December 1994 the horse made its last parade at the King's Squad pass-out of 674 and 675 Troops.

Throughout all the changes, the distinctive hallmark of the Royal Marine Commandos has been the green beret. It has been worn by generations of successful recruits who will tell you that their famous headgear comes in just one size – proud.

EIGHT

BRITAIN'S AMPHIBIOUS FORCE

'When a crisis looms the planners will say, "Where is the Amphibious Ready Group?"'

Brigadier Rob Fry RM

A strong amphibious task force that can be at sea ready to deploy a Commando battlegroup to an area of conflict within hours or days is an attractive asset for any government, particularly in a global environment where the next flashpoint is often hard to predict. Amphibious forces have the freedom to advance, withdraw or concentrate in international waters without violating frontiers and can be used as a potent political tool. The mere departure of amphibious forces from their home bases can demonstrate political intent. The force can put to sea early, with much publicity, to demonstrate capability. It can resolve or sail out without statement and form up at sea. Once in theatre, amphibious forces can be held poised to intervene while alternatives to military action are explored; their sheer presence can exert favourable pressure on negotiations. Should it be necessary, this period of poise may be sustained almost indefinitely.

It was perhaps the 'threatening intent' that amphibious forces can deliver that helped persuade politicians to secure the amphibious capability of the Commandos in the government's Strategic Defence Review of 1999, which fundamentally influenced the future of the Corps. Never before in their history have the Royal Marines been assigned so much new equipment and resources to ensure that the amphibious capability of the Commandos is retained for the present and prepared for the future. From delivering humanitarian relief, to peace support operations or working alongside NATO and the United Nations, 3 Commando Brigade RM is in permanent readiness for these tasks and for its core function of 'war fighting'.

Since the Second World War the Commandos have had to struggle to maintain their role with limited amphibious resources and have been forced constantly to promote their ability. Today, amphibious operations are in vogue and the Commandos have an extensive range of new equipment scheduled to be delivered over the next decade. In addition, they have a key role in the Joint Rapid Reaction Force and as an expeditionary force they are in demand more than at any other period in their history.

It has taken almost half a century for Britain to develop its amphibious pedigree after decades of indecision and 'make-do' policies to utilise and convert existing hardware. By 2003 it will have the dedicated shipping that will deliver a fully fledged amphibious capability and if the decision-makers look to history they will never again allow the UK's amphibious capability to decay as it did in the postwar years when the Royal Navy was starved of cash and the concept was dismissed.

During the Second World War more than 600 amphibious operations were carried out, ranging from small raids to full-scale divisional assaults, and while most were successful, with the exception of Dieppe in 1942 and Dakar in 1940, the military enthusiasm for seaborne assaults appeared to wither after 1945. A lack of investment combined with the fact that many senior officers believed amphibious operations would not be required in future conflicts. The general attitude was summed up in 1949 by the chairman of the US Joint Chiefs of Staffs, General Omar Bradley, who said: 'I predict that large scale amphibious operations will never occur again.' Less than a year later, US forces were conducting amphibious landings during the North Korean offensive when General Douglas MacArthur, the US commander of the combined force, devised a plan for a bold seaborne assault against the port of Inchon.

Shortly after the Korean campaign the UK started seriously to review amphibious operations, thanks to the work of Major-General Jim Moulton. He had vast operational experience from the Second World War where he commanded 48 RM Commando and he was later appointed Major-General Royal Marines. In the 1950s Moulton noted the US Navy's decision to convert the carrier USS *Thetis Bay* into Landing Platform Helicopter (LPH) to ferry the US Marines. Impressed with the potential of the new vessel's role he formed a special projects team to review the benefits of adopting the capability for the Corps. The Major-General highlighted the flexibility afforded by helicopters in mounting assaults from an LPH, but the concept was criticised by senior officers who claimed that the aircraft were too vulnerable. The Commandos had access to helicopters via the Fleet Air Arm and planned to demonstrate their role on exercise, but again the new tactic was overlooked. Then, in 1956, the first helicopter assault was mounted by 45 Commando RM at Suez, when the unit deployed from aircraft carriers poised 7 miles off the Egyptian coast. The aircraft proved to be a vital asset to the assault force, but helicopters were in short supply and this style of assault was new and still being developed.

The use of aviation at Suez added a new dimension to amphibious assault, but the Royal Navy's ability to mount seaborne landings in Operation 'Musketeer' (Suez) was put severely to the test when 40 and 42 Commando, as well as 2nd Battalion the Parachute Regiment, and supporting armour were put ashore in outdated Second World War landing craft. However, the success of the helicopter landings and Major-General Moulton's enthusiasm for their role resulted in an Admiralty decision in 1957 to convert the light fleet carrier HMS *Bulwark* into an LPH or what was originally called a 'Commando carrier'. In 1961 the conversion of HMS *Albion* to the same task was approved.

HMS *Bulwark*, one of the first former aircraft carriers to be converted for a new role as a Commando carrier, sails into wind as her troop-carrying helicopters deploy from the flight deck. The carrier took part in the withdrawal from Aden in 1967 with 45 Commando aboard and in exercises around the globe before she retired in 1976 after twenty-one years of service.

By the early 1960s it was clear that if the UK was to maintain any significant capability of global military intervention, then its force had to include a substantial amphibious element. This fact resulted in a review of amphibious shipping. Major-General Moulton, now Chief of Amphibious Warfare, lobbied hard for specialist shipping and he saw the future in Landing Platform Docks (LPDs) that could incorporate a stern harbour from which landing craft could operate. To generate support for development of the amphibious fleet, Moulton canvassed the Army, highlighting the fact that landing ships could pre-position armour and would be of great value to operational effectiveness. In 1961 the Army, on Moulton's advice via the Commander-in-Chief Middle East, had deployed armour aboard old tank landing ships which had been pre-positioned at Bahrain in case of Iraqi aggression against

The Landing Platform Dock (LPD) HMS *Intrepid*. The arrival of *Fearless* and *Intrepid* with well docks at their sterns significantly enhanced the capability of amphibious operations. Landing Craft Utility (LCU), which could carry heavy stores and tanks, Landing Craft Vehicle Platform (LCVPs), which could ship troops and light artillery, and raiding craft, now operated from these ships.

Kuwait. When Iraqi forces massed on the Kuwaiti border in July that year, the tanks were ideally placed for deployment. HMS *Bulwark*, on a visit to Karachi, sailed for Kuwait and flew 42 Commando ashore by helicopter; 45 Commando was flown in by RAF transport aircraft from Aden. The 'fortunate' decision to pre-position a tank squadron to go ashore in Kuwait highlighted the 'flexibility of an amphibious force for on-call operations'.

By 1962 Moulton's proposals were gaining increased support and the first LSL, *Sir Lancelot*, was approved, as was the first LPD, HMS *Fearless*. An LPD could carry a force of more than 400 troops, along with vehicles, stores and logistics support, and a specialist operations room, which was a command-and-control facility for the embarked force. A helicopter deck provided the capability for limited air assault while landing craft could operate from a flooded well dock at the stern. HMS *Fearless* entered service in November 1965 and HMS *Intrepid* in March 1967.

The Commandos now had access to the largest concentration of specialist shipping available for amphibious operations since the Second World War and in 1968 Royal Navy Commando carriers played an important role in the withdrawal of the last British troops from Aden, as well as in operations in Kuwait and Cyprus. However, while the Corps had secured new shipping in the form of the LPDs, the converted Commando carriers were far from ideal. Messdecks had been crudely arranged and offered little space for a Marine's kit, passageways were not wide enough to allow a Marine to move forward to assault stations while wearing his bergan (large backpack), and the galley for the embarked force was so small on HMS *Bulwark* that troops regularly used to spend an hour queuing for a meal in a line that would stretch to the quarterdeck. There was no below-deck space for vehicles or containers of specialist kit and instead lorries, Land Rovers and 105 guns had to be parked on the flight deck and lashed down against the weather. The funding available for the conversion of the aircraft carriers (HMS *Bulwark*, HMS *Albion* and HMS *Hermes*) was limited. As a result important facilities, such as a command centre for the embarked force commander, were inadequate. The carriers failed to address the requirements of an expeditionary force and its command element.

During the 1960s and '70s, 3 Commando Brigade often found itself diverting a unit aboard a carrier or assault ship away from an exercise to potential operational deployment, such as Cyprus in 1974. In the main, however, the limited amphibious force was used to transport Commandos from one area to another. The full potential of a floating expeditionary force able to remain at sea, on-call, ready to support political intent was probably never grasped by the Ministry of Defence; neither was it needed, perhaps. In the 1970s ministers were preoccupied with the problems of Northern Ireland and with ensuring that British forces were prepared for a Soviet assault both across Europe and through northern Norway.

In 1970, 45 Commando RM prepared for its first deployment to Norway at Evergardsmoen Camp near Narvik. It joined Norwegian, Dutch and US forces, all tasked in a new role to protect NATO's northern flank. Here the Marines began their arctic warfare training, learning how to scale ice-covered mountains, become expert skiers and survive hidden in the snow for days before mounting a surprise attack in freezing temperatures while carrying more than 100lb of weapons and equipment. There were initial teething problems. The need for cold-weather gear had not been taken into account and, unlike today's Commandos, they deployed with only a few basic additional items of clothing. Lessons had not been learned from November 1968 when 41 Commando took part in exercises in Norway. Within days of returning to their Plymouth base from exercise 'Blue Hill', the local *Sunday Independent* paper reported that a 'number of marines received medical treatment as a result of the cold weather'. Later, specialist clothing was developed and after years of experience the

Commando Brigade became Britain's leading exponents of mountain and cold weather warfare training. Today Royal Marine Commandos oversee all mountain training for the Army, write the doctrine concerning cold-weather warfare and even train special forces units.

While units of the Commando Brigade supported a wide range of operations during the 1950s, '60s and '70s, it was the Falklands War in 1982 that suddenly put the force in the public spotlight and once again brought the importance of the amphibious capability to the attention of military commanders. The outstanding and decisive action taken under the command of General Jeremy Moore and Major-General Julian Thompson ensured that the Marines would not have to advertise their skills again. Ironically, just prior to the operation, codenamed 'Corporate', the then Conservative government clearly indicated that it had lost its belief in amphibious operations. There had not been a major seaborne assault since Suez and in 1981 Defence Secretary John Nott announced wide-ranging cutbacks to the Royal Navy's surface fleet and in particular its amphibious ships. Following the Argentine invasion, Nott and his staff were pessimistic about the Navy's ability to mount a task force to sail south and retake the islands. However, the First Sea Lord Admiral Sir Henry Leach persuaded Prime Minister Margaret Thatcher that it could be done. Leach stressed that the task force should include two aircraft carriers and the Commando Brigade and could be ready to sail within days. The straight-talking Admiral impressed the Prime Minister with his confident and forceful advice and she gave her approval for Operation 'Corporate' to go ahead. The 8,000-mile dash to the South Atlantic highlighted the importance of naval power and the decision to scrap the assault ships HMS *Fearless* and *Intrepid* was revoked.

In the post-Falklands 'wash up' the urgent requirement for new assault vessels and a helicopter carrier was highlighted and while politicians promised new shipping, they delivered little to enhance the Commandos' amphibious role. The amphibious capability began to decline.

Following Operation 'Corporate' the Corps continued with a strong presence in Northern Ireland. During the 1970s and '80s, Commando units deployed on regular tours, while at the same time maintaining a strong commitment to mountain and arctic warfare with regular training in Norway, but throughout this period there was little opportunity for full-scale amphibious exercises. Shipping for winter warfare training included an LPD supported by a large number of commercial vessels tasked to ferry vehicles and troops to Norway. In some years, an aircraft carrier provided a platform for helicopter operations, but in the main shipping was used only in a transit role. The post-Falklands period was an uneasy time for the Corps: its amphibious resources had slowly drained away and the converted Commando carriers had made their final deployments for the Mediterranean and the USA before being paid off. Politicians promised replacements for the two ageing assault ships, but there was no sign of firm orders.

While the Commando Brigade escaped the heavy cutbacks of two Conservative defence reviews ('Options for Change' and 'Frontline First') there was no move to introduce new

Main picture: Royal Marines from 40 Commando take part in NATO exercises in Turkey in 1976. The Marines had been flown ashore from the carrier *Bulwark*. *Inset:* The Commando carriers HMS *Bulwark* and HMS *Hermes* pictured at Malta in 1976. At the time these ships gave the Navy a strong amphibious element on paper, but the ships were old and built for carrying fixed-wing aircraft not Commandos and their helicopters.

Main picture: By the late 1980s the Navy's amphibious shipping was in desperate need of replacement. An out-of-area exercise in Oman was supported by one of the 'Invincible'-class carri̶ but a lack of an LPD (Landing Platform Dock) to support the exercise resulted in a lack of logistical support as *Invincible* had no landing craft and all stores had to be flown ashore, taking̶ more time. *Inset:* HMS *Fearless*, an 'Invincible'-class carrier, will have served more than thirty-five years by the time she is withdrawn from service.

specialist shipping. The first of the new 'Invincible' carriers had arrived in time to take part in Operation 'Corporate' (Falklands), and ministers claimed she could carry a Commando unit. Unfortunately that was all she could do; there were no landing craft as there had been on HMS *Bulwark*, *Albion* and *Hermes*, and no room for Commando equipment. HMS *Invincible* and her sister ships were aircraft carriers: the Navy did not want them spoilt by bergan-carrying Marines. Their only use to the Corps was as transit ships.

At the time of the defence reviews ministers had decided with good reason to invest their budgets in armour and the development of the Challenger 2 main battle tank, which would be based on the Rhine, the EH101 anti-submarine helicopter to search for Soviet submarines, and a new conventionally powered submarine, also to shadow the Russians. Then the Berlin Wall came down in 1989 and everything changed overnight. There was no longer a need for submarine-hunting helicopters or new tanks to be based in Germany. Neither was there a role for the super-quiet 'Upholder'-class submarines. The dramatic developments in Germany ushered in a new strategic era.

The so-called 'New World Order' brought hopes of global peace and economic stability, but the power vacuum created by the break-up of the Soviet Union left many

Aboard the aircraft carrier HMS *Invincible* there was little space for Marines and any large force which embarked had to be accommodated on camp beds in the hangar. There were no landing craft to support an amphibious operation and few facilities for the Commando group.

Marines of 42 Commando are raised to the flight deck of HMS *Illustrious*. These 'lifts', primarily built to move helicopters from the flight deck to the hangar, provided the perfect platform to put sixty troops quickly onto the flight deck. Lifts were used aboard *Hermes*, *Bulwark* and *Albion* and are fitted on the new helicopter carrier.

countries isolated and threatened by their neighbours. Conflicts were inevitable. Several former Soviet states demanded total independence from Moscow and the Balkans ignited into battle as warlords fought for control of the region. The United Nations and NATO were dragged into the fighting as the conflict spread like a cancer across the Balkan region and later into Kosovo.

The end of the Cold War was followed by a proliferation of nuclear weapons. Regional instability combined with economic, social and political tensions to threaten security across the globe. Many countries opted to enhance their own military capability. Iran procured submarines from the former Soviet navy, India and Pakistan increased their naval forces and demonstrated their nuclear capabilities, while Iraq attempted to spread its military influence and invaded Kuwait.

The poor health of the Royal Navy's ageing amphibious shipping had been exposed during the Falklands conflict and while plans were drawn up for replacements, delays and commercial battles over build costs left the Commandos with little reliable shipping. As a consequence they were limited in their ability to mount amphibious operations during the Gulf War. In 1990 when allied forces massed to remove the Iraqis from Kuwait the US Marines poured amphibious resources into the northern Gulf in a deception plan that forced Iraqi commanders to commit five divisions to defend Kuwait from maritime attack. The Royal Navy's minesweepers were at the forefront of the deception, clearing a way through mine-fields, but the UK had no assault ships to assign to this mission. The two key assault vessels, HMS *Intrepid* and HMS *Fearless*, were so old that it was not possible to ensure they could be fully sealed against a gas attack – a major concern during the 1990 war – and as a result Britain did not deploy any of its front-line amphibious vessels to the conflict. Neither did it send a Commando battlegroup to support the Gulf campaign. It did use landing ships from the Royal Fleet Auxiliary who played a vital role in ferrying armour to the Middle East, and elements of 539 Assault Squadron RM did deploy into the Gulf aboard the hospital ship RFA *Argus*. However, the inability to send assault ships exposed a massive breakdown in the UK's amphibious capability – all the politicians could offer was that they would maintain their commitment to ordering new ships.

After the Gulf War the Commandos seized an opportunity to go into action when thousands of Kurdish refugees were stranded in the mountains between northern Iraq and Turkey, hunted by Saddam Hussein's forces and not welcomed by Turks. As in the

A Royal Navy Wessex helicopter prepares to lift off as a full-scale Commando assault gets under way from the deck of the converted Commando carrier HMS *Hermes*. *Hermes* not only carried landing craft as part of her conversion but was also later fitted with a ski-ramp so that Harriers could operate from her deck. But she was too old and was sold to the Indian Navy.

The Commandos were selected to go into the mountains of northern Iraq primarily on the strength of their 25-year record in cold-weather and mountain warfare, which they had achieved in Norway. They were, and remain, Britain's mountain and arctic warfare (MAW) experts.

Falklands, it was their mountain warfare pedigree that ensured 3 Commando Brigade RM was the first choice of the defence chiefs for the humanitarian mission, codenamed Operation 'Safe Haven'.

However, a year after 'Safe Haven' the political intent to build new ships was still at the paperwork level. Many senior officers in the Corps regard this period as one of the most dangerous in its history. 'At several times during the 1980s and '90s we were hanging on to our amphibious capability by our fingertips. Only the guile of the Royal Marines to improvise and make the best of the assets available kept us in business', said one officer.

Opposite: The then Defence Secretary George Younger, pictured second from the right during a visit to the assault ship *Intrepid* in 1986, when indications were given that the old amphibious fleet was to be replaced, but it was not until the late 1990s that the first new amphibious ship HMS *Ocean* entered service.

The first plans for replacements for HMS *Fearless* and HMS *Intrepid*, the Landing Platform Docks (R), were formulated after the Falklands War but the Conservative government dragged its feet over taking a decision. In the mid-1980s verbal statements were made about the future of specialist shipping. In March 1986 during Exercise 'Anchor Express', Defence Secretary George Younger visited elements of 3 Commando Brigade aboard HMS *Intrepid* where it was expected he would announce orders for new ships. Instead Mr Younger simply stated that 'a number of options were available to the MoD, but no decisions have been made'.

The end of the Cold War saw the Royal Navy suddenly concerned about its own future and this changed the way ahead for the Commandos. For years the Navy had focused its attention on the important task of monitoring Soviet submarine activity in the northern North Sea. Now it feared cutbacks because the Russian bear was no longer the enemy the West had prepared to face. The Senior Service looked towards out-of-NATO-area operations which in a future, more unstable world would offer fresh opportunities for amphibious forces. Specialist shipping and other new equipment would be needed to meet the requirements of escorting and protecting these forces. In addition, maritime operations need air support and any future amphibious force would require carrier enhancement to ensure combat air patrols could be made.

The view of some retired Royal Marine officers was that for years the Navy had only paid lip service to the amphibious role of their sea soldiers. But whatever had happened in the past, the Navy was now prepared to develop its Royal Marines and fully endorsed the Corps' plan for future operations. A helicopter carrier was given the procurement seal of approval and orders for replacement assault ships quickly followed. In 1991 the decision to replace HMS *Fearless* and HMS *Intrepid* was announced, but the project was severely delayed by financial problems and appeared to many observers to lack political commitment. Cynical observers claimed that the announcement had only been made to keep the amphibious lobby quiet. Finally, in 1993 the order for HMS *Ocean* was placed with an in-service date (ISD) of 1999. The eventual order for the two LPD(R)s was not made until 1996 with the first steel cut in 1997. The new ships will be named HMS *Bulwark* and HMS *Albion*.

After a long period of development the UK's twenty-first-century amphibious forces are held in high esteem as the country's leading exponents of expeditionary warfare. The highly flexible style of their operations replaces the 'stand-off' readiness of the Cold War period. Today, the threat to British interest overseas is global, and the demand for reaction and vigilance has never been greater. For the planners, coups that could see UK nationals trapped or held hostage are not as easy to predict as they were during the Cold War and the ability to mount national evacuation operations (NEOs) has never been more relevant. As well as being prepared for a variety of peace support operations, the Commando Brigade's primary role is its capability to mount seaborne or helicopter assaults into hostile environments anywhere in the world. In a worst case scenario it must be able to deliver a punch out of all proportion to its size. Former Royal Marine officer Lieutenant-General Sir Robin Ross, who commanded 3 Commando Brigade, summed up the strength of the Marines when he said: 'We have the capability to go where we are not invited and kick down the door.'

The Commando Brigade now has a key role in the UK's Joint Rapid Reaction Force. Formed in 1996, the force's core elements are 3 Commando Brigade RM and 5 Airborne Brigade, later re-formed as 16 Air Assault Brigade. Applying a concept known as the Amphibious Ready Group (ARG) a Commando battlegroup can now deploy aboard HMS *Ocean*, the new helicopter carrier, or one of the new assault ships and head to an area of potential crisis identified by intelligence staff at the Permanent Joint Headquarters (PJHQ). The ARG can then wait in international waters.

The ARG provides amphibious forces based around a Commando group with supporting joint assets. These can include RAF Chinook helicopters, specialist Army units and RAF Harrier GR7s, which can join the force aboard an aircraft carrier. The ARG is deployed as far forward as possible and is capable of meeting a wide range of warfighting and non-warfighting tasks. It is not a flag-waving opportunity for British arms companies to advertise their weapons overseas, but is rather an operational force putting the Commandos at the forefront of the UK's deployable assets. ARG elevates Brigade members to the same expeditionary status as their cousins in the US Marines. During its period afloat, potentially a three-month operation, the embarked Commando battlegroup will deploy ashore to exercise with host nations of the NATO alliance while maintaining constant readiness to return to the ship or be flown forward to mount operations in an area where the carrier can rendezvous with them. HMS *Ocean* provides the capability to manoeuvre the embarked battlegroup 300 miles in twenty-four hours and poise over the horizon. It is therefore an immense military asset.

In 2000 the newly created ARG sailed for the first time, destined for routine exercises in the Mediterranean. HMS *Ocean* – with 42 Commando RM, artillery and engineering assets – was scheduled to take part in a series of NATO amphibious exercises while under orders to be prepared to react to a number of potential flashpoints, including a reinforcement of the Balkans. Within two months of the

Opposite: The new helicopter carrier HMS *Ocean*, her flight deck packed with Sea King, Gazelle and Lynx helicopters. *Ocean* frequently operates with Chinook twin-rotor helicopters. *Ocean* has dedicated facilities for an embarked force and during her first year on operations deployed on two occasions to Sierra Leone as the lead element of the Royal Navy's new Amphibious Ready Group.

carrier's departure from her base port at Plymouth in Devon the ARG was redirected by the Permanent Joint Headquarters to Operation 'Palliser' in west Africa. Here the force and its Commando battlegroup poised offshore in support of the Parachute Regiment who had seized the airport in a rapid air land (RAL) operation. The ARG was able to demonstrate its ability to wait off the coast, provide logistic support for ongoing operations, act as a platform for joint helicopter operations, and finally to deploy a Commando battlegroup ashore and sustain it with everything from aircraft to medical and communications skills.

The ARG divides into three parts – specialist amphibious shipping, supporting naval forces, and the landing force. The size and composition of each part of the force is 'mission orientated'. To supplement the sea-lift operation, commercial shipping is chartered. Known as STUFT (Ship Taken Up From Trade), such craft were used during the Falklands War and again in the seatail logistics operation to support forces in Bosnia and Kosovo. The chartered ships can carry the bulk of follow-on stores and vehicles, and may include passenger vessels for personnel, ro-ro ferries, hospital ships, primary casualty receiving ships (PCRS) and tankers, as well as specialist lift assets, including semi-submersible ships to transport additional landing craft.

The jewel in the crown of the fleet's amphibious and aviation capability is undoubtedly the helicopter carrier HMS *Ocean*. This 20,500-tonne LPH was launched in 1995 and is the lead naval asset of the ARG. She can accommodate an embarked force of 800 men and operates twelve support helicopters (enough to airlift one full company group) and four Mk5 LCVPs. In addition she can carry six battlefield helicopters (Lynx and Gazelle). Chinook helicopters can also operate from HMS *Ocean* and the new Apache is due to join the ship's operational aviation package. The vessel can also provide a landing and take-off platform for Sea Harrier FA2s and RAF GR7 Harriers. Inside she has deck space for forty vehicles which can be airlifted off the carrier by helicopter or can leave by the stern loading ramp and ferried ashore by landing craft.

Lieutenant-Colonel Simon Guyer, who commanded the amphibious squadron based aboard HMS *Ocean* in 1998 and early 1999 and was involved in the development and acceptance of the carrier into service, says that for once the designers have taken into account the requirements of an embarked force:

The project team took on board a lot of the lessons from the old HMS *Hermes* aircraft carrier converted into commando role which had the troops living three decks away from their assault stations, resulting in chaos when it came to deploying forces ashore.

There was never enough room, but in *Ocean* the carrier has been built around the Marine's bergan. We have stacks of space, sensibly thought out design and plenty of capability to enhance our stores or bring on more personnel.

The ship can inload vehicles into below deck areas and offload them via a stern ramp, there is a small hospital on board and all the facilities that an embarked force could ask for. We even have a small arms trainer which is basically a computer linked to an SA80 or pistol which connects to a film scenario. It is very realistic.

Ocean has tremendous capability. There are 50,000 man days of food on board and enough fuel to circumnavigate the world one and half times and we could achieve it in 100 days. Well, that's what the engineers claim.

The new LPD(R)s (HMS *Bulwark* and HMS *Albion*) will replace HMS *Fearless* and HMS *Intrepid*. They will be 171 metres long and have a displacement of 6,500 tonnes as well as accommodation for an embarked force of 600, four Landing Craft Utility (LCU) and four Landing Craft Vehicles and Personnel (LCVP). *Fearless* and *Intrepid*, the two 11,582-tonne Landing Platform Docks will be replaced by 2005. Each provides a key command-and-control centre for amphibious operations, and carries four LCUs in an integral dock and four LCVPs on davits. The vessels can land Commando equipment, vehicles and Marines, as well as armour.

The amphibious force also includes Landing Ships Logistic (LSLs), which are currently being overhauled. They provide additional sea lift for amphibious personnel and materiel. There are currently five in UK service operated by the Royal Fleet Auxiliary. Each LSL accommodates seventy vehicles with trailers and other logistics support. They have stern and bow offload ramps. The LSLs can operate support helicopters and, because they have a very shallow draft, can run directly onto the beach for rapid on and offload.

A seaborne operation can also call on support from 539 Assault Squadron Royal Marines which provides a dedicated fleet of small craft for raids in coastal areas and inland waters. Nos 4 and 6 Assault Squadrons are permanently based on the two assault ships *Fearless* and *Intrepid* to give greater lift, and thus speed up the offload. 539 can provide a wide variety of assault craft to the Commando battlegroup, including LCUs, which are 27 metres long and are capable of carrying a full rifle company of 120 Marines, two lorries or four ATV/Land Rover and trailer combinations. An LCU has a speed of 9 knots and a range of over 200 nautical miles. The current LCU, the MkIX, is being replaced by a ro-ro version. LCVPs are 13 metres long and capable of carrying a full troop of 28 Marines, an ATV or a Land Rover and trailer. They have a speed of 14 knots and a range of 150 nautical miles. Landing Craft Air Cushion (Light) or LCAC(L) are 12-metre hovercraft capable of over 30 knots across water and land, and with an endurance of 12 hours. They can carry 16 Marines or 2 tonnes of stores.

539 can also deploy Rigid Raiding Craft (RRC), which are 8-metre raiding boats capable of carrying a section of eight Marines with full kit. They travel at speeds of 25 knots fully laden to a range of 80 nautical miles. The RRC MkII is being replaced by the RRC MkIII, which has an inboard diesel engine giving a greater range and speed. Inflatable Raiding Craft (IRC) are 5 metres long and can carry four Marines with full kit. They are capable of 8 knots for up to two hours. Large pontoons called

Mexeflotes are used for moving heavy logistics vehicles and equipment from ship to shore. They may be linked together, allowing a floating quay to be constructed over which vehicles can be directly offloaded from ships. Two are carried by each Landing Ship Logistic.

Finally, Ramped Craft Logistic (RCL) are 33-metre landing craft operated by the Army. They have a range of 1,000 nautical miles at a speed of 8 knots and have a similar capacity to the LCU. Sub-units of 17 Port and Maritime Squadron Royal Logistic Corps usually support an amphibious operation. Based on Landing Ships Logistic, squadrons from the regiment operate RCLs and Mexeflotes, predominantly for offloading the heavy logistic sea tail to sustain the operation.

Brigadier Rob Fry, who commands 3 Commando Brigade RM, summed up his opinion of the Corps' position. He said:

> We were rudderless in the late 1980s and '90s. The amphibious fleet was in a pretty sorry state, it was old and dying on its feet. In the main the ships were being used as transporters of troops and not for amphibious operations, but that is what the market demanded [transit from UK to Norway during NATO training].
>
> During the Cold War our operations were focused on Northern Ireland and reinforcing Norway's northern flank in support of NATO. Then suddenly at the end of the 1980s the Wall came down and the world changed. It was during this period and up to the late 1990s that we lost the operational handle to the field army.
>
> The delivery of HMS *Ocean* and the new assault ships is a major factor. We are no longer rudderless. As we enter the twenty-first century, we are a fully fledged amphibious force with bespoke shipping. We have a significant capability and are second only in force capability to the US Marines.
>
> The Strategic Defence Review was without doubt the most significant event to affect the Corps since World War Two. It sought mobile forces which could rapidly deploy or be 'on call', and we were the natural answer. We are in a growth industry. There are potential flashpoints all over the world which we could be directed to.
>
> We are a force for the future, highly capable and ready for operations. When a crisis looms I expect one of the first questions planners will ask is where is the Amphibious Ready Group.

In an operational environment the task force commander will focus his plan on the ship-to-objective manoeuvre (STOM), or the method he will adopt to put the first wave of his assault force ashore, while at the same time assessing the support his men will need once ashore – artillery, for example. The ARG will be joined by a carrier group to provide air power, by a mine countermeasures squadron to clear the waters ahead of the assault force, and by additional escorts such as air defence ships and frigates to provide naval gunfire support (NGS), which may be used in support of the assault force or to

Main picture: The Mortar Troop of 45 Commando RM carries out a live firing mission with its mortar baseplates mounted in the back of all-terrain vehicles. The troop's role is to give the Marines flexibility and constantly move the mortars before the enemy can locate and engage them. *Inset:* Commandos on the deck of the helicopter carrier HMS *Ocean* board a Chinook helicopter during operations off Sierra Leone.

The Amphibious Operations room aboard HMS *Ocean*, which allows the Commandos to command, control and coordinate the progress of an amphibious assault. Each arm of the force taking part in the assault will be represented here by liaison officers who come from the engineers, artillery and air defence as well as staff officers to plan and prepare key movements of troops as the operation develops.

mount a deception, or both. Depending on the environment, a communications warship may act as an offshore secure satellite platform for the Commando group. Once the force has established itself ashore the demands on the communications warship will reduce but during operations, such as Operation 'Palliser' in Sierra Leone in 2000, a naval vessel coordinates all secure communications. The assault force, the first wave ashore, is likely to fly in and take possession of key objectives as a second wave arrives by sea. In most cases seaborne assault is likely to take place in darkness.

Most major campaigns and deployments are conducted under a joint command, involving forces of the same nation combining their capabilities to meet a variety of threats. Carried out under a tri-service commander, such a mission is known as a 'purple' operation. The first truly joint operations headquarters was probably established by the UK during the Second World War to organise amphibious operations. It was known as the Combined Operations HQ, although in today's terminology it would be called Joint.

The Amphibious Operations Area (AOA) is a so-called sterile area in which the force commander will deploy assets to 'steal a corridor' of air, sea and underwater space and land mass which his forces will dominate and prevent others from entering. Operating in an AOA requires naval (surface and sub-surface), land and air components to be assigned to the ARG. All three components are commanded by individual maritime, ground and air commanders and are brought together under a single purple commander, normally of two-star rank. He can come from any of the three services, is known as the Joint Force Commander (JFC), and works from a headquarters in the theatre of operations. Overall national command is exercised from the Permanent Joint Headquarters.

In a phased amphibious campaign naval forces provide a secure and capable communications headquarters at sea for joint forces, offering flexibility and mobility. Joint Command can be moved ashore at the relevant stage of the campaign and, if necessary, return to sea during a withdrawal, redeployment or evacuation. The commander of the Amphibious Ready Group is the Royal Navy's Commodore Amphibious Warfare (COMAW). During an operation he becomes the Commander Amphibious Task Force (CATF), commanding not only the amphibious shipping and the embarked land forces at sea, but also other ships assigned to the ARG by the Joint Commander. Command of the landing force moves to the Brigade Commander once the Brigade deploys ashore. Air power from the Maritime Group, including Royal Navy Sea Harriers and RAF Harrier GR7s, contributes air defence and air interdiction for the amphibious force, and is supplemented by other land-based aircraft, if they are in range.

On a wider joint task 3 Commando Brigade can be assigned to the Army's 3 (UK) Division. This provides a balanced formation for deployment overseas, or for assignment to the Allied Command Europe (ACE) Rapid Reaction Corps. Together 3 Commando Brigade and 16 Air Assault Brigade form the core elements of the Joint Rapid Reaction Force, which is underpinned by other units assigned to it on a rotational basis. The JRRF is Britain's force in permanent readiness, equipped and prepared to deploy up to reinforced brigade strength of more than 5,000 at a moment's notice anywhere in the world. As part of a deploying JRRF force 3 Commando Brigade would be able to draw on RAF transport aircraft, assigned support and battlefield helicopters and the amphibious fleet for its mobility. The Brigade is ideally suited to this role, being capable of a broad spectrum of missions from full amphibious assault through evacuation operations to peace support. As a light amphibious brigade it is able to project military power quickly and at short notice in support of British interests.

The Brigade trains and exercises regularly with the amphibious forces of allied nations in order to maintain an appropriate level of combined readiness, and to enhance inter-operability. While primarily within a NATO structure, such exercises can also support Western European Union operations and are often based on United Nations' scenarios. 3 Commando Brigade's primary link is with the Royal Netherlands Marine Corps (RNLMC), formed in 1665, a year after the Royal Marines. The RNLMC joins with 3 Commando Brigade in its NATO role to form the United

Kingdom Netherlands Landing Force (UKNL LF). This is a potent amphibious force including in its organisation additional marine infantry, artillery, landing craft, air defence, reconnaissance, engineer and logistic assets from the Dutch, as well as additional amphibious shipping.

In its NATO role as part of the UKNL LF, 3 Commando Brigade is assigned to the Supreme Allied Commander Atlantic (SACLANT), a four-star US commander based in Norfolk, Virginia. Under his direction, the UKNL LF may reinforce any number of NATO contingency plans and trains to do so, working to a variety of NATO commands. These include the Supreme Allied Command Europe (SACEUR), Maritime Control Force Atlantic (MARCONFORLANT), Strike Force South – Mediterranean (STRIKFORSOUTH) and other area commands, such as Allied Forces Baltic Approaches (BALTAP) and Allied Land Forces Schleswig-Holstein and Jutland (LANDJUT). The UKNL LF is also earmarked for inclusion in the NATO ACE Rapid Reaction Corps (ARRC) and may form part of a multinational maritime force or a multinational amphibious task force (MNATF).

The Brigade has strong links with the US Marines and a Marine Expeditionary Unit (MEU) has come under the command of the UKNL LF on exercises; 3 Commando often subordinates to an MEU, for example annually on arctic exercises in Norway

The modern-day 3 Commando Brigade is a sought-after military commodity. But it is facing increasing overseas commitments both on operations and as a directed force to NATO, while at the same time maintaining its availability for service in Northern Ireland and training for its role as one of the core forces within the UK's Joint Rapid Reaction Force (JRRF).

and during Exercise 'Purple Star' in America in 1996. The Brigade also operated under US command on Operation 'Safe Haven' in Kurdistan, northern Iraq, in 1991.

It may also form part of the Combined Amphibious Force Mediterranean (CAFMED). This is not a standing NATO force, but a means for amphibious forces from the UK, US, Greece, Italy, Netherlands, Spain and Turkey to train together to achieve maximum inter-operability under NATO command. Amphibious landing forces from these nations came under command of 3 Commando Brigade in Mediterranean exercises in 1994 and 1995.

The Commando Brigade also has a twinning agreement, signed in 1995, with 9th Division d'Infantrie de Marine (9e DIMa), the amphibious light-armoured element of the French rapid reaction force, the Force d'Action Rapide. This agreement involves regular exercises, and exchange of personnel and observers.

But while the Commandos are seen as the 'force for the future', there is a clear danger of overcommitment. In addition to its requirement to allocate a Commando battlegroup to the JRRF, the Brigade also has a list of what are known within the Corps as 'programme drivers'. It must supply a unit for the Spearhead list; it provides mountain and arctic warfare skills to the Ace Mobile Force (Land) (AM(L)) and must exercise the role twice a year; it must take part in the Army's operational tour plot (primarily in Northern Ireland), undertake exercises within the Partnership for Peace programme and maintain its amphibious warfare skills by mounting major exercises, as well as finding time for routine training. Such a demanding schedule must also include time off. In 2000, 40 Commando was in Northern Ireland, 42 Commando in Sierra Leone and 45 Commando in Kosovo. The biggest danger for the Corps today is that the demand for its expertise may outgrow its capability. Following 42 Commando's return from Sierra Leone the Royal Marines sought approval from Land Command to remove the unit from the Spearhead list for a short period. Without approval for this plan the unit would not have enjoyed any leave before sailing again in the autumn with the ARG.

The UK government's massive commitment to amphibious forces comes at a time when many other countries are also strengthening their naval capability. The Dutch are increasing the size of their marine forces and have recently taken delivery of a purpose-built assault ship. The French are investing in amphibious ops, as are the Spanish and the Americans.

In the twenty-first century the military may appear to be obsessed with the development of new procedures and 'doctrine speak', such as the 'manoeuvrist approach' and 'power projection' – two terms used to explain the direction of the seaborne assault and the ability to put military power ashore. But while these are fundamental to success the Corps always has a fall-back plan and Lieutenant-Colonel Gordon Messenger, the Chief of Staff at 3 Commando Brigade in 1999, adds a note of reality to modern planning with a concept which has served the Commando Brigade well since the Second World War: 'Never underestimate the combat high boot as a method of manoeuvre.'

NINE

US AND DUTCH MARINE CONNECTIONS

The US Marines have had a long association with the Royal Marines. They fought alongside each other at Chosin reservoir in Korea in 1950, they have trained together for many years in Arctic warfare and in 1991 the two forces deployed on Operation 'Safe Haven' in northern Iraq to protect thousands of Kurds who fled from Saddam Hussein's military forces. This close bond has resulted in many exchange drafts between the two Corps with selected instructors from the USMC spending several years at the Commando Training Centre where they have been fully integrated into training teams. Others have joined the mountain and arctic warfare course and other branches of the Royal Marines.

Ironically the US Marines were formed in 1775 to fight the British at sea and were modelled on the Royal Marines. US and British Marines clashed again in 1812, but ever since they have fought on the same side. Since its creation the USMC has fought across the globe – in the Boxer rebellion in China in 1900, in the Philippines, then in the Second World War they took part in the famous battle of Iwo Jima. In the postwar years they saw action in Korea, evacuated US nationals from Egypt in 1956, then deployed into Vietnam. In 1979 US Marines took part in the abortive 'Desert One' raid to free US Embassy staff held hostage in Tehran. They joined the invasion force in Grenada in 1984 and then played a major role in the Gulf War. In addition, they have deployed to Bosnia and supported the advance by NATO forces into Kosovo in June 1999.

Since the early 1970s, after the US pulled out of Vietnam, the men of the British Commando Brigade have carried out regular exercises with their cousins in the USMC, deploying units to training areas such as Vieques, an island off Puerto Rico which was used by the USMC as a training ground prior to deployment to Vietnam.

At that time British converted Commando carriers were still in service and entire Commando units would exercise seaborne assaults, but as the UK's amphibious asset slipped away in the 1980s and '90s the Royal Marines deployed smaller company groups to train with the US Marines. These partnership exercises focused on tactics and operations in order to give the two forces the opportunity to understand each other's 'standing operational procedures' and weapon systems. Such understanding enhanced joint force operations in areas such as NATO deployment.

While the Royal Marines have suffered from a shortage of recruits, the US Marines do not seem to have encountered the same problem. More than any other part of the

Above: US Marines head into Kosovo during the multinational operation in the Balkans in June 1999. Here a column of light armoured vehicles rolls towards the border as the Serbian stranglehold on Kosovo is broken. *Below*: A US Marines CH53 Sea Stallion helicopter during reinforcement operations in Bosnia. The USMC served in Bosnia both as part of IFOR (Implementation Force) and SFOR (Stabilisation Force).

US's armed forces the Marines symbolise valour, patriotism and military virtue. They are, in fact, the military face of the USA. However, US Marine NCOs reveal that they believe training is now too 'sanitised' and that instructors should be given more slack. 'The kids that appear at bootcamp are overweight and out of shape and when they arrive at Camp Lejeune they are supposed to be Marines, but I am not so sure', said one cynical NCO.

Training on the Royal Marine Commando course is three times longer than for US Marines and Americans who have served at Lympstone and passed the Commando course are the first to state that it is the hardest infantry test in the world – what better recommendation could there be!

The US Marines are structured and equipped for projecting American military power onto hostile shores from the sea and for rapid deployment to hot spots around the world. They are unique among fighting forces in that they have their own integrated artillery, armour, aviation and logistics to support the front-line infantry.

The Corps is geographically positioned to operate across two oceans. It covers the Pacific largely from Camp Pendleton in southern California, where the 1st Marine Division is based. The Atlantic is managed by Camp Lejeune, in Jacksonville, North Carolina, where the 2nd Marine Division is based. These camps are huge compared to

The US Marines are unique in that they have their own integral artillery, aviation and logistics, and have a wide range of amphibious vehicles, manned by the US Navy, to support their amphibious operations. Here a hovercraft is marshalled to its landing site.

barracks in the UK – Lejeune, for example, has 61,000 acres of training real estate, 9 miles of beach and more than 45,000 Marines. The force commander can mount seaborne assaults without leaving camp!

While the Royal Marines of 41 Independent Commando fought with the 1st Marine Division in Korea, it is the 2nd Marine Division whose sub-units often exercise with today's Royal Marines. The 2nd Marine Division is the direct descendant of the 2nd Marine Brigade which was activated on 1 July 1936 and saw service in China in 1937 and 1938. As the prospect of war increased and the Marine Corps expanded, division-sized organisations were created. Accordingly, the 2nd Marine Division was officially activated on 1 February 1941 at Camp Elliot, California, dropping its earlier brigade designation. The Division was built around the 2nd Marine Regiment which had protected American interests in Latin America and the Caribbean. (The 6th Marine Regiment had established combat records known round the world; the 8th Marine Regiment had seen action in Haiti and the Division's artillery arm, the 10th Marine Regiment had also been very active.)

Initially, support was provided by service, medical and engineer battalions and transport, tank, signal, chemical and anti-aircraft companies. These supporting organisations have evolved into the six separate battalions within the Division. They are: Headquarters Battalion, 2nd Assault Amphibious Battalion, 2nd Combat Engineer Battalion, 2nd Light Armoured Infantry Battalion, 2nd Tank Battalion and the Reconnaissance Battalion.

In May 1941 the 6th Marines and the 2nd Battalion 10th Marines along with support detachments formed the 1st Provisional Marine Brigade and sailed for Iceland. Similarly, the 2nd Combat Engineer Battalion was sent to Hawaii and helped defend Pearl Harbor during the Japanese attack on 7 December. Immediately after Pearl Harbor, the Division deployed along the west coast of the USA to defend it against a possible invasion. In January 1941 a new 2nd Marine Brigade was formed around the 8th Marines and deployed to American Samoa. By 1942 the Division had been relieved of its defensive duties and began to reorganise for amphibious operations.

The US Marines have always been in the vanguard of US military action and as such have been among the first to trial, test and develop new equipment for US forces. At the start of the twenty-first century the USMC began a special programme aimed at developing 'non lethal' weapons such as glue guns for use in future riots and internal security operations.

In 1942 the 2nd Marine Division saw its earliest action in the first US ground offensive of the Second World War – the Guadalcanal campaign. It is this action, fought under the stars of the Southern Cross, that provided the pattern for the five stars in the Division emblem.

Later, during the Cuban Missile Crisis in 1962, the Division was deployed to Guantanamo Bay and the waters off Cuba, remaining there until December of that year. Over the next few years units of the Division were deployed in the Caribbean in response to unrest in the region. In April 1965, elements of 2nd Division landed in Santa Domingo, Dominican Republic, to protect the lives of American citizens and aid the evacuation of refugees after a communist-inspired coup. From the end of 1967 until July 1973, the ground defence force of the US Naval Base at Guantanamo Bay was the responsibility of a battalion from the 8th Marines. Later, in October 1979 President Jimmy Carter directed that forces from the Division should again return to the area following Soviet activities in Cuba.

The Marines acted as the ground combat element of the US contribution to the multinational peacekeeping force in Beirut. It was here that the force headquarters was attacked by a suicide bomber in October 1983. In the same year the 2nd Marines provided the lead element of invasion of Grenada.

During the Iran–Iraq War 2nd Division Marines were again in action, serving as the assault force in a raid against an Iranian oil platform. In 1989 elements of the Division deployed to Panama to protect US rights under the Panama Canal Treaty in Operation 'Just Cause'.

In the Gulf War the entire 2nd Division deployed for the first time since the Second World War. Later, forces from the Division deployed on reinforcement operations in Bosnia and supported the advance into Kosovo.

Today a battalion landing team from the Division remains continuously deployed with the 6th Fleet. Other forces within the formation are regularly deployed on exercises, support counter-drug operations, train with NATO partners and maintain readiness for global operations.

THE ROYAL NETHERLANDS MARINE CORPS

Britain's Royal Marine Commandos and the Royal Netherlands Marine Corps (RNLMC) have worked together in a special joint amphibious group since the early 1970s, developing a unique partnership in a seaborne landing force.

The first meeting between the two forces took place in 1965 when a company of Dutch Marines came to the UK to exercise with 43 Commando RM. In 1972 both formations deployed on winter warfare training to Norway. This was followed by further joint ventures before the partnership was made official in 1973. On 9 May that year the defence ministers of the UK and the Netherlands signed a memorandum of understanding to formalise the establishment of closer military cooperation and Whisky Company of the RNLMC joined 45 Commando RM at Arbroath in Scotland.

Above: The RNLMC was deployed in Bosnia in 1995 with the United Nations Protection Force (UNPROFOR) working on Mount Igman as part of the multinational brigade and served in the Albania and Kosovo multinational force.

Right: The RNLMC wear a blue beret with anchor-shaped cap badge on a red background. These Dutch Marines are wearing British-pattern camouflage and are armed with US-produced M16s.

The Dutch company remained under 45's operational control at Condor barracks for many years as the UK/NL project developed. The Netherlands Marines were totally integrated into the Commando group as the concept of a joint amphibious landing force matured. By the late 1970s the 'cloggies' as they were affectionately known were exercising all over the world with the Royal Marines and in 1979 a much larger contribution to the UK/NL Landing Force was made when the battalion-sized 1st Amphibious Combat Group was assigned to operate as part of 3 Commando Brigade on NATO operations.

It was in June 1977 that the Royal Netherlands Marine Corps mounted its most overt operation: the unit's anti-terrorist specialists were called in to resolve a hijack situation in which armed South Moluccans had seized a train and taken eighty passengers hostage. The train, a commuter service on its way between Rotterdam and Groningen in northern Holland, had been hijacked on 23 May and halted at De Pont. The terrorists wanted the Dutch government to exert pressure on the Indonesians to grant independence to South Molucca. They demanded that a Boeing 747 be made available at Amsterdam's Schipol airport and to demonstrate their violent intent they shot dead the train driver and threw his body onto the rails. After nineteen days of siege negotiation the authorities handed over control of the incident to the Marines. On 11 June, seconds before the Dutch Marines stormed the train, a pair of Dutch Air Force F-104 Starfighters screamed in low and fast to confuse the hijackers. As they peeled away, charges on the carriage doors were detonated and the assault teams moved in. In total six hijackers were killed and seven arrested. Sadly two passengers also died.

In 1991 a substantial reorganisation of the RNLMC resulted in all operational units being incorporated into what is called the Group of Operational Units Marines (GOUM) which enhanced the forces' ability to support the UK/NL landing force and resulted in the commander of the GOUM being made deputy commander of the joint amphibious force. The GOUM consists of four infantry battalions. One of these is a reserve battalion, another partly reserve, of which the sub-units are stationed in the Dutch Antilles and Aruba on a permanent basis while two operational infantry battalions are based in the Netherlands (1st and 2nd Marine Battalions).

Also in 1991, just a year after the Gulf War, the many years of joint training and exercises came to fruition when the UK/NL force had its first joint operational deployment to northern Iraq during Operation 'Safe Haven' – a humanitarian mission to provide relief and protection for thousands of Kurds fleeing Iraq.

Then in 1992 and 1993 the Dutch Marines deployed three battalions to Cambodia on United Nations duty. At the end of 1994 they took part in a UN mission to Haiti which was followed in 1995 by a rapid reaction force to support UNPROFOR (United Nations Protection Force) in Bosnia. Later a heavy mortar battery was deployed with IFOR/SFOR (Implementation Force/Stabilisation Force) in Bosnia.

RNLMC manpower currently stands at just over 3,000 and the Marine Corps' headquarters is located in the centre of Rotterdam. A recruit's training takes

The HNLMS *Rotterdam*, a Landing Platform Dock, can carry 600 Marines and mount seaborne and helicopter assaults at the same time.

approximately twenty-five weeks and the centre runs six courses per year. It is here that various specialist training also takes place, such as sniper and mortar work. Additional parachuting, commando and special forces training is undertaken elsewhere in the Netherlands, as well as overseas where jungle warfare, combat skiing and climbing courses are held. The Dutch Marines also have a specialist amphibious training school at Texel.

Perhaps the single most important event for the RNLMC in the late 1990s was the delivery of a specialist assault ship which has given the force the flexibility to mount a broad spectrum of operations and increase its profile within NATO and alongside the UK/NL landing force.

The HNLMS *Rotterdam* is a Landing Platform Dock similar in concept to the Royal Navy's assault ships, which can carry 600 Marines and mount seaborne and helicopter assaults at the same time, while encompassing all the state-of-the-art technology that many commanders in the early 2000s can only dream about.

TEN

THE MODERN BRIGADE

'The whole value and essence of the Royal Marine Commandos is that they can undertake any kind of military or security job under any conditions anywhere in the world at a moment's notice.'

HRH The Duke of Edinburgh, Captain-General Royal Marines.

Britain's modern-day Commando Brigade is a priceless national security asset that can poise at sea, ready to strike as a lethal weapon or offer the diplomatic hand of humanity in situations of international disaster. In the twenty-first century the 'go anywhere role' of the Amphibious Ready Group provides the operational platform for the Commandos to be constantly at a high state of readiness for deployment. They can regard themselves as the UK's 'masters of flexible response'. Based on three front-line Commando units and reinforced by specialist units, the Brigade is on permanent standby for deployment. Its operational remit is broad and constantly changing in order to be ready for the 'unexpected' in today's unstable world.

In addition to being Britain's amphibious force, the Brigade has twenty-five years' experience in Norway and is the UK's leading exponent of mountain and arctic warfare. Its Commando units are prepared for operations in all potential theatres of

HRH The Duke of Edinburgh pictured during one of his many visits to the Corps' Commando units. This visit in the early 1980s took place shortly after 42 Commando became the first unit in the British forces to be issued with the SA80.

warfare and regularly train in the desert with deployments to Egypt, Jordan and Oman. They also maintain a high level of jungle warfare expertise, sending troops to Belize and Brunei every year.

The Brigade consists of approximately 4,500 personnel and includes the three front-line Commando units as well as specialist artillery, engineers and a light-armoured squadron. Until 2001, when a reorganisation programme was introduced, each Commando unit consisted of three fighting companies, a support company and a headquarters company. The fighting companies are the first troops into action. Their formations consist of approximately 120 men who are split into separate sub-units called troops. The three companies are only lightly armed and when required they can draw on heavier firepower from the Support Company. This group is a collection of specialists providing mortar, anti-tank, surveillance, electronic warfare and signals skills,

All Royal Marine Commandos wear the 'Commando flash' on their combat uniforms and those serving in Commando units wear the Commando dagger on their left arm.

as well as assault engineers and a reconnaissance unit, but all on a limited basis. It, too, is approximately 120 strong and is the backbone of the Commando unit. The Headquarters Company provides administration, medical and communications support to the commanding officer.

This format was established in the postwar years and shaped the organisation of each Commando unit until the early twenty-first century when a project codenamed 'Commando 21' was introduced. It delivered the biggest change to the structure of the Corps' front-line Commando units since their creation during the Second World War. Changes included the introduction of a fourth fighting company, the renaming of Support Company to Logistic Support and HQ Company to Command Company. In addition, the manning level of each Commando increased from 650 personnel to 692.

In 1996 the 4,500-strong Commando Brigade was selected as a core component of the UK's Joint Rapid Deployment Force (JRDF) which was formed in August 1996 as an on-call force, permanently ready for global operations. (The framework for the JRDF was developed in 1994 and it was renamed Joint Rapid Reaction Force (JRRF) in 1999.) To prove its readiness for the JRDF, elements of 3 Commando Brigade, under command of Brigadier Tony Milton, took part in a testing exercise in America during 1996 to demonstrate its capability to mount a strategic deployment. Called 'Purple Star' the exercise involved numerous amphibious and helicopter assaults just months prior to the JRDF being officially formed.

Above: Green Beret gunners from 29 Commando Regiment Royal Artillery in Bosnia using M-STAR — a surveillance radar which helps identify the source of mortar attacks and movement of forces.

Left: A Marine from 42 Commando is pictured during a high abseil (220ft) onto the deck of the assault ship HMS *Fearless*. This type of training often takes place while the ship is on passage between exercises and waiting off a coastline for a potential operation.

New specialist amphibious shipping has sharpened the military capability of the Brigade and allowed it to mount expeditionary operations for longer periods with sustained logistics. These are often launched in a joint environment in which RAF helicopters and Harriers can be deployed to operate in what is called the Amphibious Ready Group. As noted in Chapter Eight, the ARG is an on-call Commando battlegroup which has the ability to deploy twice a year and mount exercises while at the same time maintaining its readiness for operations. Based aboard the helicopter carrier HMS *Ocean*, the 'embarked force' can remain at sea for an indefinite period or can be pre-positioned in a friendly country.

For the Brigade commander of the future, the kind of amphibious assault that involved mass storming of beaches, such as the operations at Dieppe and Normandy, has passed. Present-day hi-tech defensive systems would compromise such an operation and make it potentially costly both in men and shipping. Today, the Brigade commander's job is much more complex than it was in the Second World War. His remit must encompass a wide range of tasks from full-scale landings to evacuation operations in support of diplomacy (which might not actually involve committing forces to action). In addition, the Brigade can be called upon to undertake peace support operations, such as those mounted in Kosovo and Sierra Leone in 2000, as well as constabulary tasks where forces are used to enforce law (again Kosovo is an example), and benign operations in an area of disaster relief.

A key aspect of any modern seaborne assault is to strike at the enemy's weakest point, his Achilles' heel. Helicopters play a major role in modern amphibious operations, their pilots using night-vision optics to fly in pitch darkness and make a rapid attack, delivering the first wave of Commandos as landing craft deliver more troops, possibly at an alternative target. This tactic of punching combat forces, men and heavy weapons ashore is known as 'projecting power from the sea'.

The sequence of events that leads directly to the deployment of the Amphibious Ready Group or a Commando battlegroup on its own starts at ministerial level. Approval provides the catalyst for military involvement and the Chiefs of Staff then pass the requirement to the Current Operations Group (COG) which directs the format of the operations and 'mission feeds' the relevant force structure. The Permanent Joint Headquarters at Northwood commands and coordinates the deployment and may, depending on the situation, deploy its own command cell as it did in Sierra Leone in 2000.

A seaborne assault requires advance force operations to collate intelligence about potential landing areas, both for helicopters and landing craft. Aspects of this reconnaissance work are carried out by the Brigade Patrol Troop, which includes teams from engineer and artillery recce. These forces can be landed by raiding craft, helicopter or parachute – the method is decided by the commander on advice from BPT. Electronic warfare experts and other key communications teams may also be included in these advance operations.

Following a decision to mount a landing, artillery forward observation teams also land ahead of the assault force, ready to direct naval gunfire to suppress enemy activity and support a diversionary plan. At the same time units assigned to the Brigade will be ashore identifying key targets and locating potential hazards.

An assault could take place in several different formats but a likely scenario would be the first wave of troops being airlifted ashore in darkness to an area up to 5 miles inland. Pilots would fly on NVG (night-vision goggles), avoiding the use of any lights to increase the element of surprise. A second wave of landing craft would then land on identified beaches while the logistics seatail could either move ashore to support the force as it advanced inland or remain afloat and provide resupply in a helicopter 'fly forward' operation. Every operation is different and the deployment of any assault is complex.

Amphibious operations are totally dependent on good planning and preparation from the outset. Assault ships and support vessels must be loaded correctly so that when the landings take place priority equipment is readily available. Reserve stores and logistics vehicles go on first, while the Scimitars of the Blues and Royals, if embarked, are loaded last to ensure they are first off.

While a dedicated land force has only one command formation, an amphibious operation requires two command groups. These provide the command and coordination of troops leaving the ships, troops on the ground and the correct delivery of rations, fuel and ammunition to those units already ashore.

Assault ships are vulnerable to air attack and while RAF and Royal Navy fighter aircraft can provide protection, the amphibious force commander will also seek to deploy his air defence assets very early.

The helicopter carrier HMS *Ocean* has the capability to airlift Marines into action by Sea King helicopters and landing craft. The assault will usually take place in darkness, perhaps at or just before first light. But aboard *Ocean* the Marines involved in the operation will have been ready hours earlier. They will be called forward to their assault stations and into the hangar of the carrier where they will be issued with ammunition and given last-minute briefings, then they will rest on their bergans to await the call to the flight deck (if it is an air assault).

The combat units of the Brigade include: 40 Commando RM, raised on 14 February 1940; 42 Commando RM, formed in October 1943 and based at Bickleigh in Devon; and 45 Commando RM, which was formed in the first week of August 1943 and is based at Arbroath in Scotland.

The Brigade's three Commando units regularly carry out amphibious training and are constantly developing new tactics for transporting Marines by helicopter and landing craft. Each Commando unit has a specialist anti-tank unit and mortar troop within its Support Company which can provide the commander with firepower additional to the light weapons carried by the fighting companies. Also, every Commando unit has a mounted machine-gun troop.

Within the Commando unit a commander can call upon his own assault engineers to clear mines or work alongside Royal Engineer specialists. He can deploy his own reconnaissance force to parachute ahead of the main force and gather intelligence or assign them to work with the Brigade Recce Force (BRF). The Commandos have their

Opposite: Sergeant Paul Rees, a mountain and arctic warfare leader and jungle warfare instructor, leads a patrol across a river during training in Brunei. The Royal Marines send a company to the jungle every year on what is called Exercise 'Curry Trail'.

own medical resources for 'first line' care and these personnel can also be detached to work with larger formations within the Brigade.

When a Commando unit deploys on operations it works as a battlegroup and is joined by a specialist unit of Army Commandos who provide artillery support in the form of a battery of 105mm light guns, engineers to clear minefields, and Scimitar armoured reconnaissance vehicles. This additional level of firepower provides a significant boost to the fighting capability of the battlegroup.

Within the Brigade based at Stonehouse barracks the forty-strong Brigade Patrol Troop (BPT) forms the Commandos' reconnaissance force. Those serving in this special unit are all mountain experts and many have completed jungle warfare and survival courses. While not special forces, the BPT provides an interface between the Brigade and advance forces and is trained by a small body of mountain and Arctic warfare instructors, formerly known as the Cadre. Its key mission is to collate intelligence prior to an amphibious landing and relay it to the force commander. Brigade Patrol Troop consists of five six-man teams and a ten-strong command element. Each member of the troop has several skills, for example in communications or medical training, and generally they are trained to the same standard as special forces units. They favour using the Armalite against the SA80 and do not wear qualification badges or rank slides on their smocks when in the field. Their arsenal also includes two .5 rifles (ISWs). BPT draws its manpower from across the Brigade's Commando units, but more often than not from reconnaissance units. All members are trained in the full spectrum of insertion methods, from parachuting to high abseil, heli-casting and covert assault from the sea. During a deployment or operational task the Brigade Patrol Troop will be augmented by engineer and artillery personnel to form the Brigade Recce Force.

Communications and electronic warfare skills play a fundamental role on today's battlefield and a team of electronic warfare specialists form Y Troop. They provide a 'countermeasures' capability at the highest level. A small team from Y Troop supported the Kosovo operation in June 1999. An additional communications troop, known as 501 Detachment, maintains specialist satellite communications for Brigade headquarters from any location in the world to a rear link command, such as PJHQ or seaborne headquarters; 501 Detachment works closely with Y Troop.

Air defence for the Brigade is provided by Royal Marines equipped with Javelin ground-to-air missiles. Their deployment is directed by the mission 'air threat' and in recent years elements of Air Defence have been located aboard warships in the Gulf and have supported Commando groups on operations. A secondary asset from 20 Commando Air Defence Battery also provides support to the Brigade using the Rapier anti-aircraft missile system. However, this unit is scheduled to be disbanded under the Strategic Defence Review, leaving the Brigade exposed in the area of air defence. While a number of solutions to the loss of 20 Commando Air Defence Battery are being considered, the main option open to the Brigade is to form its own larger air defence squadron manned by specialists from the Royal Artillery and equipped with the most advanced Rapier system, which will be required by 2005.

e classic night-time cliff assault is still a key aspect of Commando operations. A team from the Brigade Patrol Troop (Mountain Leaders) can lead a raid by climbing the cliff face and ablishing rope lines for the raiding force. In some situations a method called 'roller haulage' may be used to pull men and equipment up a cliff face at speed.

nmandos are trained to race wn a cliff at speed in order to ke their exit from a raid. The ning is overseen by instructors m Brigade Patrol Troop or the all pool of climbing instructors in Cadre who will also be the last eave the site of a raid.

Air Defence Battery fires a Javelin missile from the deck of a Landing Ship Logistics (LSL) off Scotland. The air defence capability has grown in importance and in future an enhanced air defence unit supported by specialists from the Royal Artillery is scheduled to be established.

In order to maintain convoy discipline and vehicle movements the Brigade has its own Royal Marines police who also provide close protection for the Brigade commander. Air coordination of fighter aircraft from both Royal Navy and Royal Air Force close air support is the responsibility of the Brigade's Tactical Air Control Parties. These units played a major role in Bosnia in the mid-1990s and during an amphibious assault can be deployed ashore with advance forces, ready to direct air strikes as the main force lands.

New colours were presented to all three Commandos in 2001. 45 Commando RM played a leading role in the Second World War and in particular the Normandy landings on 6 June 1944. In the postwar years the unit was deployed to the Far East. After several years it was withdrawn and redeployed to the Mediterranean where it undertook amphibious training. The Cypriot emergency in 1955 saw the Commando

Opposite: A Royal Navy Sea King helicopter drops a rigid raiding craft of 539 Assault Squadron into the sea off Norway. The assault squadron, which is a vital aspect of the Brigade's assets, includes Landing Craft Utility (LCUs), Landing Craft Vehicle Platforms (LCVPs), hovercraft and a variety of inflatable boats. The unit is regularly put on standby for operations and was among the first of the Brigade's units to go ashore in Sierra Leone in 2000.

in action against the EOKA terrorists in the Kyrenia and Troodos mountains. In 1956, 45 Commando took part in the Suez operation and mounted the first heliborne assault. The 1960s were mainly spent in Aden, Radfan and a counter-insurgency operation in Tanganyika, later known as Tanzania. In the 1970s, 45 spearheaded the Brigade's mountain and Arctic warfare role when it was the first unit to deploy to Norway in preparation for the Corps' NATO responsibility to reinforce and protect the northern flank against a Soviet invasion. Then, in 1982, the unit took part in the Falklands War. It continued to deploy to Northern Ireland. In 1991 it was sent to northern Iraq in defence of the Kurds and in 1994 it deployed to Kuwait as a rapid reaction force to deter Iraqi aggression. In 1996 it took part in the test exercise for the Joint Rapid Deployment Force. In 1998 while on exercise in Belize 45 Commando was diverted to Nicaragua and Honduras after Hurricane Mitch caused widespread devastation – Operation 'Tellar'. In 2000 the formation deployed to Kosovo.

42 Commando RM was raised from the 1st Battalion Royal Marines and spent much of the Second World War in India where it was part of 3rd Special Service Brigade. After the war the Commando remained in the Far East and was deployed to the Malayan emergency. In September 1954 the unit returned to England to establish a training unit at Bickleigh near Plymouth for Commando and specialist courses. Then, in 1956, 42 was sent to Suez. Throughout the 1960s it was deployed in the Far East and in 1967 it covered the withdrawal of British troops from Aden. The unit has seen considerable service in Northern Ireland and in 1982 took part in the Falklands War. In 2000 42 Commando deployed to Sierra Leone and was the first Commando unit to do so as part of the newly created Amphibious Ready Group.

40 Commando RM suffered heavy casualties at Dieppe in 1942 just months after being raised. In the postwar years the Commando served in Palestine, Malaya and Cyprus. After a decade in the Far East 40 returned to Plymouth and established itself at Seaton barracks in Plymouth until the late 1970s when it moved to Taunton. The unit has won the Wilkinson Sword of Peace three times. It played a leading role in both the Falklands War in 1982 and the protection of the Kurds in 1991.

The Brigade's vital combat support units include 59 Independent Commando Squadron Royal Engineers, re-formed at Plymouth in 1971 to support the Brigade, having been initially raised as 59 Field Company in 1900. 59 is based at Chivenor in north Devon. It provides vital engineer support and in the 1980s formed its own reconnaissance troop, which works closely with the Brigade Patrol Troop in order to provide advanced engineer intelligence; 59 Squadron's Support Troop provides the machinery used in survivability tasks, and the boats and divers who carry out underwater engineering tasks, including EOD (Explosive Ordnance Demolition) skills. The Squadron can also call upon No. 2 Commando Troop (EOD) of 33 Field Regiment to provide bomb disposal skills to the Brigade. General engineer support skills in the Brigade's rear area are provided by 131 Independent Commando Squadron Royal Engineers (V). Commando engineers have deployed on operations all over the world from Northern Ireland to the Congo and in 2000 the Squadron served in

Opposite: Gunners from 29 Commando Regiment Royal Artillery. Based at the Citadel in Plymouth, the unit's three gun batteries are assigned to the front-line Commando units and deploy with them all over the world. A fourth, 148 Battery, is a specialist forward observation unit primarily trained to direct naval gunfire from ship to shore. This unit, which is based at Poole, is the only non-American force in NATO with the skill to direct fire from every warship within the organisation.

Bosnia. A small unit, 59 has a proud reputation within the British Army and many of its sappers have served with the SAS.

The Royal Artillery is vital among the Brigade's combat support units and has been with it since 1961 when the Army agreed to a request for support from the Royal Marines. It was decided that 29 Field Regiment should fill this role and as such should also be Commando trained. During January and February 1962 the first Commando course for the gunners was held at Lympstone and on 15 May 1962 the first Commando gunners were formally presented with their green berets. At this stage the regiment consisted of three gun batteries (145, 79 and 8 Commando Batteries) and a headquarters battery. In September 1962, 145 (Maiwand) Battery was detached to support Commando operations in Malaya and on 29 December 1962 it became the first gun battery to fire the newly issued 105mm Pack Howitzer guns in anger.

By 1963 the need for an additional Commando battery became apparent and this was formed from 95 Close Observation Battery, which became 95 Commando Regiment. From the two regiments it was decided that one should remain 'home-based' and in this capacity should train and provide men for the regiment based

Below: Since the Falklands War the Household Cavalry have supported the Commando Brigade with their light, armoured reconnaissance vehicles. They provide additional firepower and their mobility has been a major benefit. Officers and men of the Blues and Royals attend the Commando course and wear the green beret. *Opposite*: Royal Navy helicopters provide vital mobility to the Commando Brigade ranging from Eagle flights in the border countryside of Northern Ireland to operations in the Falklands, northern Iraq and Sierra Leone. Royal Marines may now train as aircrew and some naval airmen attend the Commando course.

abroad. Early in 1964, 95 Commando Regiment, with 8 Battery, took over the Royal Citadel from 29 Commando. Gunners in 7 (Sphinx) Commando Battery came to join their Commando counterparts and 148 Commando Battery also came under the same command, although it remained based in Poole. During this period 79 Battery and Regimental Headquarters moved to Singapore and 20 Commando Battery, detached to Hong Kong, came under command 29 Commando Regiment. During the following six years the Commando gunners maintained a presence in the Far East serving in Malaya, Brunei, Borneo, Sarawak and Hong Kong. In 1965–6 parts of the regiment were based in Bahrain in support of 2 Para and saw action in Aden, while those not involved carried out exercises with the Commando Brigade.

By 1970 the gunners were pulling out of the Far East and the focus of training changed to operations on NATO's northern flank in Norway and in Northern Ireland. Throughout the 1970s changes were made to the Commando gunners formation as defence cuts took effect. The Arbroath-based 145 Battery was disbanded in 1976. 95 Regiment was forced to prune itself to a battery-sized unit, with 148 Commando Forward Observation Battery remaining. Plans were made to disband 79 Battery in 1977 but it was reprieved and in addition the regiment received reserve support when 289 Parachute Battery (V) changed its role to become 289 Commando Battery (V).

Since the 1970s the Commando gunners have always detached a battery alongside a Commando unit on operations and have served across the globe with 3 Commando Brigade. During the Falklands War 8 (Alma) Battery provided fire support for 3 Para at Goose Green and in 2000 Commando gunners deployed to Sierra Leone, Ulster and Kosovo.

Combat service support – logistics – is provided by a specialist Commando regiment based at Chivenor. It was formed in July 1971 and includes a medical squadron, as well as a workshop and transport squadron. The Logistics Regiment provides stores and fuel for the formation and is equipped with special vehicles that can deliver and collect containers. The Logistics Regiment can deploy Forward Repair Group (FRG), light-dressing stations, or operate these facilities from the safety of the helicopter carrier HMS *Ocean* as the operational situation demands.

The Brigade also has medium reconnaissance support from B Squadron the Household Cavalry Regiment which can provide Scimitar and Striker armoured vehicles to the forces in a number of roles, primarily recce. B Squadron has the ability to provide highly mobile firepower and supported the Brigade on operations in the Falklands. It is regularly at 'short notice' to move in support of the Lead Commando Battlegroup during periods of JRRF readiness.

Finally, the Brigade has its own helicopter force which, while under operational control of the Joint Helicopter Command, is regularly assigned to the Commandos during deployments aboard HMS *Ocean*. Chinook helicopters can also be allocated to the force.

Opposite: Marines from Brigade Patrol Troop parachute into the arctic waste of northern Norway. This small section is using the PX4 canopy, which was replaced in 2000 by the low-level parachute (LLP) which is used by BPT who also jump with steerable parachutes.

THE FUTURE BRIGADE

The Commando Brigade of the future will be equipped with state-of-the-art assault ships and revolutionary weapons as well as hi-tech battlefield support from new aviation assets, such as Apache.

Mobility, firepower and protection are the key issues on which new procurement decisions have been made for the Commando Brigade. These enhancements will ensure that the formation is at the forefront of future operations.

The helicopter carrier HMS *Ocean* is the most obvious and important addition to the brigade's amphibious 'train set' and the procurement of two new Landing Platform Dock Replacements will further boost strategic mobility. In addition, new landing support ships will be delivered and the Royal Navy is scheduled to receive two new carriers designed for fixed-wing operations. These will provide air power, complement the Amphibious Ready Group and form a maritime task group, regarded by senior commanders as the ultimate amphibious formation. A new roll-on, roll-off landing craft will improve loading and delivery times of a seaborne assault, while new armoured all-terrain vehicles will provide limited protection for the force as it crosses a beachhead. It is unclear how these vehicles will be employed, but one idea being considered is the assignment of all 108 to one Commando unit.

A replacement for the Milan anti-tank weapon has been identified as an urgent priority and the automatic grenade launcher (AGL) is still being reviewed. But perhaps top of the shopping list for firepower, mobility and protection is the introduction of the Apache helicopter in 2001. The Apache will have the ability to fly forward to significant ranges and engage targets before the main force lands, thus offering protection from direct engagement with the enemy. It can protect forces on the ground with combat air patrols and can deliver devastating firepower when required.

The gunners at 29 Commando Royal Artillery are to be equipped with BATES (Battlefield Artillery Target Engagement System – this will enable calls for fire to be processed more quickly and thereby enhance the operational effectiveness of 29 Commando's guns). The unit is also scheduled to receive a new gun, a 155mm weapon, in the next decade.

The Sappers at 59 Independent Commando Squadron Royal Engineers will receive a replacement for the combat engineer tractor which has been in service for more than twenty years. Development is ongoing and the new vehicle is expected to be delivered by 2004.

The wide range of enhancements at all levels will deliver better hardware to the Commandos and will be complemented by the Commando 21 reorganisation, which is intended to make the most of the Brigade's landing force and best use of new equipment. Developed by staff at Headquarters Royal Marines in Portsmouth, the new structure was drawn up alongside revised naval doctrine for the Amphibious Ready Group, known as the 'Maritime Contribution to Joint Operations'. The aim is to increase the operational tempo of the Commandos to allow them to hit harder, faster and more accurately.

Opposite: Marines 'Taff' Lancaster and his colleague 'Horse' in Borneo during jungle training with 42 Commando RM.

EPILOGUE

COMMANDOS IN THE FRONT LINE: ULSTER, KOSOVO AND SIERRA LEONE

The dawn of a new millennium signalled a new era for the Corps. For the first time since the Second World War the entire Brigade was deployed on operations in three different areas of the globe. From Northern Ireland to Kosovo and Sierra Leone all Commando units deployed on operational tours in 2000. In addition, a Commando battlegroup was able to mount two tours of expeditionary duty aboard the carrier HMS *Ocean* with the Amphibious Ready Group.

In early 2000 HMS *Ocean* sailed from Plymouth on its first major deployment as the lead component of the ARG. With a Commando battlegroup embarked, the carrier was destined for a series of exercises in France and Portugal before proceeding into the Mediterranean. At all times the ARG was to be 'on-call'.

Just a year earlier the helicopter carrier, the first purpose-built Royal Navy vessel of its kind, was undergoing hot-weather trials in the West Indies with elements of 45 Commando and the Royal Netherlands Marine Corps (RNLMC) on board when she was directed to support a major humanitarian relief operation in South America, following a hurricane.

After a maintenance period back in the UK *Ocean* sailed out of Devonport in May 1999 amid press reports that she was bound for the Adriatic as a intervention force for Kosovo. In actual fact the carrier was mounting amphibious assaults off the Welsh coast, although she was part of a contingency plan for the Balkans. Later in 1999 the carrier and a Commando battlegroup mounted a full-scale seaborne exercise in Egypt to prove that the ship and the Brigade were ready for operations.

When HMS *Ocean* sailed at the beginning of 2000, Lieutenant-Colonel Andy Salmon, commanding officer of 42 Commando, and the carrier's commander Captain Scott Lidbetter were well aware of the potential flashpoints in and around the Mediterranean and of their possible missions – a reinforcement of Kosovo in respect of unrest in Montenegro, or the evacuation of British nationals from one of several African countries.

Sierra Leone has been the focus of conflict for a number of years and Royal Marines from the Fleet Standby Rifle Troop (FSRT) had been in Freetown a year earlier on a

Main picture: Royal Marines of 42 Commando RM pictured in special Land Rovers, known as WMIKs (Weapons Mounted Installation Kits), as they enter Freetown at the port. The Marines deployed into Sierra Leone from the helicopter carrier HMS *Ocean* which had been sitting off the coast with the Amphibious Ready Group. *Inset:* A Royal Marine Commando sniper of Brigade Patrol Troop operating in Kosovo. The Marines developed this 'urban' sniper suit themselves to enhance their surveillance in Kosovo.

Lieutenant-Colonel Andy Salmon, the commanding officer of 42 Commando RM, briefs his key staff at his headquarters in Sierra Leone. The Marines had been waiting off the coast to support the initial British force in Freetown and finally moved in after three weeks to take over the security operation.

deployment named Operation 'Resilient'. The FSRT teams from 45 Commando RM had flown in with Brigadier David Richards, the then head of the Joint Headquarters at Northwood. They were sent in after the British Embassy had been evacuated following increased violence in late 1998 as the Revolutionary United Front (RUF) moved into Freetown, but their deployment went unnoticed by the UK press. The force, consisting of just twenty-two Marines, supported by elements of 539 Assault Squadron and a Navy Lynx, went ashore to deliver medical supplies after rebels left hundreds of mutilated victims in the capital, hacking off the limbs of men, women and children. The Marines used vehicles from the British High Commission and worked in liaison with Nigerian UN forces. In early 1999 the FSRT teams pulled out, although Sierra Leone remained most definitely listed as an 'area of conflict' by the planning teams at the Permanent Joint Headquarters.

Then in early May 2000 the British High Commissioner in Freetown, Alan Jones, warned that the situation in the capital had deteriorated and advised London that an evacuation of British nationals should not be delayed. Lead elements of 1 Para flew

As they arrived in Freetown, the Commandos were able to rely on the support of Sea King troop-carrying and Lynx (pictured) battlefield helicopters which were fitted with anti-tank missiles. The WMIK Land Rover in the foreground is fitted with an infrared sight on top of the machine gun.

into the capital of Sierra Leone on 8 May to assist in the evacuation of 500 British people as fears grew that the rebel RUF was preparing to mount an attack. Smaller renegade groups, later identified as the West Side Boys, had already raped and murdered. The situation was described as 'grave' by the UK media.

Aboard HMS *Ocean* the embarked force was spearheaded by 42 Commando RM and included elements of 29 Commando Royal Artillery and engineer support from 59 Independent Commando Squadron Royal Engineers. In addition, the force included Sea King helicopters and the full suite of logistics support available from stores on board the carrier and from the flotilla of naval support ships and warships escorting her.

In the first week of May the carrier docked at Marseilles for a planned programme of cross-training with French forces but within days the visit had been abandoned and HMS *Ocean* put to sea. Her commander Captain Lidbetter had received an 'eyes only' signal regarding the growing unrest in Sierra Leone and was directed to 'stand off' the Ivory Coast.

The Marines arrested several members of the notorious West Side Boys (WSB), a group of rebel soldiers high on a diet of drugs and alcohol who fought alongside the Sierra Leone Army one day and the opposition Revolutionary United Front the next. Armed with a collection of British, American and Soviet weapons the WSB were responsible for some of the appalling injuries inflicted on women and children in Freetown prior to the arrival of British troops.

Marines of 42 Commando on a river patrol in Sierra Leone. The inflatable boats were manned by 539 Assault Squadron and provided amphibious support to the parachute battalion in Freetown, which was relieved by the Commandos.

een Beret engineers from 59 Independent Commando Squadron RE carry out maintenance on a road outside Freetown. A Commando Engineer Troop always operates with a Commando unit d deployed as a squadron on specific tasks in the Falklands and Bosnia.

Royal Marine from 42 Commando escorts children to school at a lage on the outskirts of Freetown. Prior to the arrival of British rces many children had missed school fearing attack by the WSB.

A Chinook helicopter lifts two 105mm light guns of 29 Commando Regiment Royal Artillery. This picture illustrates the 'joint concept' of the Sierra Leone operation with an RAF helicopter and Army guns being lifted from the deck of the Navy's helicopter carrier HMS *Ocean*.

Back in London the Defence Secretary Geoff Hoon approved plans to divert the aircraft carrier HMS *Illustrious* to the area. At the time *Illustrious* was off Lisbon and heading back to the UK. The French media reported the departure but international agencies failed to pick up on the story and as HMS *Ocean* headed south her redirection was announced by the Ministry of Defence in London. At Gibraltar the carrier was joined by the Type 22 frigate HMS *Chatham*. Aboard were men from 148 Forward Observation Battery of 29 Commando RA as well as boats from 539 Assault Squadron, which had been flown out to the Rock. More Royal Marines from the Fleet Standby Rifle Troop, now sustained by Comacchio Group, deployed aboard the Type 23 frigate HMS *Argyll* (Royal Marine Protection Party 3) to support the task, named as Operation 'Palliser'.

Back in 1996 when the Joint Rapid Reaction Force (initially the Joint Rapid Deployment Force) was formed, both 3 Commando Brigade and 5 Airborne Brigade (later 16 Air Assault Brigade) were assigned to the formation to provide a light battalion for immediate readiness on alternate periods of standby. A host of additional specialist units were also assigned to the force to be used in a 'mission requirement' role. Now in West Africa the two units were to take part in a peace support operation that would demonstrate for the first time the full benefit of UK joint operations working within the JRRF. The Kosovo deployment by the 1st Battalion Parachute Regiment in June 1999 had demonstrated RAF and Army cooperation, but Sierra Leone was truly tri-Service.

As HMS *Ocean* sailed for the West African coast paratroopers flew direct from the UK and seized Sierra Leone's airport at Freetown. The Paras then evacuated British nationals before mounting high-profile patrols in the capital to restore calm and confidence to the community.

HMS *Ocean* and HMS *Illustrious* arrived off the Ivory Coast to establish a maritime task group. This group was able to provide a Commando battlegroup from 42 Commando, to launch combat air patrols by Harriers aboard the carrier and to act as a secure environment for operational briefings.

The source of the problem in Sierra Leone was focused on the rebels of the RUF and rogue gangs armed and high on drugs who had been 'at war' with President Kabbah's government forces for several years. The British military intervention was made after British UN observers were detained by the rebels amid fears that the RUF was preparing to attack Freetown. This would have threatened the lives of British nationals living there.

Within days of arriving the Marines deployed inflatable raiding craft in support of the Paras. They mounted river patrols on the key waterway which separates Freetown from the airport at Lungi. The Marine coxwains had been ordered to remove their Commando flashes, worn on the shoulder of Combat 95 uniform, so that the media would not be alerted to the fact that the Commando group was ashore.

As the Paras pulled out after three weeks of living out of their bergans, 42 Commando officially rolled into Freetown. The operation was more of a media event than a tactical arrival, as many of the Commando group had already been

Opposite: 40 Commando RM deployed to Northern Ireland on yet another tour of duty with the unit working across the Province in support of other units and making a major contribution to the continuing peace process. The picture shows a Marine and a Para on patrol. The two units have worked together on numerous occasions since the Second World War.

working with the Paras – either alongside them collating intelligence in preparation for the handover or preparing accommodation and identifying resources for the unit.

The handover was made on 24 May at Lungi and Freetown. The 105mm light guns of 8 Battery 29 Commando RA were positioned at Petify junction and Lungi airport. The WMIK (Weapon Mounted Installation Kit) Land Rovers provided a highly visible presence on the streets while, more importantly, ensuring a significant level of firepower with .50 mounted machine guns and GPMG.

Just days before 42 Commando took over, three British officers and a New Zealander escaped from their captors – one of them was a Royal Marine; Major Philip Ashby telephoned his wife from the UN base where they were held and she alerted PJHQ. Then the four made their escape, trekking 40 miles through the bush at night to a rendezvous with an RAF special forces Chinook.

The deployment into Sierra Leone had been a pertinent reminder to ministers of the 'on-call' capability of the newly formed ARG, allowing the Commando Brigade to demonstrate its inherent flexibility to be ready for operations.

As 42 Commando returned to the UK, Taunton-based 40 Commando was preparing for yet another tour of duty in Northern Ireland. As peace seemed to evaporate across the Province, the unrest at Drumcree and increased violence in Belfast saw the Commandos back on the streets in June 2000. The unit's tour saw Support Company and its intelligence cell deployed in Belfast and other elements of 40 tasked to support operations at Drumcree. Many in the unit felt that this might be the last time Royal Marines would patrol the streets of Ulster, but only time will tell. Since 1969 fourteen Royal Marines have made the ultimate sacrifice in Northern Ireland.

Throughout the early part of 2000, Brigade HQ, 45 Commando RM, Commando Logistics Regiment, as well as elements of 29 Commando RA and 59 Independent Commando Squadron Royal Engineers, prepared for peace support operations in Kosovo, which involved numerous

exercises and United Nations training. This was the first peace operation for the Commandos, although they did spearhead the humanitarian operation in northern Iraq in 1991. The Green Berets, who train for rapid intervention in hostile environments, have for many years deployed on 'policing operations' in Northern Ireland. Despite the nature of the Kosovo PSO the Brigade commander, Brigadier Rob Fry, made sure his battlegroup maintained a high level of manoeuvrability so that they could react to tasks.

Maintaining the peace in Kosovo. A Marine of Zulu Company, 45 Commando RM questions a local Albanian while his colleague checks his identity card. Although the war in Kosovo was already over, the Marines' major effort was directed towards protecting Serbs from attacks by former members of the Kosovo Liberation Army, which was ordered to disband after the conflict.

Brigadier Fry commanded a force of 6,500 from his base in the Kosovo capital Prestina, including the 1st Battalion the Princess of Wales's Royal Regiment, a squadron of Queen's Dragoon Guards, 26 Engineer Regiment, 1 Regiment Royal Horse Artillery with AS90, 22 Battery with Phoenix and Puma and Gazelle helicopters from the Joint Helicopter Command (JHC). The force was also significantly enhanced by Finnish, Norwegian, Swedish and Czech units.

The Commandos' mountain and arctic warfare training proved a significant advantage in the cold Balkan winter and the Brigade tracked all terrain vehicles proved very useful. The Brigade Recce Force was used to support the intelligence mission and was regarded as a significant enhancement to the force capability. The six-month tour in Kosovo was hectic. In the weekend the Commandos arrived a man was murdered. Then just days later a municipal worker was killed and within the first week arms finds were being logged regularly.

As in the early years of Northern Ireland, the Commandos introduced new concepts to the Kosovo peace-keeping mission which were adopted by other formations. They steered away from the idea of static vehicle checkpoints and manned tower observation posts and introduced a policy of mounting snap vehicle checkpoints.

Brigadier Fry believes fixed locations give targets for terrorists to manoeuvre around and as the force commander his aim was to maintain a security structure based on the absolute minimum of static installations. Around that the Commandos built a programme of patrolling, partly overt and covert, which operated in several dimensions to allow offensive air operations, air observations and ground movement, all of which were designed to create fear in the minds of prospective terrorists that they would be caught.

During 2000, 78 per cent of the strength of 3 Commando Brigade was committed to operations, reflecting the growing demand for its skills and professionalism. The Royal Navy has clearly put amphibious warfare at the top of its new doctrine and senior officers confidently predict the future is secure for the Commandos. But the Brigade must be careful not to fall foul of its own success and overstretch its manpower with commitments that overshadow its core skills.

For generations the public has had little respect for military personnel during peacetime, although, as Rudyard Kipling's poem 'Tommy' reflected, the country praises them during war. Today's 'politically correct' society has little stomach for the reality of Commando training and has little regard for or understanding of the importance of maintaining high standards of recruit training.

In the early twenty-first century the emphasis is on peace support and humanitarian operations, otherwise known as 'police work and baby hugging'. As these roles increase there may be calls to limit the more aggressive aspects of the thirty-week Commando course with the aim of cutting costs in an era when 'warfighting' may seem remote. But if history repeats itself, as it has so often, at some point in the next decade British troops will face combat just when it is least expected. Then, armed with new weapons or delivered into battle from a fleet of new assault ships, the cold reality of the reason for the Royal Marines' training will become apparent – to kill the enemy.

CHRONOLOGY

S ince their formation in 1942 the Royal Marine Commandos have deployed on operations every year except 1968. At the beginning of the twenty-first century all units of the Brigade were on operations in three different areas of the world: Northern Ireland, Sierra Leone and the Balkans.

1942 – Formation of Royal Marines Commando role   40 RM Commando raised at Deal on 14 February 1942. Operations followed at Dieppe. 41 Commando also formed in 1942 from men of the 8th Battalion Royal Marines. After the war 41 was disbanded but re-formed in 1950 for the Korean operation, and disbanded after Korea. The unit was re-formed again in 1960 and disbanded in 1981. Towards the end of 1942 senior officers of No. 1 Commando decided that headdress should become standard across all ranks and opted for the beret as the most practical. The Royal Tank Regiment had worn a black beret for many years and the recently formed Parachute Regiment and airborne forces had chosen a maroon one. No. 1 Commando's flash showed a green salamander walking through fire, which provided a choice between green, red and yellow for its beret. Green was chosen.

1943 – Expansion of commando role   Operations in Sicily and Italy. Termoli landing on 3 October 1943. More RM Commando units were formed. Training at Achnacarry: the Commando Training School at Achnacarry turned out 40, 42, 43, 44, 45, 46, 47 and 48 Commandos – 40 and 43 to serve in Italy, 42 and 44 in Burma and the remainder were assigned to work up for the invasion of France. The invasion was a significant development in Royal Marines history as it marked the start of the Corps' involvement in Commando operations. 43 Commando formed from 2nd Royal Marine Battalion and disbanded after the war; in 1961 the unit was re-formed and then disbanded in 1968. 44, 46, 47 and 48, who were formed in 1943, were disbanded after the war.

1944 – Normandy and operations across Europe   Royal Marine Commandos took part in Normandy landings – D-Day. In 1944 there were four Special Service Brigades (also known as Commando Brigades). 1st Special Service (under command of Brigadier the Lord Lovat) was in Britain preparing for 'Overlord' and included Nos 3, 4 and 6 Army Commandos as well as 45 (Royal Marines) Commando. 2nd Special Service was in the Mediterranean and consisted of Nos 2, 9, 40 and 43 Commandos. 3rd Special Service was about to depart for the Far East and included Nos 1, 5, 42 and 44. Finally, 4th Special Service was also in the UK and

Right: Commando training in the war years took place at Achnacarry, where instructors ensured that the volunteers underwent a realistic programme of training to prepare them for operations. Today a Commando memorial at nearby Spean Bridge stands as a lasting reminder to the formative years of Britain's Green Berets.

Below: Marines of 45 RM Commando digging in at Pegasus Bridge after landing on Sword Beach with Lord Lovat's 1st Special Service Brigade and advancing through to link up with the 6th Airborne Division. Members of the Royal Marine Association attend a ceremony at the bridge every year to pay their respects to the Commandos who fought there in 1944.

preparing for D-Day and under the command of Brigadier 'Jumbo' Leicester. The latter was a dedicated Royal Marine brigade consisting of 41, 46, 47 and 48 Commandos. In total there would be three Army Commando and five Royal Marine Commando units taking part in the landings. Commandos also spearheaded the assault on Walcheren in November 1944.

In the Far East, the 3rd Commando Brigade (formerly Special Service Brigade) took part in operations to clear the Arakan in Burma. Here the Brigade saw fierce fighting and experienced the brutality of the Japanese. In December 1944 as the Japanese began withdrawing, British forces launched Operation 'Talon' to cut road and sea routes and prevent the enemy re-forming in central Burma. At the village of Kangaw in January 1945, 44 RM and 42 RM Commandos fought a bloody battle which culminated with the defence of Hill 170; 31 January 1945, the day of the battle, is known in the Corps as 'Kangaw Day'.

1945 – Advance across the Rhine and into Germany   Commandos fought at Montforterbeek (VC awarded to RAMC orderly Lance Corporal Harden). Captain Barry Pierce of 46 Commando RM was killed on 13 April 1945. His grave states that he was the first British soldier over the Rhine. He served with Y Troop in the operation to cross the river on 23 March 1945. The eventual success in north-west Europe contrasted with the fighting stalemate in Italy, where the Germans yielded ground but never looked like totally collapsing. Various attempts were made to crack the front. In April 1945 at Lake Comacchio in north-east Italy, 43 and 40 RM Commandos fought a battle to dislodge the Germans from their strongly held positions. Here Corporal Thomas Hunter of 43 Commando was awarded the Victoria Cross. 42 and 44 RM Commandos took part in bitter fighting at Akyab and across the Far East until late 1945. In October 1945 Army Commando units were disbanded and the role was transferred exclusively to the Royal Marines, which retained a single brigade. 3 Commando Brigade, made up of 44 (later known as 40), 42 and 45 Commandos, was sent to Hong Kong to supervise resettlement after the Japanese occupation.

1946 – Hong Kong   The Brigade undertook police work, quelling riots and breaking up gangs, and went on anti-smuggling patrols. (The Commandos returned temporarily in 1949 because of fears over the communists' rise to power in mainland China.)

1947 – Hong Kong   Continued internal security operation. The Brigade departed in summer 1947 for Malta.

1948 – Palestine   This year saw the end of the British mandate in Palestine and increasing conflict between Arabs and Jews. From January 40 Commando was involved in internal security operations, keeping the two sides apart and coming under attack from both. The Commandos patrolled extensively, searched for arms and cleared underwater mines. They also attempted to halt unauthorised Jewish immigration. 40 Commando evacuated Arab refugees. The British presence was reinforced by the arrival of 42 and 45 Commandos at the beginning of May, but the force eventually left on 27 June 1948. Royal Marines were the last British troops to leave Palestine. The area degenerated into civil war and a wider Arab–Jewish conflict led to the founding of the modern Israeli state.

1949 – Jordan   In April 1949 45 Commando provided part of a British garrison force between Israel and what was then known as Transjordan during a time of border tension. The unit was withdrawn to its base in Suez in June.

1950 – Malaya   41 Independent Commando was raised for operations in Korea. In May and June the Brigade began a two-year tour of duty in Malaya to carry out counter-insurgency operations against the mainly Chinese guerrillas of the communist Malayan Races Liberation Army. The Brigade was based in Perak state for most of the tour, with 40 at Kuala Kangsar, 42 at Ipoh and 45 at Tapah. The Commandos patrolled over 8,000 square miles of jungle up to the Thai border, operating with Chinese and Iban trackers on long jungle patrols and having occasional gun battles with guerrilla groups.

1951 – Grenada   From 2 to 14 February HMS *Devonshire*'s detachment was deployed in support of local police to quell serious rioting, and to protect the hospital and airport.

1952 – Malaya   Operations against the mainly Chinese guerrillas of the communist Malayan Races Liberation Army. Main Malayan campaign ends. 40, 42 and 45 Commando served in Malaya. A total of thirty-three Royal Marines died in operations there.

1953 – Global operations   Marine Commandos on operations at the Suez Canal Zone, completion of operations in Malaya and 41 Independent Commando returns to UK. In August 1953, after a serious earthquake had devastated the Greek island of Zankinthos, the detachments of HMS *Gambia* and *Bermuda* and elements of 45 Commando provided assistance with rescue operations, supplying food, shelter and medical services in a joint operation with the Royal Navy, the British Army and the US Marine Corps.

1954 – Suez Canal   Continued Operations.   The Brigade had been ordered to the zone in May 1953 after talks between Britain and Egypt on the future of the British-administered area had broken down. Royal Marines were employed on internal security duties, protecting convoys and enduring occasional ambushes and guerrilla attacks. The Brigade was withdrawn in September and October, although British forces did not finally leave until March 1956.

1955 – Cyprus   In September 1955 the Brigade, less 42 Commando, moved to Cyprus to counter the increasing threat from the Greek-Cypriot independence movement EOKA. Cyprus was to become a regular deployment for the next three and a half years, as Marines of Brigade HQ, 40 and 45 Commandos carried out the familiar tasks of patrolling, arms searches, road blocks, riot controls and ambush.

1956 – Suez   When the Egyptian President Nasser ordered the nationalisation of the Suez Canal in August 1956 a combined British and French force was formed to recover it. The British seaborne invasion, supported by a parachute landing, was spearheaded by 3 Commando Brigade. 40 and 42 Commandos landed on Port Said's bathing beaches in landing craft, accompanied by 6th Royal Tank Regiment; 45 Commando was flown ashore by Whirlwinds and Sycamores from HMS *Theseus* and HMS *Ocean* in the first-ever helicopter-borne assault. The Commandos fought their way into the city, but plans to advance were halted by a ceasefire, and British forces were replaced by United Nations troops.

The attack on Port Said in Egypt in November 1956 saw the first military helicopter assault. It was carried out by 45 Commando RM in Whirlwind helicopters. Both 40 and 42 Commandos landed on the beaches at Port Said. This was the first major seaborne assault since the Second World War and it was a very successful operation. In the face of international criticism the Anglo-French operation was short-lived; the initial force was quickly withdrawn and replaced with United Nations troops.

1957 – Cyprus   From January to May 40 Commando was based in the Troodos Mountains of Cyprus on internal security operations against EOKA. This role was taken over for the second half of the year by 45 Commando.

1958 – Persian Gulf   Royal Marines of ship's detachments were involved in patrols in the Gulf, particularly as tension heightened following the fall of the Iraqi government. Their duties included providing boarding parties, which searched ships suspected of gunrunning for Arab nationalist groups. They also attempted to stop drug smuggling and slave trading. Ships of the Amphibious Warfare Squadron also operated in the Persian Gulf in the late '50s.

1959 – Cyprus   40 Commando continued operations in the Troodos Mountains from January to April.

1960 – Aden   45 Commando moved to Aden and was based there for the next seven and a half years. Drafting gave Marines from other units a one-year-long tour of duty in the protectorate. Aden was the scene of a complex series of political struggles as British forces countered radical Arab independence movements which had Egyptian and Soviet backing. Royal Marines also operated against incursions from Yemen to the north. 45 Commando was initially based in the built-up area of Little Aden, with troops on rotating desert patrols in the Dhala Mountains to the north.

1961 – Kuwait   Commandos were sent to the newly independent state of Kuwait in July 1961, following threats of invasion by the Iraqi leader General Kassim. 42, on the newly converted commando carrier HMS *Bulwark*, was flown to Kuwait City by Whirlwinds, while 45 was carried from Aden in transport aircraft. They were joined by the Royal Marine detachment of HMS *Loch Alvie* and deployed in the searing desert heat of Mutla Ridge alongside tanks of the Queen's Dragoon Guards. This was enough to deter the Iraqis and the Commandos were withdrawn within a few weeks.

1962 – Brunei revolt   Britain hoped to establish a federation of states on withdrawal from Malaya, but this plan met considerable opposition, both internally and from the Sukarno government in Indonesia. In December 1962 the first open rebellion occurred in the British region of Brunei. Rebels took over several towns, and at Limbang held Western hostages and threatened to execute them. The hostages were rescued on 12 December 1962 in a daring raid by 42 Commando's L Company, which had been flown to Singapore, and then travelled up the Limbang River on converted lighters. The revolt quickly collapsed as Brigade HQ, 40 and 42 Commandos patrolled the jungles of Brunei until 1963, but opposition to the federation flared into a wider conflict which became known as the 'Borneo Confrontation'.

1963 – Borneo   In April the confrontation began in earnest as guerrillas began to cross into Sarawak from Indonesia. 40 and 42 Commandos, on alternating tours, were based in either Brunei or Sarawak throughout the year, fighting a jungle campaign of long patrols and ambushes, and trying to win hearts and minds. The rebels, unlike the British forces, could cross and recross the Indonesian border with impunity, but did not have major advantages in their use of river patrol craft and helicopters. The SBS also carried out clandestine operations.

1964 – East Africa   At the beginning of the year mutinies seemed likely in several new East African states, and the governments of Kenya and Tanganyika (now Tanzania) asked for British assistance to contain them. In January 41 Commando was sent to suppress an expected revolt in Kenya, which did not materialise. The unit then joined 45 Commando in Tanganyika to put down a mutiny there. 45 had been transported to East Africa from Aden on the strike carrier HMS *Centaur*. Its timely arrival meant the insurrections were quickly suppressed, and 45 returned to Aden in February; 41 Commando remained until April.

1965 – Borneo   Royal Marines continued the campaign, coming into occasional contact with Indonesian regulars, who had been thrown into the conflict alongside the guerrillas at the end of 1963. In 1965 40 and 42 Commandos were based in Borneo, while an experimental Royal Marines unit used hovercraft on active service for the first time. (Marines also still in Aden.)

1966 – Borneo   42 Commando carried out anti-guerrilla operations in Lindu until May, when 40 Commando took over. When the confrontation was successfully concluded in August 1966 40 returned to Johore in Malaysia, while 42 were based at Sembawang in Singapore.

1967 – Aden   45 Commando continued operations in Aden throughout the early 1960s, and had been increasingly involved in the flight against the dissident tribesmen of the Radfan Mountains in addition to countering urban terrorism in Aden City. By 1966 45 had completed eleven major tours 'up country' and in June finally handed over control – if such a thing had ever been possible in the Radfan – to the South Arabian Army. In October, 42 Commando arrived to cover the British withdrawal from the protectorate as it gained independence. On 28 November, 42 and 45 left Aden – the last British forces to do so.

1968 – Quiet year   This was a relatively quiet year, although 40 Commando was still based in Singapore, while 42 saw service on Commando carriers. The usual round of exercises continued unabated.

1969 – Northern Ireland   Since the beginning of the current conflict Royal Marines have been deployed on internal security duties in the Province on a regular basis. The first Royal Marine unit to become involved was 41 Commando, which was Spearhead battalion of the Strategic Reserve in 1969, and in September was sent to the Divis area of West Belfast. The Commando spent six weeks policing riots before returning to the UK.

1970 – East Pakistan (now Bangladesh)   The Ganges delta was devastated by a tidal wave on 18 November 1970. Royal Marines from 40 Commando were immediately sent from Singapore on HMS *Intrepid*, *Triumph* and the RFA *Sir Galahad*, while detachments from Amphibious Training Unit Royal Marines at Poole and the 2nd Raiding Squadron were flown in with their gemini rubber boats. In Operation 'Burlap' the landing craft and raiders were used to carry food, medical supplies and shelter,

Marines of 45 Commando crouch beside a digger in the early 1980s. Both men are wearing the old-style DMS boots, with the Marine on the left wearing puttees and his colleague wearing hosetops, which at the time were a favourite item with members of the MAW Cadre (before it was reorganised on the formation of BPT). The need for units to deploy regularly, or be ready for operations, in Ulster continues in the twenty-first century. However, troop levels have reduced and there is hope that peace will return to this divided Province.

providing invaluable relief to the local population. Marines deployed to Northern Ireland. 45 Commando commenced first Arctic warfare training.

1971 – Northern Ireland   45 Commando Group was moved to Northern Ireland for its third tour, arriving on 10 August, the day after the introduction of internment. The group was based in the Belfast area, but also patrolled in and around Newry. 42 Commando, meanwhile, arrived in Armagh in October and carried out patrols in rural areas near the Irish Republic. 41 Commando was in Malta.

1972 – Northern Ireland   In June 1972 40 Commando began a four-month tour, while 45 was temporarily deployed for the marching season. 45 was relieved at the end of July by 42 Commando, stationed in the Province for a short period during Operation 'Motorman'. This was, at the time, the largest British military operation since Suez. On 31 July 22,000 troops moved into the 'no-go' areas, removing barricades which had previously hindered security work. 40 and 42 Commandos played a full part in this operation, while landing craft from *Fearless* carried the Royal Engineers' tanks, fitted with bulldozer blades, ashore.

1973 – Northern Ireland   From February to June 1973, 42 Commando was based in North Belfast. It was relieved by 40 Commando, accompanied by 7 (Sphinx) Light Battery Royal Artillery, for a tour which lasted until October.

1974 – Cyprus   40 and 42 Commandos deployed to reinforce the British garrison at the time of the Turkish invasion. In November 41 Commando began a six-month tour in Cyprus on peacekeeping duties with the United Nations. The Commando was accompanied by Royal Engineer and Royal Artillery Commando units, and administered the Limassol district for United Nations forces in Cyprus. Its duties included monitoring the ceasefire between Greek-Cypriot and Turkish forces, and administering humanitarian aid to Turkish-Cypriot and Greek-Cypriot communities.

1975 – Northern Ireland   From February to June 1975 42 Commando was based in the Anderstown area of West Belfast. In October 42 Commando, as Spearhead, completed a short tour in the 'bandit country' of South Armagh before returning to the mainland at the end of November.

1976 – Northern Ireland   From February to June 1976 42 Commando was based in the Anderstown area of West Belfast for its sixth tour. From August to December 40 Commando was in South Armagh. HMS *Bulwark* made her last commission with 40 Commando embarked in spring 1976.

1977 – Northern Ireland   From June to September 45 Commando with 79 Commando Battery RA, were based in Anderstown. Montforterbeek Flight was also deployed in the Province in this year, and small detachments of Royal Marines operated raiding craft and provided boarding parties on vessels patrolling the loughs and coasts of Northern Ireland, a role they have performed virtually continuously. First 'Oilsafe' commitment to guard North Sea rigs was mounted.

1978 – Northern Ireland   41 Commando was in West Belfast from February to June and 42 Commando on an emergency tour of Armagh from July to November. There were fire-fighting duties at the beginning of the year during the firemen's strike on mainland UK, when over 2,000 Marines were deployed in Strathclyde and the West Midlands.

1979 – Hong Kong   In July 1979 a training team of raiding craft specialists was sent to Hong Kong. It was followed in September by 42 Commando – reinforced by thirty members of the Royal Marine Reserves – on a two-month tour; 42's duties included patrolling the border with the Chinese mainland to prevent illegal immigration. L Company came under Royal Navy command because it was used as a fast patrol boat unit which intercepted illegal immigrants at sea. The raiding craft proved so successful that the specialists remained after 42's return to the UK in November, and in

1980 formed the nucleus of the new 3rd Raiding Squadron, which was permanently based in Hong Kong until 1988. 1979 saw the first full Brigade-sized deployment to Norway. 41 Commando went back to Cyprus.

1980 – New Hebrides   Early in the year a revolt broke out in the New Hebrides, a colony jointly administered by Britain and France, during the run-up to independence. M Company and the Tactical HQ of 42 Commando, Spearhead at the time, were deployed to the islands in June in an attempt to prevent clashes between English- and French-speaking groups. They were joined by French paratroopers and stayed for two months without encountering major disturbances. The Royal Marines took part in the independence celebrations at the end of July and then returned to the UK. Comacchio Company, later Comacchio Group, was formed this year.

1981 – Hong Kong   3rd Raiding Squadron continued its deployment, intercepting drug smugglers and illegal immigrants. 41 Commando was disbanded.

1982 – Falklands   On 2 and 3 April 1982 Argentine forces invaded the Falkland Islands and South Georgia, capturing the small defending parties of Royal Marines. All elements of 3 Commando Brigade played vital parts in the massive operation to recover the islands. The three Commandos were landed on East Falkland, together with two parachute battalions and supporting groups, on 21 May. SBS teams had already been ashore on enemy-occupied territory for some weeks, while other parties took part in daring raids on Argentine installations. Royal Marine landing craft crew and members of the Brigade Air Squadron were used to move men, equipment and casualties, while 40 Commando provided the reserve at Ajax Bay. 42 Commando was airlifted to Argentine forward positions, while 45 completed an epic 'yomp' across East Falkland. Aggressive patrols probed the Argentine defences and deterred counterattacks, and then in successful night assaults on Mount Harriet and Two Sisters 42 and 45 Commandos captured these virtually impregnable defensive positions that dominated Port Stanley. The Argentine will was broken by these and later attacks and the war ended on 14 June.

1983 – Northern Ireland   From January to-June 1983 40 Commando was based in South Armagh. Additional Commandos were deployed as part of training teams across the globe.

1984 – Cyprus   From June to December 40 Commando was based in Cyprus, on a split tour that entailed 'blue beret' duties with United Nations forces in Cyprus as a peacekeeping force and 'Green Beret' protection of the British sovereign base areas. Royal Marines from 539 Assault Squadron maintained operations in Northern Ireland and there were continued deployments in the Province.

Opposite: A Marine from the Brigade Intelligence Cell escorts a captured Argentine observer away for questioning. The man was one of four captured by 40 Commando near San Carlos Water, Falklands, who had been directing Argentine fighter aircraft to attack Royal Navy warships disgorging men and supplies in support of the operation. The landing in San Carlos Water on 21 May 1982 is a principal date to remember for the Corps while the attack on Two Sisters by 45 Commando on 11/12 June, the assault on Mount Harriet by 42 Commando on 11/12 June and the critical logistics support on 22 May by the Commando Logistics Regiment, are remembered by the respective units.

1985 – Hong Kong   3rd Raiding Squadron continued its patrols searching for illegal immigrants in Hong Kong, while Naval Party 1002 was on Diego Garcia in the Indian Ocean. Royal Marines have acted as police and customs officers on the island since 1982. Continued deployments to Northern Ireland.

1986 – Northern Ireland   45 Commando was in West Belfast from June to November. At the beginning of the year the RM detachment of HMY *Britannia* assisted with the evacuation of British subjects in Aden during an emergency in South Yemen. 40 Commando on London duties (guarding Buckingham Palace).

1987 – Northern Ireland   42 Commando, as Spearhead, was sent to Northern Ireland on an emergency tour in May, and was based in rural locations. The Commando returned in July, although Recce Troop's stay was slightly extended.

1989 – Northern Ireland   40 Commando was deployed in South Armagh from February to July. 3rd Raiding Squadron ceased operations in Hong Kong in July. The Diego Garcia party continued customs and security duties. C Company 40 Commando undertook first raiding trials with HMS *Ocean* in Plymouth Sound. 42 Commando deployed to West Belfast from June to October – this was during the twentieth anniversary of the troubles and media attention on the unit was intense. The Diego Garcia party continued its duties.

1990 – Gulf War   Air Defence Troop deployed teams to provide additional air cover for the maritime task force. Commando Helicopter Unit also deployed, as did elements of 539 Assault Squadron. 40 Commando deployed to Northern Ireland.

1991 – Northern Iraq   3 Commando Brigade deployed to northern Iraq for Operation 'Safe Haven'. 45 Commando RM deployed to Northern Ireland – South Armagh.

1992 – Northern Ireland   42 Commando was in Ulster. Royal Marine boarding parties were in the Adriatic enforcing UN operations to stop weapons being smuggled into Bosnia.

1993 – Northern Ireland   40 Commando in Northern Ireland. 45 Commando in Belize. 59 Independent Commando Squadron Royal Engineers in Bosnia. 148 Forward Observation Unit (29 Commando RA) in Bosnia. Fleet Standby Rifle Troop in Hong Kong. Team of Tactical Air Controllers (TACPS) also in Bosnia.

1994 – Kuwait   45 Commando was deployed to reinforce Kuwait. 40 Commando was in Northern Ireland. 42 also deployed in same year. 148 Battery deployed to Bosnia, TACPs also in Bosnia.

The Commandos of the future. Training at Lympstone starts with daily gym work and then quickly transfers to the outside assault course, the 30 foot ropes and the Tarzan course as recruits are slowly prepared for the Commando selection tests, which include a 30-mile yomp across Dartmoor and the endurance course across Woodbury Common.

1995 – Northern Ireland 40, 42 and 45 Commandos were all in Northern Ireland. Logistics Regiment deployed to Montserrat; 148 Battery was in Bosnia and RM Boarding Teams were in Hong Kong.

1996 – Northern Ireland 40 Commando in Ulster. Elements of 29 Commando in Bosnia. Fleet Standby Rifle Troop in Hong Kong.

1997 – Congo and Northern Ireland 59 Independent Commando Squadron Royal Engineers in Ulster. Alpha Company 40 Commando RM deployed to Congo in Operation 'Ladbrook'.

The look of the future Royal Marine Commando – helmet-mounted camera allowing the Commando to relay everything he can see to his commanders, lasers, helmet communications and hi-tech body armour. The new system is called FIST (Future Infantry Soldier Technology) and is expected to enter service by the end of the decade.

1998 – Northern Ireland   42 Commando deployed in Northern Ireland (Armagh). 45 Commando provided troops for FSRT. A boat group from 539 deployed to the Adriatic on Operation 'Swanston' – a potential non-combatant evacuation of British nationals from Albania. Other RMs deployed to Bosnia, and as members of the OSCE in Kosovo.

1999 – Northern Ireland   42 Commando in Northern Ireland. FSRT in Sierra Leone. Specialists from 3 Commando Brigade in Kosovo. TACPs in Bosnia. 20 Commando Battery in Cyprus. 59 Independent Commando in the Falklands.

2000 – Sierra Leone, Northern Ireland and Kosovo   42 Commando deployed as ARG and was directed to Sierra Leone. 40 Commando was in Northern Ireland. 45 Commando was in Kosovo where 3 Commando Brigade RM took armour under command for the first time since Suez.

2001 – Presentation of new colours to all Commando units on Plymouth Hoe. 45 Commando in Kosovo.

ACKNOWLEDGEMENTS

The author has made every effort to ensure that facts and figures in *Commando* are correct and has received considerable assistance from Matthew Little of the Royal Marines Museum in this matter. While the Foreword by Countess Mounbatten of Burma and the Preface by Commandant-General Royal Marines Major-General R.H.M. Fulton are highly valued, they do not endorse these facts and figures in any way. The book is entirely the author's work.

Commando would not have been possible without the support of the Royal Marines, the Commandant-General Major-General Sir Robert Fulton RM and Countess Mountbatten, who very kindly wrote a fitting foreword which is itself a tribute to the Commandos.

Thanks must also go to Brigadier Rob Fry RM at 3 Commando Brigade, Lieutenant-Colonel Kevin de Val and WO2 Richard Scott and WO2 Paul Hugil at Headquarters Royal Marines, Major Mark Benting at the Corps Historical Record Office, and C/Sgt Neil Warrington at Public Relations, CTCRM.

In addition I would like to thank:
Lieutenant-Colonel Simon Guyer RM, the first amphibious operations officer on HMS *Ocean*
Matthew Little at the Historical Records section of the Royal Marines Museum
Patrick Allen, for his commando aviation knowledge
George Gill, whom I first met in 40 Commando's Recce Troop – and who is one of the most professional men in the Corps
Andy Taylor, another great soldier and good friend who was able to remind me of a few dits (stories) I had almost forgotten
Peter Holdgate, the Commando photographer whose outstanding photographs recorded the Falklands War
Ian Perkins, a young Marine in the Falklands who is a mine of anecdotes
Major-General Julian Thompson, my commanding officer in 40 Commando whose contribution was much appreciated
Lieutenant-General Robin Ross, whose quotes about the Commando Brigade's capability have been used time and time again
Alan Saunders and Ken Morris, who served at Dieppe and spoke from the heart
Ken Parker and Cyril Penberthy, who took part in the D-Day landings; Ken also took part in the action at Walcheren and the helicopter assault at Suez with 45 Commando

Fred Hayhurst of the 41 Independent Commando Association

Tom 'Jan' Webber, who served with 42 Commando at Suez

Falkland islander Fred Ford, who was one of the unsung heroes of the Falklands War

Graham Bound, who was in the Falklands as a civilian during the invasion

Major Jeff Moulton, who as a lieutenant trained recruits at Lympstone

'Yorkie' Malone, who saw action with 45 Commando in the Falklands

Rod Boswell, the commanding officer of 40 Commando's Recce Troop in 1976 and the OC of the MAW Cadre at Top Malo House in the Falklands, a great bloke

Geoff Page-Bailey, another former Marine full of anecdotes

I consulted the Historical Records department at the Royal Marines Museum in Portsmouth regarding all aspects of Royal Marines history, in particular the historical accounts of Normandy from Marine Bill Andrews, Major Dan Flunder, Corporal Arthur Hines, Captain Matthew Oliver, Captain John Oven (later Major-General), Sergeant Arthur Gray, Lieutenant Paddy Stevens (later Colonel), Lieutenant-Colonel Peter Young; background on the Far East and the account at Suez by Captain Derek Oakley MBE, RM; the records concerning Aden, Brunei and Cyprus; the Falklands accounts of Lieutenant-Colonel Whitehead RM and Lieutenant-Colonel Vaux RM. Information was also provided by the US Marines Public Affairs Office in Washington and the Royal Netherlands Marine Corps PR staff at Den Helder.

A note of special thanks needs to be made to Matt Little and Fred Hayhurst who assisted in reading and checking facts and figures – thank you very much.

PICTURE CREDITS

Andrew Chittock, Dil Banerjee, Simon Kelly, Richard Spake, Tom Ross, David Wotton, and Harry Steele of The Defence Picture Library.

Matthew Little of the Royal Marines Museum, Patrick Allen, the aviation specialist photographer, Steve Lewis, Teddy Neville, Peter Holdgate.

The Defence Picture Library is a specialist military photo agency. To obtain prints of the images published in the book contact: Picture Editor, The Defence Picture Library, Sherwell House, 54 Staddiscombe Road, Plymouth, Devon PL9 9NB.

BIBLIOGRAPHY

Ballantyne, Ian, David Reynolds and Steve Brumwell, *The Falklands War* (Northcliffe, 1992)

Barzilay, David, *The British Army in Ulster* (all volumes) (Century Services, 1975)

Dear, Ian, *Ten Commando* (Leo Cooper, 1987)

Dewar, Michael, *The British Army in Northern Ireland* (Arms & Armour, 1985)

Directorate of Naval Studies, *British Maritime Doctrine BR1806 HMSO* (Crown, 1995)

Harnden, Toby, *Bandit Country* (Hodder & Stoughton, 1999)

Hastings, Max , *The Battle for the Falklands* (Michael Joseph, 1983)

History of the Commandos (The Commando Association, 1993)

Hunter, Robin, *True Stories of the Commandos* (Virgin, 2000)

Jackson, Robert, *Suez, The Forgotten Invasion* (Airlife, 1996)

Jeffrey, Keith, *Northern Ireland, The Divided Province* (Crescent Books, 1985)

Keegan, John, *Who's Who in World War II* (Routledge, 1995)

Ladd, James, *Commandos and Rangers of World War II* (David & Charles, 1978)

——, *By Land, By Sea, History of the Royal Marines* (Harper & Collins, 1998)

Marix Evans, Martin, *Encyclopaedia of the Boer War* (ABC-CLIO Books, 1988)

Neillands, Robin, *By Sea & Land, The Story of the Royal Marine Commandos* (Orion, 1987)

Oakley, Capt Derek, MBE RM, *Suez Commando* (Orbis Publishing, 1986)

——, *The Royal Marines into the Nineties* (DNR, 1993)

Reynolds, David, *3 Commando Brigade RM* (Royal Navy, 1996)

——, *Lympstone, The Commando Training Centre* (Royal Navy, 1997)

Royal Marines of the 1970s and 1980s (Dept of Commandant-General, 1981)

Ripley, Tim, *Operation Deliberate Force* (CDISS, 1999)

Smith, John, *74 Days, An Islander's Diary of Falklands Occupation* (Century, 1984)

Snelling, Stephen, *Gallipoli* (Sutton Publishing, 1994)

Steeles, Mark, *Operation Neptune* (Ministry of Defence reprint, 1994)

Thomas, Lt Col Peter, *41 Ind Commando, Korea* (Royal Marines Historical Society, 1960)

Thompson, Julian, *No Picnic* (Leo Cooper Publishing, 1985)

——, *The Royal Marines, From Sea Soldiers to a Special Force* (Sidgwick, 2000)

Turner, John Frayn, *Invasion 1944* (Airlife, 1959)

Underwood, Geoffrey, *Our Falklands War* (Maritime Books, 1983)

Vaux, Nick, *March to the South Atlantic* (Buchan & Enright, 1986)

Wells, Mike and David Reynolds, *Across the Beach* (Newgate Press Limited, 1995)

Working Together to Police Northern Ireland (Royal Ulster Constabulary, 1988)

Index